More Ghost Towns of Texas

ALSO BY T. LINDSAY BAKER

(with Steven R. Rae, Seymour V. Connor, and Joseph E. Minor) *Water for the Southwest: Historical Survey and Guide to Historic Sites* (New York, 1973)

The Early History of Panna Maria, Texas (Lubbock, Tex., 1975)

The First Polish Americans: Silesian Settlements in Texas (College Station, Tex., 1979)

Historia najstarszych polskich osad w Ameryce [History of the Oldest Polish Settlements in America] (Wrocław, Poland, 1981)

The Polish Texans (San Antonio, 1982)

A Field Guide to American Windmills (Norman, 1985)

Building the Lone Star: An Illustrated Guide to Historic Sites (College Station, Tex., 1986)

Ghost Towns of Texas (Norman, 1986)

(with Billy R. Harrison) *Adobe Walls: The History and Archeology of the 1874 Trading Post* (College Station, Tex., 1986)

Lighthouses of Texas (College Station, Tex., 1991)

Blades in the Sky: Windmilling Through the Eyes of B.H. "Tex" Burdick (Lubbock, Tex., 1992)

(with Julie P. Baker) *The WPA Oklahoma Slave Narratives* (Norman, 1996)

(with Julie P. Baker) *Till Freedom Cried Out: Memories of Texas Slave Life* (College Station, Tex., 1997)

The Texas Red River Country: The Official Surveys of the Headwaters, 1876 (College Station, Tex., 1998)

North American Windmill Manufacturers' Trade Literature: A Descriptive Guide (Norman, 1999)

The 702 Model Windmill: Its Assembly, Installation and Use (Lubbock, Tex., 1999)

More Ghost Towns of Texas

T. Lindsay Baker

University of Oklahoma Press : NORMAN

Library of Congress Cataloging-in-Publication Data

Baker, T. Lindsay.
    More ghost towns of Texas / T. Lindsay Baker.
        p.   cm.
    Includes bibliographical references and index.
    ISBN 0–8061–3518–2 (alk. paper)
    1. Ghost towns—Texas—Guidebooks.   2. Historic sites—Texas—Guidebooks.   3. Texas—History, Local.
  4. Texas—Guidebooks.   I. Title.

  F387 .B353 2003
  917.6404'64—dc21

                                                                                                    2002040921

To my mother, Mary Lois Miller Baker,
who has always been patient with my various projects.

Contents

vii

Preface

Some of the most enjoyable research that I have ever undertaken has been visiting and documenting ghost towns. Twenty years ago, when I first began making field investigations for the initial *Ghost Towns of Texas* (1986), these sites drew me into their mystique, and I have never escaped their appeal. Unanswered questions about the places where people no longer live repeatedly draw me to the abandoned towns, empty houses, and scattered debris that document lives of the past.

When I wrote *Ghost Towns of Texas*, I felt that there would eventually be a sequel. During those years of research, I traveled over 5,000 miles within the state of Texas, visiting over 300 sites of former towns. The first book, however, was limited to just 86 sites. During my fieldwork and library research, I discovered far more places than I could include. In the meantime, colleagues, friends, and readers have been generous in suggesting additional sites that did not "make it" into the first book. During travels for other studies I stumbled across even more sites. My latest field research identified some "new" ghost towns, communities that died recently and, up to this time, have not been considered "ghost towns." It is even possible to find Texas ghost towns on the Internet at a website that critiques the places in my writings and in those of others, describing them as "Baker towns" and "non-Baker towns." Again I have found more abandoned towns than will fit into one book. So, how did I make the final selection?

Through the years I have used one definition for a ghost town: a town for which the reason for being no longer exists. This definition does not necessarily exclude populated sites. Many such places are totally abandoned with no residents whatever, but some of them do retain skeleton populations. Towns for which the reason for being no longer exists typically have died for economic reasons. They have been bypassed by

railroads or major roads and thus have been unable to compete with neighboring communities. The mineral resources on which they depended were depleted. Or they have ceased to serve as government seats. Some were destroyed by fire, flood, or—in one instance here—land subsidence along a seacoast. For whatever reason, these are places that no longer have a rational reason for existence.

The criteria for sites to be included in *More Ghost Towns of Texas* have remained the same as in the first book. Each site must meet all three requirements: 1) there must be tangible remains for visitors to see, 2) the sites must have public access, and 3) the locations must be distributed evenly across the state. All of the places described on the following pages have something to see: foundations, well-preserved buildings, abandoned structures, or maybe just a really interesting cemetery. The sites I have chosen are spread across the state so that at least one ghost town could be visited in day's trip from any point in Texas. At the time of writing, all sites in this book were either on public property or could be accessed by way of public rights-of-way such as county roads or highways. Private property may lie across a barbed-wire fence or off the roadway, so visitors should respect the rights of landowners and not trespass. Certainly the removal of any artifacts or materials from private or public land without permission is prohibited by law.

Just because places are identified in this book does not mean they are entirely safe for visitation. Children should always be attended, for abandoned towns are not playgrounds. Ghost-town travelers must be aware that mining- and petroleum-related sites may contain dangerous mine shafts, equipment, chemicals, gasses, and other hazardous materials or conditions. Abandoned buildings should not be entered, as often they are unstable and liable to collapse. They may also contain dangerous materials. Many of the roadways identified on the following pages have low water crossings that can fill with enough floodwater during rains to stall or wash away a motor vehicle. This is not to mention the possibility of becoming stuck in mud both on and off unpaved roads after precipitation. Ghost-town travelers are advised to carry extra tools, spare tires, bedding, water, food, and a first-aid kit when traveling to remote areas, especially during extremes of temperature. In addition, wild animals, insects, and plants have returned to many areas abandoned by humans. Visitors to these places should at all times be aware of the possibility of poisonous snakes, sometimes aggressive mammals, biting and stinging insects, and poison ivy or thorny plants.

A number of friends and colleagues have called to my attention sites that appear in this book. Without their knowledge of Texas and its history and their willingness to share their expertise, *More Ghost Towns of Texas* would have neither the breadth nor the depth that it has. Among these generous helpers have been Garnell A. Baker of Cleburne; LeAnna S. Biles, Dan K. Utley, Jim Steely, Jack Jackson, Gene Fowler, and Barry Hutcheson of Austin; John W. Crain of Dallas; Tom Christian of Claude; Tom Shelton of San Antonio; Dr. William C. Griggs of Houston; Dr. Diana D. Olien and Dr. Roger M. Olien of Odessa; Al Lowman of San Marcos; Jimmie Ruth Picquet of Kingsville; Calvin Smith, Thomas Charlton, and Rebecca Sharpless of Waco; Larry Francell of Alpine; Billy R. Harrison, Fred Rathjen, Jack T. Hughes, and Bill Green of Canyon; Barry Stone of Amarillo; Jason Schubert of Cimarron, New Mexico; H. Allen Anderson of Lubbock; Fain McDaniel of Sidney; and Dr. Bobby D. Weaver of Oklahoma City, Oklahoma.

Over the years many people have shared with me their historical documentation and photographs as well as their particular knowledge of the sites that appear in this book. Some of these people have been associated with libraries, archives, and museums, whereas others have been individuals who opened their personal files. Among the librarians, archivists, and curators who have gone out of their way to be of assistance have been Tom Shelton and Chris Floerke, University of Texas Institute of Texan Cultures, San Antonio; Kent Keeth, Ellen Brown, Michael Toon, and Dorothy Copeland, Texas Collection, Baylor University, Waco; Donaly Bryce and John Anderson, Texas State Library and Archives Commission, Austin; Betty Bustos, Claire Kuehn, Lynne Guy, Lisa Lambert, and Bill Green, Panhandle-Plains Historical Museum, Canyon; Janet Neugebauer, David Murrah, and Tai Kreidler, Southwest Collection, Texas Tech University, Lubbock; Dora Guerra, Daughters of the Republic of Texas Library, San Antonio; Verna Ann Wheeler, Crosby County Pioneer Memorial Museum, Crosbyton; Brenda Lincke Fisseler, Friench Simpson Memorial Library, Hallettsville; Daisy Harvill, Akin Regional Archives, Paris Junior College, Paris; Mrs. Peggy Fox, Harold B. Simpson History Center, Hill College, Hillsboro; Elizabeth Heath, Ward County Historical Commission, Monahans; Melleta Bell, Archives of the Big Bend, Sul Ross State University, Alpine; Kevin Ladd, Wallisville Heritage Park, Wallisville; Cindy Rosser, J. Conrad Dunagan Library, University of Texas of the Permian Basin, Odessa; Vanessa Vallez, West of the Pecos Museum, Pecos; Todd Houck, The Petroleum Museum, Midland; and Terri M. Grant, Border Heritage Center, El Paso Public Library, El Paso.

In addition to librarians, archivists, and curators, a large number of individuals have shared valuable and often one-of-a-kind documents and photographs with me as I researched this book. All of these individuals, whether they are historians, historic preservationists, genealogists, or general researchers, are working to preserve the Texas past. Among these colleagues have been William Osborn and John B. Meadows of Austin; Margaret Waring and Samuel J. C. Waring of Comanche; Glen Justice of Midland; Skipper Steely of Paris; Doug Braudaway of Del Rio; Dr. John Miller Morris of San Antonio; Viola Doebbler of Grapetown; G. R. LaMaster of Perryton; and Allen Ehresman of Endee, New Mexico.

Upon my arrival at various ghost towns, local experts helped me understand the remains that I found. Among these essential individuals have been Opal Hunt of Bradshaw; W. C. Smith III of Baytown; Carl Larson of Danevang; Mary Cross and Lee Morgan of Justiceburg; Mrs. Ernest Boulware of Kiomatia; Debby Opdyke of Lipscomb; Green Boyd of Medicine Mound; R. M. "Bob" Helton of Wichita Falls; James McReynolds of Chireno; Bob Siekman of Pyote; and Jim Herold of the Caddoan Mounds State Historical Park.

As I have grappled with roll after roll of photographs, boxes filled with papers, and a sometimes contrary computer, my wife, Julie, has encouraged me throughout this project. Not only has she supported my time "in the office" rather than with the family, but she has even prompted me into the field at times when I otherwise might have found less fatiguing activities. She reviewed the entire manuscript, making invaluable suggestions, and throughout its compilation has been an ever-dependable emotional support.

Whatever errors appear on the pages that follow lie completely in my hands. I encourage readers to let me know about other sites they have discovered and also to inform me of any mistakes or changes in status they find as they visit these fascinating places.

T. LINDSAY BAKER
Rio Vista, Texas

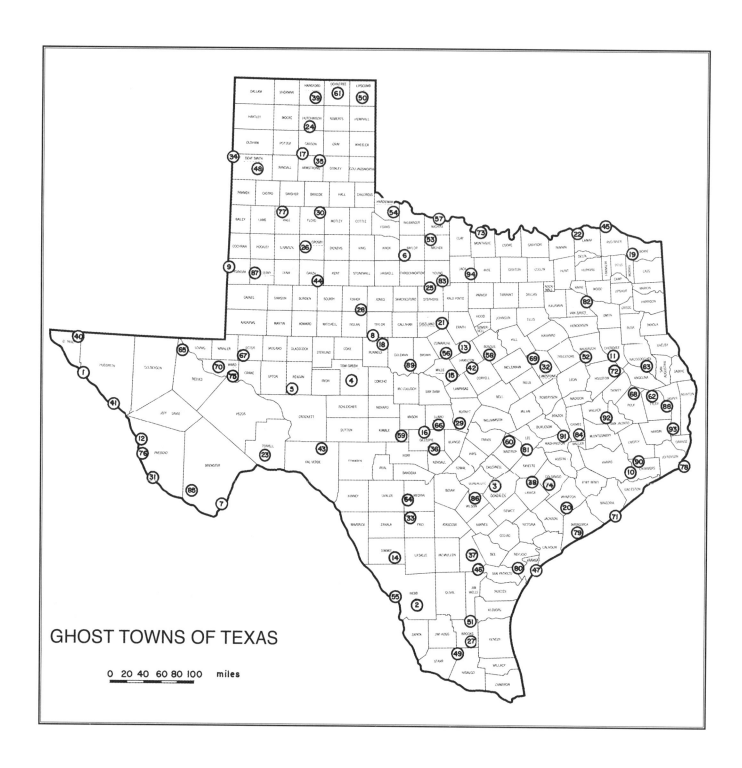

GHOST TOWNS OF TEXAS

0 20 40 60 80 100   miles

1. Acala
2. Aguilares
3. Belmont
4. Ben Ficklin
5. Best
6. Bomarton
7. Boquillas
8. Bradshaw
9. Bronco
10. Brownwood
11. Caddoan Mounds
12. Candelaria
13. Carlton
14. Catarina
15. Center City
16. Cherry Spring
17. Conway
18. Crews
19. Dalby Springs
20. Danevang
21. Desdemona
22. Direct
23. Dryden
24. Electric City
25. Eliasville
26. Emma
27. Encino
28. Eskota
29. Fairland
30. Flomot
31. Fort Leaton
32. Fort Parker
33. Frio Town
34. Glenrio
35. Goodnight
36. Grapetown
37. Gussettville
38. Hackberry
39. Hansford
40. Hueco Tanks
41. Indian Hot Springs
42. Ireland
43. Juno
44. Justiceburg
45. Kiomatia
46. Lagarto
47. Lamar
48. La Plata
49. La Reforma
50. Lipscomb
51. Los Olmos
52. Magnolia
53. Mankins
54. Medicine Mound
55. Minera, Santo Tomás, and Dolores
56. Newburg
57. Newtown
58. Norse
59. Noxville
60. Oak Hill
61. Ochiltree
62. Ogden
63. Oil Springs
64. Old D'Hanis
65. Orla
66. Oxford
67. Penwell
68. Pluck
69. Prairie Hill
70. Pyote
71. Quintana
72. Ratcliff
73. Red River Station
74. Rock Island
75. Royalty
76. Ruidosa
77. Runningwater
78. Sabine
79. St. Francisville
80. St. Mary's of Aransas
81. Serbin
82. Silver Lake
83. South Bend
84. Stoneham
85. Study Butte
86. Sutherland Springs
87. Tokio
88. Town Bluff
89. Trickham
90. Wallisville
91. Washington-on-the-Brazos
92. Waverly
93. Weiss's Bluff
94. Wizard Wells

More Ghost Towns of Texas

Looking northeast along an irrigation canal toward the center of Acala. Photograph by the author, 2000.

Acala

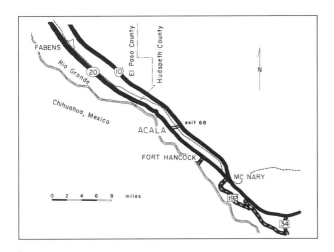

Straddling what once was the coast-to-coast Bankhead Highway, Acala came into existence early in the twentieth century. It was supported by irrigated cotton crops in the lower El Paso Valley of the Rio Grande where it passed through Hudspeth County. The victim of eco-nomic changes, Acala prospered and then withered away quickly.

The valley of the Rio Grande above and below El Paso has been a site of agricultural cultivation since long before written records. The earliest Spanish visitors to the area reported that Native people used Rio Grande floodwater to irrigate plots of corn, squash, and beans. During the late nineteenth century, while settlers began constructing large canals to carry river water to more distant fields, where they raised wheat, alfalfa, fruit, and vegetables for the market. All this time, however, the land downstream from El Paso, around what would soon become Acala, remained a scrub-brush desert. That all changed with the introduction of a new crop—cotton.

In 1917 three agricultural entrepreneurs, Louis J. Ivey, J. B. Dale, and Will T. Owen, combined their resources to plant experimental cotton plots in the lower El Paso Valley. The trial produced twelve bales of cotton from their eight acres, which they considered a superb rate of production.

The next year they purchased six hundred acres of scrub-brush land below Tornillo. There they planted and irrigated cotton, with a yield of 686 bales. The success, at a time when cotton prices were high because of industrial needs during World War I, led to a boom in cotton-raising in the lower El Paso Valley.

A former rice farmer from Matagorda County, Texas, named W. T. Young came to El Paso in 1904. There for a number of years he operated a sand, gravel, and building-stone business. His trade slowed during World War I, leaving him with hungry mule teams to feed but little work for them to do. Young turned his dilemma into a solution by purchasing a large acreage of cheap desert land in the Rio Grande valley near the Southern Pacific Railroad tracks about thirteen miles below Tornillo. Using his mules to clear the brush and break the soil for the first time, he planted the Acala variety of cotton seed that was imported from Mexico. The fields proved fertile, and Young earned a handsome profit from his fluffy, white fiber, which was much in demand by textile mills during the war. He raised so much cotton, in fact, that he built his own cotton gin to remove seeds, stems, and leaves from the lint. In time other farmers joined Young in the area, which came to be known as Acala from the Mexican variety of cotton. Young himself became a cotton breeder.

A northwest-southeast road through the new community of Acala connected El Paso with Fort Hancock. During the 1910s this road became known as the Bankhead Highway and was eventually declared U.S. Highway 80. This major highway, in conjunction with a siding from a transcontinental railway, provided ideal opportunities to ship Acala's irrigated agriculture. Acala in the 1920s and '30s boomed into a town that boasted a general store, tourist courts, a restaurant, a gasoline service station and garage, and a post office. By 1929 Acala had an estimated fifty residents. This number dropped during the Great Depression of the 1930s but rose again to an estimated one hundred during the late 1950s.

Then the number of residents dropped again. Increased mechanization of cotton-raising had reduced the need for field laborers to till and pick the crop, so most of the farm workers who had lived in and around Acala moved elsewhere during the 1950s and '60s. The railway removed its spur to the town, and then Interstate Highway 10 replaced the old, two-lane U.S. Highway 80 through Acala, bypassing the town. Today Acala contains about two dozen scattered residences; the former tourist court, store, and restaurant; an abandoned garage; the ruins of the adobe building that housed W. T. Young's cotton gin; and several impressive irrigation canals that still carry Rio Grande water to agricultural fields of cotton, alfalfa, and other crops.

LOCATION: *Acala is located in Hudspeth County on Texas State Highway 20 at a point that is 4.8 miles northwest of Fort Hancock and 13.2 miles southeast of Tornillo. Acala can also be reached via Interstate Highway 10. Take exit 68 and drive 1.3 miles southwestward on the roughly graded county Acala Road through open range and across the tracks of the Southern Pacific Railroad. This road will intersect with Texas State Highway 20 at a point that is 0.1 miles southeast of the townsite.*

Aguilares

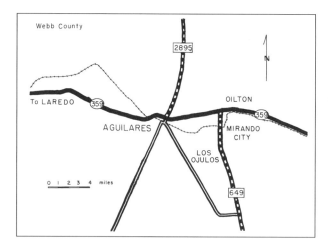

The town of Aguilares sprang to life in the 1880s on a siding of the Texas-Mexican Railway east of Laredo in Webb County. Not only was the town's economy based on ranching, it was even named after a local pioneer livestock-raising family. Aguilares served as a market for the surrounding ranch country before improved highways directed its business to other towns.

An abandoned Laredo city bus gradually deteriorating in a vacant lot in Aguilares. Photograph by the author, 2000.

Locario, José, Francisco, Próspero, and Librador Aguilar settled on ranches east of Laredo during the early 1870s. They created a ranch headquarters known as Rancho los Aguilares. Then in 1881 the Texas-Mexican Railway expanded westward through the Aguilares family holdings, connecting Corpus Christi with Laredo and the Mexican National Railroad across the Rio Grande. The line became a principal link between the railroads of Mexico and the Southern Pacific Railway system in the United States. Aguilares originally served as a water stop for steam locomotives hauling freight and passengers, but the railroad town almost automatically became a distribution center for the surrounding ranches.

As early as 1890 Aguilares had received its first post office but it closed within a matter of months, reopening only in 1895. By 1907 the community had several stores and two schools. Catholic priests visited from Hebronville or Laredo to conduct religious services. In that year the schools had

eighty-nine pupils and two teachers. An exaggerated report claimed 1,500 residents for Aguilares in 1910, but an estimate of three hundred residents in 1914 is probably closer to the truth. As groundwater in the area was not potable for humans, all drinking water had to be hauled in by the railroad.

An unexpected story of buried treasure comes from this ranching community. According to stories heard by Texas ghost-town enthusiast Grover C. Ramsey, it was near Aguilares that a cowboy's horse stepped into a hole and down into a rotted wooden box. The cow puncher discovered gold coins in the buried container, stuffed all that he could into his pockets and hat, and rode away with his loot. He returned to the area the next day to load up more but never could relocate the hole full of money.

Although Aguilares received an infusion of people when oil was discovered in nearby Mirando City in 1921, by the end of the 1930s its population dwindled to an estimated ten residents. The post office closed in 1930. Then when Texas State Highway 359 was rebuilt in the area, its route shifted three blocks north—away from the remnant of the commercial district—essentially bypassing the town. The older concrete highway still parallels the railway tracks through the former town.

Today Aguilares still lingers, but with only a handful of residents. Most of the town stands abandoned. The site has multiple vacated residences, a historic brick school that has been converted into a dwelling, a closed store, a church marked only by its still-standing stucco entryway, a maintained cemetery, and a grid of paved and gravel streets that are still marked by street signs but pass mostly vacant lots, foundations, debris, and disturbed ground that marks the sites of former structures.

LOCATION: *Aguilares is located in Webb County on Texas State Highway 359 at its intersection with Farm Road 2895 at a point that is 26.5 miles east of downtown Laredo and 6.9 miles west of Oilton.*

Playground swings outside the long quiet Belmont school. Photograph by the author, 1999.

Belmont

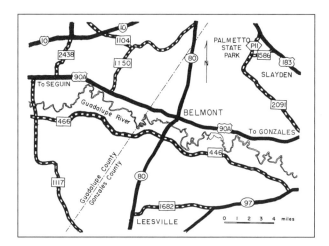

Located on a slight rise overlooking the Guadalupe River valley, Belmont has lived astride an important east-west thoroughfare since its founding in the 1840s. Originally called Centerville and established as a stagecoach stop, the community lies midway between Gonzales and Seguin on what historically was known as the San Antonio-Gonzales Road.

Due to its location near a ferry crossing on the Guadalupe River, Belmont gradually grew to local importance. It received its first post office in 1848, and by the 1860s the area had enough people to muster a ninety-man company in the Confederate Army. The community was more noted, however, for providing a volunteer relief party that carried aid to far West Texas. There the volunteers cared for defeated members of the ill-fated Confederate Texan expedition that in 1862 had attempted to invade Union-held New Mexico.

The construction of the Galveston, Harrisburg and San Antonio Railway through Belmont in the early 1880s insured years of future prosperity. More and more people moved to the Belmont area, giving it a population of one hundred. Enterprises at the time included various stores, a steam sawmill, two ferries, a cotton gin, daily mail service, a flour mill, several saloons, a blacksmith, a wheelwright, a school, and both Baptist and Methodist churches. People living on farms and ranches in the surrounding area supported these businesses in Belmont. Growth continued and the population reached a high of about 125 around the turn of the twentieth century.

Belmont is best known in the annals of Texas as the site of the so-called Battle of Belmont that took place in 1901. Events leading up to the incident focus on Gregorio Cortez, a Mexican ranch hand who became a folk hero among Mexican

Gregorio Cortez, Mexican-American folk hero, who shot Gonzales County sheriff Robert M. Glover near Belmont in 1901. Courtesy of the Texas State Library and Archives Commission.

Americans during the early twentieth century. On 12 June 1901, Karnes County sheriff W. T. "Brack" Morris and two deputies approached Cortez and his brother on a ranch west of Kenedy. In an incident sparked by miscommunication between English and Spanish speakers, Sheriff Morris shot and wounded Gregorio's brother. Cortez then fired a shot that killed the sheriff and fled the scene on foot.

Two days later Gregorio Cortez showed up at the home of Martin and Refugia Robledo, who lived on Henry Schnabel's property outside Belmont. Sheriff Robert M. Glover of Gonzales County, a friend of Sheriff Morris, had interrogated members of Cortez's family just after the shooting. From them he learned that Gregorio

would likely seek shelter at the Robledo home, so he headed back to Gonzales County, organizing a posse on the way. By the time Cortez arrived at the Robledo house near Belmont, Sheriff Glover and his posse were already in the neighborhood. The sheriff's posse included property owner Henry Schnabel, who was a county constable.

Sheriff Glover and his men rushed the Robledo house from several directions, shooting their guns. From the porch Cortez returned the fire as three other men ran from the house into the brush. Glover and Cortez kept firing at each other until the sheriff fell from his horse. Then Cortez took cover in the woods, but the posse kept firing into the house, where only a woman and some boys were hiding. Somehow in the fray one of the posse members accidentally shot Henry Schnabel. Cortez made good his escape—despite bloodhounds on his trail—walking a hundred miles before securing a horse. Lawmen eventually apprehended him near Laredo. After years in prison and multiple trials and appeals, in 1913 Gregorio Cortez received a conditional pardon from Texas Governor Oscar B. Colquit.

The otherwise quiet town of Belmont maintained its size into the early years of the twentieth century, but the depopulation of the surrounding rural area due to technological advancements in agriculture spelled its doom. By 1937 the town had only seven school-age children, and most places of business had closed. Today the community has a combination store-filling station, a volunteer fire department, and an active church, but most of the townsite lies abandoned—a derelict stone commercial building, a vacant brick school, and concrete footings that support the impressive engine of a cotton gin.

LOCATION: *Belmont lies at the intersection of U.S. Highway 90A and Texas State Highway 80 in northwestern Gonzales County at a point that is 17.7 miles east of Seguin and 14.4 miles west of Gonzales. The Belmont Cemetery—with an impressive Woodman of the World marker that comemorates Henry Schnabel's death in the 1901 Battle of Belmont—is on the north side of Belmont, west of Texas State Highway 80 just 0.3 miles north of where that road intersects with U.S. Highway 90A.*

Ben Ficklin

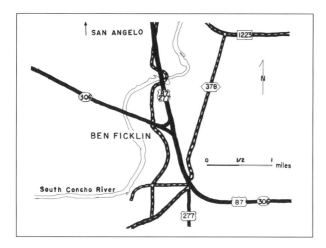

Founded in 1873 at a fresh-flowing spring along-side the stagecoach road between San Antonio and El Paso, the town of Ben Ficklin washed away in a high flood on the Concho River in August 1882, never to be rebuilt. Today only some archaeological evidence and the town's cemetery, which contains the burials of flood victims, mark the site of the original seat of Tom Green County.

Two communities sprang up near Fort Concho, the military garrison established on the Concho River in 1867. The one nearest the post took the name San Angela and became the "scab town" filled with saloons, bordellos, and gambling dens that were frequented by soldiers. The second was Ben Ficklin, which was near a major stagecoach stop and outfitting point located upstream from the fort on the South Concho River. The name Ben Ficklin was borrowed from Benjamin F. Ficklin, who initially had operated the stagecoach line.

When Tom Green County was organized in 1875, the town of Ben Ficklin was chosen as its seat of government. Eventually local residents erected a two-story stone courthouse and a stone jail on a point overlooking the river. Around the courthouse they built a loose assemblage of stores and residences. Some of the buildings were wooden, but most were adobe. In time the community had a subscription school, a union Sunday school serving all denominations, and plots of land that has been donated for the construction of churches. In addition to various stores, there were blacksmith shops and the logistical base for the extensive stagecoach services that extended west-

ward to El Paso and eastward to San Antonio. Little did the residents of this burgeoning community know that in August 1882 their town would cease to exist.

The summer of 1882 was unusually wet. Grass for grazing was green and the soil in all the stream valleys remained saturated with moisture. Then on the evening of 23 August 1882, heavy rains fell into the valleys of Dove Creek, Spring Creek, the Middle Concho River, and the South Concho River, all of which converged above Ben Ficklin. By dawn the next morning the water had started rising, and it continued to rise until the middle of the day. More quickly than people could believe possible, their homes and businesses were surrounded or covered by water that rose an estimated forty feet. Wooden houses lifted off their foundations and floated away. Adobe structures dissolved as if they had been built from sugar cubes.

An estimated sixty-five people drowned in this flood—the greatest natural disaster in the history of Tom Green County. In a situation representative of the incident, members of the Metcalfe family and others sought refuge in the wood frame Metcalfe home. C. D. Foote drove to their home in his carriage to rescue them, but Mrs. Metcalfe mistakenly thought that the water had reached its highest point and believed they would be safe. Her daughter Zemula told Foote, "My place is with mother." The waters continued to rise. Next, S. C. Robertson approached the Metcalfe house in his carriage. This time the occupants did attempt to leave in the vehicle, but the horses balked at the rising waters. The stranded residents then retreated by way of a ladder to the roof of the house, which began to shake and was soon floating downstream in the torrent, carrying on its roof seven humans. It eventually broke in half, sinking into the waters. Only Robertson survived.

The aftermath of the flood was devastating to the survivors. *The Tom Green Times* in nearby San Angela reported, "Ben Ficklin, our county seat, is almost wholly destroyed." It went on to describe how the Concho River, spread two to three hundred yards beyond its banks, carried with it "chairs, goods, trunks, boxes, and furniture of all kinds," as well as noting that "hundreds of carcasses of sheep and other stock are scattered over the prairies" together with "wagons, blankets, clothing and all sorts of furniture."

The grave for Zemula L. Metcalfe, a teenage victim of the 1882 flood that washed away the town of Ben Ficklin. Photograph by the author, 2000.

After the great flood, most of the surviving residents of Ben Ficklin moved downstream to San Angela, which soon assumed the position of county seat. The next year it received a post office under the name of San Angelo. Since that time San Angelo has thrived, becoming a major marketing and distribution center for West Texas. The site of Ben Ficklin has been lost to all but local history buffs. It is marked only by the rock-walled cemetery and historical markers located near a large highway interchange on the south side of present-day San Angelo.

LOCATION: *The site of Ben Ficklin is in the general area of the modern highway interchange for U.S. Highway 87/277 and Loop 306 on the south side of San Angelo in Tom Green County. To reach the Ben Ficklin Cemetery, with its graves of the 1882 flood* victims, *drive south from San Angelo on U.S. Highway 87/277 and take Ben Ficklin Road, the first exit south of the Concho River Bridge. Proceed 0.4 miles on the paved southbound access road to the cemetery and several historical markers, which are located at a sharp westward turn in the access road. To view a 1936 Texas Centennial historical monument for the Ben Ficklin townsite, continue from the cemetery about 0.2 miles on the access road to the intersection with paved Ben Ficklin Road. Turn south on Ben Ficklin Road under the Loop 306 overpass and drive 0.2 miles to the grey granite marker just west of the road.*

Best

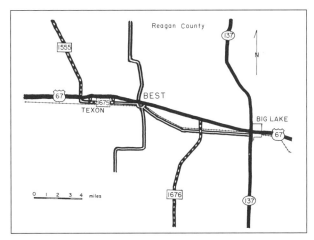

Best was an oil field boomtown that served the Big Lake Oil Field. It grew up around a railway siding into a town of 3,500 residents in 1924–25. As petroleum production began declining in subsequent years, however, these inhabitants moved on to other locales, and by 1945 Best had no more than a dozen families. Today the site lies abandoned.

When the Kansas City, Mexico and Orient Railway laid tracks across Reagan County in 1912, it placed a railroad siding ten miles west of Big Lake. It called the siding "Best" in honor of Tom Best, a company stockholder. Local ranchers in the sparsely settled country used the siding to ship livestock to market in railway cars.

The hulk of a 1950s automobile rusting away amid the ruins of Best. Photograph by the author, 2000.

Then on 28 May 1923, oil-well driller Carl Cromwell struck petroleum on land belonging to the University of Texas just four miles west of the Best siding. This discovery led to a frenzy of oil-well drilling, and the land on both sides of the Best siding became the most important local supply center for the field. A land-development company laid out a town it called Best, scraping dirt streets around creosote-bush-covered city blocks that sold quickly at inflated prices. The promoters thought that oil might be found beneath the townsite, so they reserved a space at the center of each block for one well.

Thousands of people—mostly men—flooded into Best, which had become the focal point of the oil field. An entrepreneur drilled two water wells on the hill just south of the town and laid supply lines to the wooden buildings and tents that sprang up from nowhere. Another businessman set up a circus tent and filled it with cots, renting them in eight-hour shifts to working men. Others erected tents and cheap wooden buildings in a large gravel pit, creating more flop houses as well as brothels, bars, and gambling dens.

Because Best was never incorporated, the Reagan County sheriff's department provided the only law enforcement. The officers used a still-standing concrete cubicle that had three iron-barred windows and an iron door as their jail. When the one cell was occupied, they handcuffed prisoners to a heavy chain outside. People knew this rough town in its heyday as "the town with the Best name in the world and the worst reputation." One former resident declared that "all things were said to stick, sting, or stink." Even so, Best was a place for people to make money, and its once prosperous business district reportedly included four hotels, grocery and mercantile stores, several drug stores, a school, cafés, auto repair garages, filling stations, a post office, oil-related businesses, hairdressers and barbers, two motion-picture theaters, and several dry cleaners—as there was not enough water for regular laundries to operate.

When oil production declined, the people who had inhabited Best disappeared. Former resident Clyde Ragsdale recalled, "They departed in Model Ts and Dodges and Studebakers of the era, all their worldly possessions stacked upon the top and tied to the sides. . . . Thus began the great exodus from what had been the promised land." Oil-field historian Martin Schwettman reported that by 1945 all that remained of Best was the post office, a general store, a lumberyard, an oil-field supply-house, and the jail, as well as maybe two dozen inhabitants. Today only one ranch house remains occupied at Best; the remainder of the former town lies completely abandoned. The entire area is covered with debris from and foundations of former buildings, broken glass and ceramics, unidentified metal objects, cast-off appliances, bed springs, rusted hulks of automobiles and trucks, and the empty concrete jail cell.

A prisoner's eye view through the barred window of the concrete jail at Best. Photograph by the author, 2000.

View of the sanctuary of the now empty St. John Catholic Church in Bomarton. Photograph by the author, 2000.

Much of this wreckage provides habitation for rattlesnakes and other desert animals.

LOCATION: *Best lies on the south side of U.S. Highway 67 where that road intersects gravel Reagan County Road 113 at a point that is 9.4 miles west of Big Lake and 19.2 miles east of Rankin. Visitors should be wary of rattlesnakes, stinging insects, sharp objects, and thorny plants. Visitors might also be interested in the abandoned oil field company town of Texon, just 4.1 miles west on Farm Road 1675.*

Bomarton

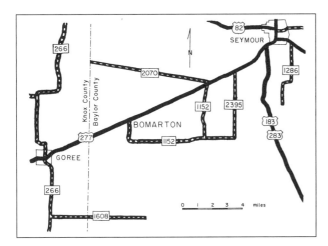

In 1906 land promoters created the town of Bomarton beside a railway line in Baylor County

in West Texas. The agricultural town thrived for a few decades in the early twentieth century before slowly declining into a dispersed rural community. Visitors today find the place visually dominated by two impressive but abandoned seventy-year-old buildings: a large red brick Catholic church with a tall steeple and an art deco school complex constructed from beautiful stone.

Bomarton owes its creation to the Wichita Valley Railroad that was built from Seymour toward Abilene in 1906. In June of that year the Wichita Valley Townsite Company auctioned lots for a new town on an open field beside the tracks. The only buildings at that time were two unpainted residences and a small lumberyard. Promoters named the place Bomarton in honor of D. T. Bomar, a stockholder in the railroad company.

While initial town lots were selling, developers divided up local ranching land to sell to farmers. Farmers could buy rural acreage around Bomarton for $7.00 to $15.00 an acre, whereas cultivated land in more developed areas of Texas sold for $40.00 to $100.00 per acre. This radical difference in price encouraged well-established families living in such areas as Waco or Hallettsville to sell their farms and reinvest the proceeds in larger holdings in West Texas. Real estate agents working either on their own or for the townsite company advertised in central Texas newspapers to promote the sale of land in Baylor County. A number of the promotions targeted areas that had been settled by Czech immigrants, leading to numerous sales to Slavic Texans. One promoter even scheduled weekly railway excursions from Waco to Bomarton in order to promote the new farmlands.

Two years of heavier-than-usual rains made Baylor County look like a garden of Eden, and the chance to buy such land at bargain prices appealed to many central Texas farmers. What was previously an open prairie beside the railroad tracks had by 1920 grown into a substantial town with 580 inhabitants. It boasted a large public school, several churches, lumberyards, automobile dealers, general stores, drugstores, a hotel, restaurants, a confectionary shop, a grain elevator, farm implement dealers, and even its own semiprofessional baseball team. In addition, the town supported two brass bands—one for the

A formerly fine home in Bomarton, its porch roof collapsed across its front. Photograph by the author, 2000.

English-speaking residents and another for the Czech residents.

Bomarton maintained a population of about 600 through 1940, but then it began a decline from which it never recovered. By 1960 the town dwindled to only 150 people, and today it is virtually deserted. The consolidation of agriculture in the 1940s through the 1960s devastated the town, when small family farms gave way to large, consolidated operations. Family after family moved away as the easy access to paved highways drew local commerce to Seymour and Munday, each larger and only about a dozen miles away on the newly paved highways. Today the majority of the surviving houses stand empty, as do the red brick St. John Catholic Church and the handsome stone school.

LOCATION: *Bomarton is located on both sides of U.S. Highway 277 at its intersection with Farm Road 1152 in Baylor County at a point that is 11.7 miles southwest of Seymour and 12.5 miles northeast of Munday. The Bomarton Cemetery, which lies on Farm Road 1152 at a point that is 1.0 miles south of U.S. Highway 277, is striking in its arrangement. A large open rectangle of grass divides the Catholic cemetery on the south from the Protestant cemetery on the north. Separate gates for each area allow funeral parties and visitors to enter either section without crossing the other.*

A cotton farmer's adobe house, erected at Boquillas about 1920, is one of the last surviving intact structures from the town. Photograph by the author, 2000.

Boquillas

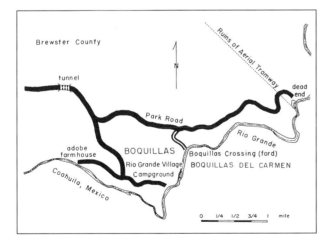

Boquillas, located on the flood plain of the Rio Grande in Big Bend National Park, has seen human activity for hundreds of years. Meaning "little mouths" in Spanish, the place-name refers to the mouths of several streams that flow into the Rio Grande from the steep Sierra del Carmen mountains in Mexico. Land-wise, the name refers to settlements on both sides of the Rio Grande as well as surrounding areas eight to ten miles north and south of the river. Rock art, stone tools, and depressions worn into rock outcroppings from the grinding of food document long-term occupation of the area by Native people.

The Mexican-U.S. Boundary Commission became familiar with the area in 1852 and so did Texan surveyors in the early 1880s. Mexican and American people began to occupy the area of Boquillas, Texas, in 1883 after the discovery of silver ore in the Sierra del Carmen south of the Rio Grande. The first known documented resident of Boquillas, Texas, was D. E. "Ed" Lindsey, who came to the area soon after 1890 as a U.S. Customs agent to check ore shipments crossing the Rio Grande. In addition to his official duties, by 1894 Lindsey had opened a store on the north bank of the river to serve miners, livestock-raisers, and teamsters from both sides of the river. Soon he began irrigating crops on the fertile floodplain with water diverted from the Rio Grande. He was even involved in mail delivery. Because the mail service through Marathon, Texas, on the Southern Pacific Railroad was faster than Mexican mail service over the rugged Sierra del Carmen, people living in Boquillas, Mexico, began using Marathon as their mailing address. Ed Lindsey provided a free service by transporting mail in his wagon on weekly freight runs between Marathon and Boquillas. In 1896 he petitioned the Post Office Department for a "Special Office" at Boquillas, reporting that the area on both sides of the river had a combined population of 1,300 people.

Ed Lindsey was not the only entrepreneur attracted to Boquillas. German immigrant Max A. Ernst in 1898 set up shop about eight miles northwest of the settlement on the river at a water hole known as Big Tinaja, or La Noria. His store thrived because of its position on the ore road from the river to Marathon. In addition to keeping his store, Ernst also became justice of the peace, county commissioner, notary public, and was even elected as a trustee for a small school near his store. In 1903 he relocated the Boquillas post office to his store, operating it with his other enterprises until his mysterious death by gunshot in 1908.

Lindsey and Ernst were the two most successful businessmen in the Boquillas area, but there was no shortage of competition. Down on the river in 1900, Martin Solis acquired a section of land he had been leasing for seven years, on which he opened a store to compete with that of Max Ernst. Solis eventually turned the store and an irrigated farm over to his son, Benito, who in turn sold it to his son, Tomas, who ran it until 1911. Yet another person, Jesse Deemer, opened a store at Boquillas. In partnership with a Marathon merchant, Deemer operated his store until 1916.

Minerals from the Mexican side of the Rio Grande were the economic lifeblood of the twin towns of Boquillas. Not only did Mexican miners extract ore at several places in the Sierra del Carmen, but for a while they even refined some of it in a crude smelter on the banks of the river in Boquillas, Mexico. The ores contained various combinations of silver, lead, and zinc, of which silver was the most valuable. Most of the ore was not refined, but was shipped, along with some of the refined metals, northward through Boquillas, Texas, to the railroad a hundred miles north in Marathon. With hundreds of people employed at the mines and smelter, merchants on the Texas

A wooden tower and steel cables from the aerial tramway near Boquillas, which in the early twentieth century transported mineral ore across the Rio Grande from Mexico to a terminal on the American side. Photograph by the author, 2000.

side of Boquillas earned handsome profits from selling food, clothing, and the other necessities of life.

In 1909 the Consolidated Kansas City Smelting and Refining Company built an aerial tramway from the Puerto Rico Mine in the Sierra del Carmen in Mexico, across the waters of the Rio Grande to Boquillas, Texas, and an additional four miles inland to a terminal. From there, teamsters driving teams of mules and burros hauled ore overland in wagons to the railroad in Marathon. Operating until 1919, the tramway provided an ingenious method of transporting the ore over rough terrain and across the river. Its ninety ore buckets could move seven-and-a-half tons of ore per hour. Now abandoned for over eighty years, its cables and mostly collapsed wooden towers may still be seen.

The long-profitable mining operations just across the river encouraged a number of Americans to acquire land in the Boquillas area for speculative purposes, leading to an increased population of Americans near the border. In 1916, during border troubles concurrent with the Mexican Revolution, Boquillas became the target for a raid by fighters from Mexico. On the night of 5 May 1916, a party of about eighty armed Mexicans crossed the Rio Grande into Texas and split into two groups. The larger party headed toward Glenn

Springs, a supply camp on a ranch ten miles northwest of the river, where they looted a general store and killed several Americans, including three members of the U.S. 14th Cavalry. Just after dawn on 6 June 1916 the smaller group struck Boquillas. Jesse Deemer and his black clerk, Monroe Payne, found themselves overwhelmed by armed attackers. By midmorning the group that had devastated Glenn Springs arrived at Boquillas, taking Deemer and Payne hostage and forcing them across the river. They were later rescued.

After most of the mines in the Sierra del Carmen were closed, the twin towns of Boquillas declined. The population dwindled, leaving only a handful of people to raise irrigated cotton on the river flats. During the 1920s and '30s, Mrs. Maria G. Sada was the last and probably the best-known of the storekeepers to serve the Boquillas area. Coming from the interior of Mexico, she met and wed her husband, Juan, in Boquillas in 1901. Mrs. Sada soon opened a small general store and café, tended a herd of goats and a flock of chickens, and farmed a small plot on the floodplain while her husband engaged in mining across the river. She became known far and wide for the delicious meals she prepared for the occasional visitors to Boquillas. After the death of Juan in 1936, Maria Sada moved to Del Rio to live with an adopted son.

With the creation of the Big Bend National Park in 1935, Boquillas changed forever. The federal government over the next several years acquired title to all of the land in the park and ended active irrigated agriculture. The National Park Service built new paved roads that allowed for the first easy vehicular access to Boquillas. Former cotton fields became a public campground in what today is known as the Rio Grande Village. Many existing structures, like the Sada store, disappeared, although a handful survived. The evidence of historic human habitation at Boquillas, Texas, however, can be seen in the non-native Bermuda grass that was introduced by American farmers, the large cottonwood and black locust trees planted in rows alongside former irrigation ditches, the use of ditch-delivered water to irrigate lawns in the present campground, the ruins of the aerial tramway, a handful of protected historic structures, and the continued use of the Boquillas

Mexican men with boats, burros, and horses for carrying people across the shallow Rio Grande between Mexico and the United States at Boquillas. Photograph by the author, 2000.

Crossing on the Rio Grande by citizens of both the United States and Mexico.

LOCATION: *The site of Boquillas, centered within the present-day Rio Grande Village Campground, is 20.3 miles east-southeast of Park Headquarters on a paved National Park Service road. A 1920s adobe farmhouse stands preserved at the extreme west end of the campground. A gravel road leading 0.3 miles to Boquillas Crossing turns south from the paved park road 1.4 miles east from the entry to the Rio Grande Village. On most days Mexican nationals will, for modest fee, carry people across the ford in rowboats or on horses and burros. These entrepreneurs will also provide transportation the short distance to Boquillas, Mexico, by pickup truck, horse, or burro. Back on the U.S. side, a parking area—for a rough foot trail that leads to the ruins of the 1909 aerial tramway—lies 2.8 miles east of the Rio Grande Village entry road. The steel cables from the tramway pass under the paved park road that is 3.9 miles east of the entry road into the Rio Grande Village area. Just upstream from Boquillas is the Hot Springs site, where park visitors still bathe in hot mineral spring waters. Its rough 1.9-mile access road, passable only in high-clearance vehicles, begins 1.6 miles west of the entry road to the Rio Grande Village.*

Bradshaw

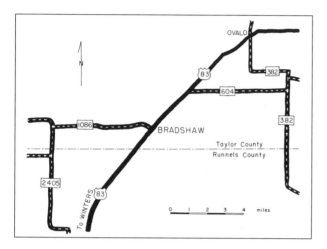

The story of Bradshaw starts with an earlier town, Audra. Located in southern Taylor County, Audra had its beginnings as a rural community in about 1900, when it received a post office that served a rural area southwest of Tuscola and just north of the Runnels County line. Audra had a general store, hotel, Methodist church, and school. Three partners, C. M. Hunt, Fred Robinson, and Frank Sheppard, established the store, but Hunt later purchased the others' shares. It was one of these partners, Frank Sheppard, who gave the town its name—that of his daughter Audra.

Audra seemed poised for further growth, but then the Santa Fe Railway, in 1909, bypassed it in constructing a railroad line between Ballinger and Abilene. Local rancher C. W. Bradshaw provided the site for a new town alongside the tracks just two miles east of Audra. Merchants and residents moved their wooden stores and houses across the prairie to the new community, which the steel rails connected to the rest of the world. C. M. Hunt put his store, rebuilt in brick, on the main street of the new town. He called it the Audra

Mercantile Company in recognition of its origin in the earlier town. Movers relocated both the hotel and the Methodist church from Audra to Bradshaw. Soon other enterprises appeared in the new town, among them two cotton gins and two additional general stores, plus a meat market, a drugstore, a blacksmith shop, and a hardware store. The Bradshaw bank began in the back of the Audra Mercantile Company, but before long it occupied its own brick building, which today stands abandoned.

The first school opened at Bradshaw in 1910. The small wooden structure stood west of town in the general area of the present-day cemetery. The first two teachers were overwhelmed by the number of children and had to teach the older pupils to instruct the younger ones. The following year a three-room brick school opened in town. It offered the students extra-curricular sports activities, including football and basketball.

During the 1920s important changes began in American agriculture that led to a general depopulation of many rural areas. Agricultural commodity prices crashed in 1921, and the Great Depression followed in 1929. Through foreclosures many farm properties ended up in the hands of financial institutions. At the same time, farm tractors with internal combustion engines made it possible for just one individual tractor driver to cultivate fields that had previously required the labor of as many as ten families using mules as draft animals. Small farms, which had dotted the countryside for years, disappeared as crews demolished farmhouses and removed fences so that men with tractors could work broad expanses of fields. As farm families left the land for the towns and cities, agriculturally based Bradshaw and towns like it began withering away. The rural population base that had been their reason for existence was lost.

From a population of 450 in its heyday in the 1920s, Bradshaw over the next decades shrank to only a shadow of its former self. By 1988 the population was about twenty-five, with children going to school in Tuscola. In 2000, Bradshaw consisted of about half a dozen occupied houses and as many abandoned. Visitors could drive the square grid plan of the town's streets. Foundations, uneven ground, and debris marked the sites of some seventy-five former homes. The

The display windows and entrance of a collapsing commercial building in Bradshaw. Photograph by the author, 2000.

commercial district had only one operating business enterprise—a fork-lift pad fabrication shop. The area had many abandoned buildings: stores, a bank, a filling station, an automobile garage, a church, and residences. The earthen embankment that once supported the rails of the Santa Fe Railway runs parallel to U.S. Highway 83 on the southeast side of the townsite.

LOCATION: *Bradshaw is on Farm Road 1086 at its intersection with U.S. Highway 83 in southern Taylor County at a point that is 10.5 miles north of Winters, 10.1 miles southwest of Tuscola, and 28.6 miles south of Abilene. The site is about 1.5 miles north of the Runnels-Taylor county line. To visit the Bradshaw Cemetery, drive southwest 0.8 miles on U.S. Highway 83 from its intersection with Farm Road 1086, and then turn sharply to the north on gravel Taylor County Road 622, proceeding 0.5 miles farther to the cemetery.*

Bronco

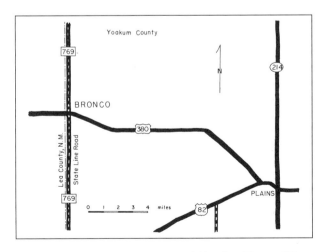

The remains of Bronco straddle the Texas-New Mexico state line in Yoakum County, west of Plains and southwest of Lubbock. The beginnings of Bronco can be traced to 1903 and the activities of a cowboy-turned-storekeeper.

Westward over building foundations to the Field family's post office-general store in Bronco. Photograph by the author, 2000.

Herschel Robert "Gravy" Field had come from his home in Arkansas to West Texas as a cowboy, where in the 1890s he worked on several large ranches, including the XIT Ranch. He had decided to move west to Arizona, but on the way he was attracted by the quality of the grazing lands he observed in extreme western Yoakum County. Field was not the first person so drawn to the area, for the nearby Pueblo Springs had served American Indians for centuries before the arrival of white settlers. Just to the south lay Sulphur Springs Draw, the headwaters for the Colorado River of Texas. Field saw this area as a place where a cowboy with limited means might start his own ranch; in 1903 he purchased a piece of land and established a store right at the Texas-New Mexico state line.

Soon after opening his store, Field applied for it to become a post office. He knew that if his store provided postal service, people from all the surrounding ranches would come there for mail and likely make purchases at the same time. Accord-ing to a 1930s interview, Field secured the post office, but agency officials in Washington had rejected his proposed name for it. About this time a traveling salesman for Peters Shoes called on him. The drummer from the East had never seen a bronco ridden, so he paid a local cowboy to ride a wild horse for his entertainment. While visiting with the storekeeper, the salesman asked, "Why don't you get a post office out here?" to which Field replied, "I've got a post office but can't get a name for it." The drummer suggested Wild Horse, but Field explained "the Government won't take no double names." Then, according to Field, the salesman proposed "Bronco." "I sent in 'Bronco,' 'Loco,' and 'Polo,' and the Government took 'Bronco.'" In time, Field acquired more land on both sides of the state line and achieved his goal of becoming a locally prominent rancher.

Settlers began to congregate around Field's store at Bronco. By 1912 about twenty-five people lived there, and three years later L. W. Walker

Interior of an abandoned tavern in Bronco, its bar and a few of its bar stools still in place. Photograph by the author, 2000.

Never-used U.S. Department of Agriculture tags for cotton bales strewn on the floor of worker housing at the Bronco cotton gin. Photograph by the author, 2000.

established a small flour mill. The population had grown enough by 1935 that local people organized a Baptist church. The expansion of cultivated agriculture into former range country brought the construction of a cotton gin in 1947. "It seemed as if everyone wanted to farm," related Mattie E.

Chambers Field, daughter-in-law of town founder "Gravy" Field.

During the 1940s, Bronco's population continued growing but the store remained the heart of the community. Each day mail came to the post office inside the store—from Brownfield, Texas, in the morning, and from Roswell, New Mexico, in the afternoon. The store, in addition to goods and mail service, offered the only public telephone for miles around. Cowboys on surrounding ranches worked for thirty dollars a month plus their housing, and much of their expendable income crossed the counters at the store.

In the 1950s Bronco began to profit from an unexpected political circumstance. Residents in areas up to a hundred or more miles to the east had voted against the public sale of beer and other alcoholic beverages. Such sales, however, remained legal in New Mexico. Two bars with restaurants soon opened at Bronco just west of the state line. According to Mattie Field, "On Saturday night, it was commonplace to see two hundred or more cars parked for people eating, dancing, and buying liquor." When people in local precincts south of Lubbock voted to open their area to sales of alcohol, the bar business in Bronco gradually dried up.

Agriculture continued to support the Bronco population, which by the early 1960s had reached a peak of 180 during cotton harvesting and ginning season. By the late '60s, however, the number had dropped to only thirty, and today the immediate Bronco area has only about half a dozen occupied houses and mobile homes. Most of the site lies completely abandoned—the empty former post office-grocery store-filling station-hardware store, the deserted cotton gin, idle meat-packing plant, vacant service station, long-abandoned housing for cotton gin workers, and closed tavern. Concrete foundations and debris from former buildings as well as the rotted hulks of wooden cotton-hauling trailers litter much of the site.

LOCATION: *Bronco is located on U.S. Highway 380 on the New Mexico state line and Farm Road 769 at a point that is 14.9 miles west of Plains in Yoakum County and 15.0 miles east of Tatum, New Mexico.*

Brownwood

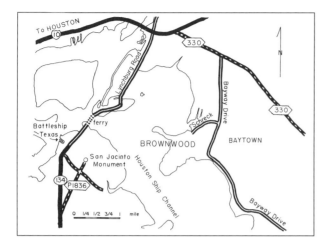

Today the site of the Baytown Nature Center, Brownwood once was an upscale residential development on a peninsula directly across the San Jacinto River and the Houston Ship Channel from the beloved San Jacinto Monument. Few communities have had such dramatic deaths as this west Baytown neighborhood.

Pottery and stone tools document human activity in the area of Brownwood and Houston for over 10,000 years. White settlers began coming to the area in the 1830s, among them one John Rundell, who raised cotton on land that later became Brownwood. Nearby, such prominent Texan leaders as Sam Houston, David G. Burnet, and Lorenzo de Zavala had residences.

In 1910 Texas rancher and investor Edwin Rice Brown, Sr., purchased 530 acres encompassing the Brownwood site. He grazed cattle on the property, where he hoped petroleum might be found. Years passed, no oil was discovered, and little happened on the quiet peninsula on the San Jacinto River. After Brown died in 1928, his widow settled the estate, placing the property into the hands of their three children.

During this time, nearby Baytown had boomed with oil discoveries and the construction of a large refinery by Humble Oil and Refining Company. In 1937 Edwin Rice Brown, Jr., subdivided his portion of the family ranch for a residential development fronting Crystal Bay. Plant managers and supervisors from the Humble refinery flocked to the development named for Brown, building imposing two-story homes facing the bay. With boathouses and landscaping that included large palms, the subdivision became the most exclusive address in Baytown.

The growing number of petroleum and petrochemical plants around Baytown required a great deal of underground water. Although no one realized it at the time, this large-volume extraction of water lowered the elevation of the entire area. A large clay deposit just below the surface compacted and then collapsed. Residents of Brownwood claimed that their area had sunk between nine and fifteen feet; other nearby areas were documented as subsiding eight to ten feet. The effects, however, had been so gradual that none of the approximately four hundred families in Brownwood realized what had occurred until it was too late. In 1961, Hurricane Carla, the largest tropical storm of record in Texas, revealed that the land under Brownwood had changed.

On 8–14 September 1961, Carla devastated much of the Texas coast. Brownwood, thirty miles inland, appeared to have taken the brunt of the storm's fury. During an eleven-foot storm surge, water flooded many Brownwood homes. Hurricane-force winds swept others completely away. The storm left over three hundred Brownwood families homeless.

Hurricane Beulah in 1967 caused more flooding, and a freak winter storm on Valentine's Day in 1969 again covered the streets and lawns with saltwater. Then came more high water with Tropical Storm Delia in 1973. Little by little, Brownwood residents realized that they were helpless victims of the land subsidence affecting the entire

One of the last four remaining homes in the Brownwood subdivision, quickly succumbing to the elements. Photograph by the author, 2000.

This abandoned sofa and set of bedsprings litter one of the paved streets once lined with homes in the Brownwood subdivision. Photograph by the author, 2000.

Texas Gulf coast. Almost from month to month they saw their retaining walls and boathouses sinking lower and lower into the bay. One former resident remarked to the author, "One day the water got up to seven or eight inches on the foundation. . . . I got out and moved up onto a hill."

In 1975 the U.S. Army Corps of Engineers offered to buy out residents of the Brownwood neighborhood. In two bond elections, in 1979 and 1980, however, Baytown residents voted against providing the necessary 20 percent matching funds. Then on 18 August 1983, Hurricane Alicia struck Brownwood's deathblow.

Despite the efforts of Brownwood residents to protect their neighborhood with an elevated levee-like perimeter road and power pumps to remove water, Alicia's ten-and-a-half-foot storm surge and accompanying winds destroyed or severely damaged over three-fourths of their homes.

The Baytown city council then voted to close the subdivision permanently due to repeated flood-ing. Municipal authorities negotiated a contract with the Federal Emergency Management Agency (FEMA) to buy out eligible homeowners. Most of the remaining Brownwood residents decided to sell, though many felt they received smaller payments than their properties were worth.

After Hurricane Alicia in 1983, city authorities agreed with FEMA to convert the former neighborhood into a public park. Since 1991 the first phases have been implemented through the conversion of part of the Baytown Nature Center to a salt water marsh and the area on San Jacinto Point to a five-acre public park. Planned for the future are a new entry, an interpretive center, a butterfly garden, a bird sanctuary, and trails to various sites and features within the nature center.

Today visitors may visit the site of Brownwood as part of the Baytown Nature Center. Some of the mid-twentieth-century paved streets remain, providing vehicular and pedestrian access to parts of the former neighborhood. In 2000, rotting hulks of four residences still stood, and the site was strewn with bricks, hunks of concrete, siding, shingles, pipe, and other debris from former houses. Plans call for the removal of the four remaining dwellings and more of the paved streets, but for years visitors undoubtedly will be able to discern the traces of what used to be "Baytown's most exclusive residential area."

LOCATION: *The former Brownwood subdivision now lies within the bounds of the Baytown Nature Center on the extreme west side of Baytown in Harris County. To reach the site, turn from Interstate Highway 10 at exit 787 westbound or exit 788 eastbound for Spur 330. Drive 1.3 miles southeastward on Spur 330 to an intersection with Bayway Drive. Turn right and then drive 1.4 miles south on Bayway Drive to its intersection with Schreck Drive. Turn right and drive southwest on Schreck Drive, passing Westwood Park, for 0.7 miles to a T intersection just inside Baytown Nature Center property. At the T intersection turn right and drive 0.5 miles farther on a paved park road to the heart of what used to be Brownwood. To reach the public park at San Jacinto Point with its picnic tables, restrooms, and fishing pier, continue on straight an additional 0.5 miles. Through all this area one may observe ornamental trees and shrubs, concrete slab foundations, and debris marking the sites of former Brownwood homes. A new entry to the Baytown Nature Center is planned to be between*

Harvey Boulevard and Foster Street directly off Bayway Drive. Visitors may observe the effects of uneven land subsidence in the form of cracks in street paving throughout this entire area.

Prehistoric Caddoan mound accessible to the public in the Caddoan Mounds State Historical Park near Alto. Photograph by the author, 1999.

Caddoan Mounds

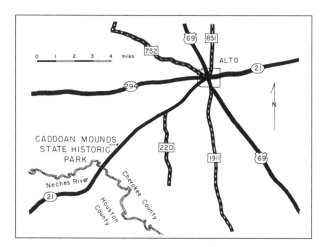

An ancient ghost town on the Neches River, the place now known as Caddoan Mounds was occupied by Early Caddoan people between approximately A.D. 800 and A.D. 1300. Its residents then departed, leaving the surrounding area to be occupied by later Caddoan people. From the 1830s onward the population of the area included white settlers and black slaves. Today Caddoan Mounds State Historic Park encompasses most of the site of the former settlement.

The Early Caddoan people who established the large community at Caddoan Mounds were part of a larger prehistoric woodland culture. Sometimes called the Mound Builders, they occupied much of the present-day United States from Georgia to Oklahoma. Their best-known ceremonial center was at Cahokia, Illinois, across the Mississippi River from St. Louis, where centuries ago they built approximately 120 earthen ceremonial mounds.

Early Caddoan people moved into the Neches River valley of East Texas about A.D. 800 during a time of population expansion. Archaeologists speculate that this population growth resulted from introduction of a more nutritious type of corn from the Southwest. After the newcomers came to the Neches Valley, they established at Caddoan Mounds the southwesternmost ceremonial center for the Mound Builder culture.

At Caddoan Mounds the Early Caddoan people created a substantial population center consisting of an "inner village" inhabited by elite rulers and priests and an "outer village" occupied by lay people. The site served as a regional trade center where surpluses were distributed and goods exchanged. As the Early Caddoan people lacked good sources of high-quality stone for tool-making, Caddoan Mounds became a location for trading foodstuffs and other materials for this much-needed commodity. By sharing surplus food with subservient groups in times of need, the elites at Caddoan Mounds maintained their influence.

The earthen mounds from which the site takes its name served two roles: as burial places for members of the elite class and as sites for ceremonies and ceremonial structures. Archaeologists have learned through excavations that the mounds were built up in multiple layers, often after burials or the intentional burning of ceremonial structures. Today three mounds remain at Caddoan Mounds, one of them rising twenty feet high above the natural terrace of the village site on the Neches River.

Amos Andrew Parker stumbled across the Caddoan Mounds while traveling along the Old Spanish Road from San Antonio to Nacogdoches in 1834. He and many other later observers puzzled over them. "I have seen no satisfactory explanation given of the origin and use of these mounds," he wrote, adding, "at this late stage of the world, their origin and use may never be fully and satisfactorily explained." It was not until the twentieth century that archaeologists began excavating and studying the evidence at Caddoan Mounds, which became known as the George C. Davis Site from the name of its owner during the 1930s. Over the decades archaeologist after archaeologist worked at Caddoan Mounds, giving us today our knowledge of the place and its past residents.

During the 1970s the Texas Parks and Wildlife Department began incremental acquisition of the land comprising the Caddoan Mounds. The agency created a state park that both protects the site and allows the public to view it. On most days of the week visitors are welcomed to a modern interpretive center, where they can learn about the role of the site in Caddoan culture, view artifacts recovered during excavations, and take a three-quarter-mile walk across much of the site.

LOCATION: *Caddoan Mounds State Historic Park is located at a point that is 6.0 miles southwest of Alto in Cherokee County on Texas State Highway 21. Two of the earthen mounds are within the bounds of the park, while the third lies on the immediate southeast side of the State Highway, from which it can be directly* *accessed. At the time of writing, the state park is open to the public five days a week, Wednesday through Sunday.*

Candelaria

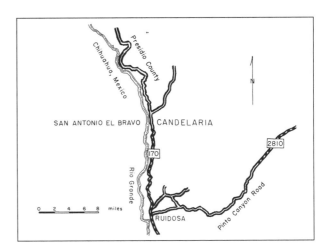

Because of its remote location in the Chihuahuan Desert, Candelaria barely survives. The paved roads leading upstream along the Rio Grande from

23
c

Candelaria viewed from the former U.S. Army camp located at the base of the mountain just northeast of town. Photograph by the author, 2000.

Pickup truck that came to rest in Candelaria. Photograph by the author, 2000.

The homemade suspension footbridge across the Rio Grande that connects Candelaria, Texas, to San Antonio el Bravo, Mexico. Photograph by the author, 2000.

Presidio end at Candelaria. There is no through traffic to keep this town alive, only the remains of a much larger historic community of Mexican farmers who for decades irrigated crops on the nearby river flats of the U.S.-Mexico border.

Written records do not tell us when American Indian or Mexican farmers began to use the waters of the Rio Grande to irrigate and raise crops of corn and squash on the floodplain of the Rio Grande at Candelaria, though archaeological evidence shows early human occupation of the area. The land along both sides of the river in Texas and Mexico in the vicinity of Candelaria lends itself to irrigated agriculture.

At least as early as 1868 an Anglo-American, William Russell, had come to the area and established a farm at Candelaria. Employing the local people to help, he raised grain to sell to the U.S. Army at Fort Davis and Fort Stockton. Irrigated agriculture remained the economic mainstay of the local population, though the supply of water was sometimes limited. In 1899 several of the local farmers argued with one another over the distribution of this essential resource. As there was no local officer at Candelaria to arbitrate the disagreement, the Presidio County Commissioners' Court merely requested reports and ordered the irrigators to refrain from any unlawful acts.

As early as 1893 Presidio County was divided into three common school districts, and Candelaria became the seat for one of them. Best-known of the early teachers at Candelaria was Mary Kilpatrick, who arrived at the village of fifteen families and one-room school in 1901. She purchased the only store in the town; her brother Dawkins Kilpatrick ran it for her. Energetic Mary Kilpatrick then bought some farm property in the little community, and J. J. Kilpatrick, Jr., another brother, came to operate it. He held the important distinction of introducing cotton to the area, having raised ten bales of the fluffy white fiber in 1910, although the remote location forced him to haul it out overland on wagons to the Southern Pacific Railroad for shipment to market. By this time in the early twentieth century, Candelaria had grown to two stores, a school, a church, and twice-weekly stagecoach service to the railroad at Valentine. By 1911 the school precinct encompassing Candelaria had 307 pupils and a general population of 1,842, though only a small number of people actually lived in town.

With the outbreak of revolution across the river in Mexico in 1910, life grew more uncertain for both Mexican and white residents in Candelaria. Supporters of first one side and then the other used the remote ranch country as a secure locale for smuggling horses and arms from Texas into Mexico.

In July 1916 a troop of U.S. Cavalry established at Candelaria what in time became an impressive army post. Located first on the floodplain of the river at the south end of town, the garrison soon shifted to an elevated hill that overlooked both the Texas town of Candelaria and the Mexican town of San Antonio el Bravo across the river. Eventually the soldiers built an extensive adobe and stone compound. Today the foundations, some walls, and an elevated concrete water tank remain. A number of U.S. troops remained at Camp Candelaria until autumn 1919. By that time, the revolution in Mexico had subsided, and the soldiers were no longer needed to protect American citizens along the border.

Life in Candelaria returned to that of an isolated, mostly Mexican village. Irrigated cultivation of cotton continued on the floodplain of the river; a local gin processed the fiber before it was shipped out on wagons and later on motor trucks. Plans were made for the opening of sodium and potassium nitrate mines in the area in 1928, but the onset of the Great Depression ended such discussions. In time the agricultural fields and cotton gin were abandoned. Crops grown on the small fields at Candelaria could not compete with the massive scale of cotton production elsewhere along the Rio Grande and on the Texas South Plains.

Candelaria remained remote and was little known outside Presidio County until the graded county road from Presidio was improved and became Farm Road 170 in the mid-1980s. This gave the desert community its first paved-road access. At this time the mostly Mexican village averaged ten inhabitants during the hot summer and about seventy-five during the rest of the year. It had only two telephones—one at the store and

one at the school—and mail delivery three days a week. Today it remains quiet and still relatively isolated. A traveling priest holds services in the Catholic church. The school closed in the late 1990s, and the former agricultural fields, which once supported the community, are choked with salt cedar and other invasive brush. Candelaria barely clings to life.

LOCATION: *Candelaria is located at the extreme northwestern terminus of paved Farm Road 170 about 12.0 miles northwest of Ruidosa and 47.8 miles northwest of Presidio. The cemetery is accessible via a short gravel road northeastward through the schoolyard and up a steep hill. At the river a privately-owned suspension footbridge provides pedestrian access across the international border.*

Carlton

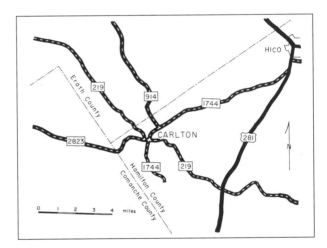

Located in rolling farm, ranch, and dairy country near Honey Creek in extreme northwestern Hamilton County, Carlton thrived just before the turn of the century. The town was an agricultural center fortunately located on main transportation routes, but it declined to a rural hamlet during the second half of the twentieth century.

Carlton occupies a rise between the heads of Honey Creek and Rocky Creek southwest of Hico and north of Hamilton. White settlers were slow to reach the northwestern part of Hamilton County. The first known among the settlers in the immediate area of Carlton was J. H. Everett, who in

Mostly quiet commercial buildings at the center of Carlton. Photograph by the author, 2000.

1865 built a log-cabin home on Honey Creek, east of the future site of Carlton. He was followed by a few other hardy souls, among them Lewis C. Smith and Dr. Francis Marion Carlton, both immigrants from Arkansas who came to Texas after the Civil War and occupied land by 1876. The next year H. R. Armstrong established the first home at present-day Carlton, using oxen to move a small frame house there from nearby Honey Creek. The existing Honey Creek post office also moved in 1877 and took the name of Carlton in honor of early settler F. M. Carlton.

The new town benefitted from an advantage it held over many of the surrounding communities. Carlton lay astride a wagon road used by teamsters hauling supplies and goods overland between Waco on the Brazos River—by way of Bosque and Hamilton Counties—and the U.S. Army garrison at Fort Concho, located over 150 miles west of Carlton. This position provided merchants in Carlton with easier access to manufactured goods than their competitors, who were farther from the freight route. The teamsters even hauled sawed lumber to the town for construction of some stores and residences, although less expensive log structures predominated at the time.

Carlton prospered in its location on the wagon road. Pioneer residents in 1878 established both Baptist and Methodist churches, to be followed later by a Church of Christ. The first school in the town met in a single-room log building with a dirt floor and split-log benches. The school was moved to a frame building in 1881 and eventually in 1916 to a two-story brick building. The first "newspaper" in Carlton never reached print. Local residents contributed articles to the editor, R. F. McKearge, who read them to audiences assembled at the schoolhouse. Later the town had two printed newspapers, one of which was published weekly until it closed in 1936.

In 1907 Carlton received its second transportation bonus, the arrival of the Stephenville, North and South Texas Railway. In 1900 the town had 161 residents, but experienced a minor boom when the new railroad brought new settlers. By 1910 the town had grown to 750 inhabitants, and it reached a high of 800 a decade later in 1920. Early in the twentieth century, Carlton boasted three general stores, three groceries, two drugstores, three churches, three cotton gins, two banks, a lumberyard, and several attorneys and physicians. People from outlying areas would congregate in town on the weekends, when business at the markets was brisk. They also brought agricultural products to be shipped out by rail. Farmers near Carlton raised crops of cotton, corn, oats, and grain sorghum, as well as vegetables and orchard fruit.

Changes in agricultural methods and transportation spelled the decline of Carlton. As the sizes of farms drastically increased and rural populations decreased during the 1930s through '60s, the town dwindled. Its hinterland no longer possessed the rural families needed to maintain its school, businesses, and churches. The railroad abandoned its line through Carlton in 1940, and with the improvement of rural roads more and more people drove for shopping to nearby Hico, Hamilton, and Dublin. Today downtown Carlton, with more buildings vacant than occupied, stands virtually deserted. The walls of a mercantile store that burned in 1929 still stand. Although about forty residences still appear to be occupied, about fifteen lie empty. Dozens of sites once occupied by structures can be identified from foundations, disturbed ground, and debris. As one local resident declared, Carlton "had the best people in the world and was the hardest place in the world to make a living."

LOCATION: *Carlton lies in northwestern Hamilton County at the intersection of Farm Roads 1744, 2823, and 219. It is 9.5 miles southwest of Hico, 17.4 miles north of Hamilton, and 16.4 miles southeast of Dublin. The Carlton Cemetery—with its interesting homemade grave marker for J. E. Pinkerton, who was killed by Comanche Indians in 1867—is located 0.3 miles west of the town on Farm Road 2823.*

1920s, only to wither away during the subsequent decades due to economic problems and lack of water. Today its mostly abandoned buildings stand in semiarid ranch country on U.S. Highway 83 between Carrizo Springs and Laredo.

For over two centuries the area around the present-day townsite has been known by the name Catarina. Spanish priest Juan Augustín Morfi, who accompanied Teodoro de Croix on an inspection in northern Mexico, visited the area on 26 December 1778. He noted that he had passed Aguaje de Santa Catarina, the water-hole of St. Catherine, which appears to have been located on what is known today as Catarina Creek.

In the early 1880s David Sinton became the owner of a ranch in southeastern Dimmit County that by the turn of the twentieth century had become known as the Catarina Ranch. His daughter, Ann, married Charles P. Taft, brother of United States president William Howard Taft. Together Ann and Charles Taft inherited and purchased a total of 235,000 acres in Dimmit County, calling their property the Taft-Catarina Ranch. The Tafts enjoyed rich grazing for stock on their lands, but they found it expensive to market their cattle. They had to drive the animals overland to the nearest railroad at Encinal almost thirty miles away. Consequently, they were pleased when land promoter Asher Richardson approached their manager about

Catarina

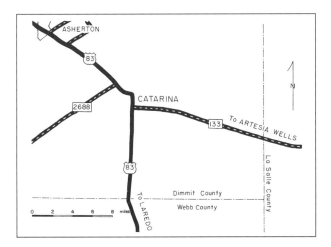

The main boulevard through Catarina as seen from under the open canopy at a former roadside business. Photograph by the author, 2000.

Originally a ranch headquarters, Catarina sprang to life as a showplace for land developers in the

building a railway line across their property. Richardson was developing a proposed community ten miles northwest at Asherton, but needed a railway connection to insure its success. He offered the Tafts an opportunity to build a station and cattle shipping pens on his proposed Asherton and Gulf Railway at Catarina if they in return would grant him an easement across the ranch in order to build the line from Artesia Wells to Asherton.

Even before the rails reached Catarina in 1910, the Tafts had begun moving their ranch headquarters to the site. They constructed a commissary, cattle shipping facilities, several homes and a bunkhouse for ranch employees, a school, and even a two-story wooden hotel. They also decided to build a winter home, and soon work began on a three-story residence that came to be known as the Taft House. The elaborate home had oversize bathtubs large enough to accommodate Charles's brother, President William Howard Taft, who tipped the scales at over three hundred pounds.

Pretty Ethel Andrews holds grapes at Catarina in 1928. Courtesy of the San Antonio Light Collection, the University of Texas Institute of Texan Cultures at San Antonio.

Ornamental entry to the long abandoned high school in Catarina. Photograph by the author, 2000.

About 1920 Kansas oilman S. W. Forrester purchased the Taft-Catarina Ranch, undoubtedly hoping to find oil beneath its pastures. Disappointed in this quest, he sold the property five years later to a group of Kansas land promoters who were interested in large-scale real-estate promotion.

In the hands of the Kansans, the Taft-Catarina Ranch in 1925 became Catarina Farms. Partner C. H. "Clint" Kearney laid out a modern townsite near the railway tracks in Catarina and began building a new two-story brick hotel, waterworks, electric lighting system, a well lit, palm-lined boulevard, and a fourteen-acre park. In the meantime his crews graded roads from the town into the surrounding brush land, where they laid out individual farm properties to be sold to prospective fruit- and vegetable-raisers.

The Kansans hired salesman Charles F. Ladd—already famous for promoting the development of Harlingen and Weslaco in the lower Rio Grande Valley—as their "general colonizing agent." Dressed in a ten-gallon hat, riding breeches, and knee-high English boots, Ladd regaled train loads of potential land buyers with stories of the wealth they could earn raising irrigated fruit and vegetables at Catarina. The master showman even ordered that an entire orchard of full-grown citrus trees loaded with fruit be shipped to Catarina. After crews planted the trees behind his house, they gave the appearance of a mature orchard.

Appearances proved inviting and by the end of the 1920s Catarina had over a hundred new homes and dozens of businesses. Its commercial district included several lumber yards, an implement dealer, ice plant, swimming pool, produce buyers and shippers, a drugstore, bakery, telephone exchange, a bank, and several cafés, filling stations, automobile garages, and grocery stores. The town also boasted two schools and one church. Street lamps and palm trees lined the boulevard through town. Although estimates vary, Catarina may have had as many as 2,500 residents at its peak around 1929.

Despite a promising start, Catarina Farms rapidly failed. Because of insufficient water resources for irrigation, marketing difficulties, and the economic problems caused by the Great Depression, Catarina disintegrated. By 1932 only 592 people lived in the town, and that number decreased to 403 in 1940. Very few businesses stayed open in downtown Catarina; most of the neighborhoods in Catarina Farms reverted to ranch land. The town council disbanded in 1950. Catarina shrank to 160 people in 1969 and a mere 45 in 1990. For decades the Taft House stood as a reminder of better times, but even it disappeared in 1981. Former Texas governor Dolph Briscoe, Jr., purchased it and moved it fifteen miles to his own ranch headquarters. Today Catarina appears to be more abandoned than occupied, with fewer than thirty occupied residences. The brick hotel still stands, as do the abandoned school, waterworks, and several empty residences. When one drives the rectangular grid plan of Catarina's streets, it is possible to envision rows of neat 1920s frame houses where today only vacant lots and foundations remain.

LOCATION: *Catarina is located on U.S. Highway 83 at its intersection with Farm Road 133 in Dimmit County* *at a point that is 19.5 miles south of Carrizo Springs and 60.3 miles north of Laredo. Visitors should watch out for both snakes and tarantulas.*

Center City

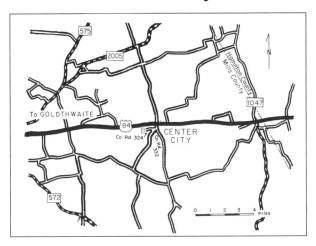

Center City, which took its name from the mistaken belief that it stood at the geographical center of Texas, was founded in the 1870s as settlers pushed the frontier westward across what later became Mills County.

For many years the residents of the area believed that a particular live oak tree stood exactly in the middle of Texas—marking the state's true geographical center. After the community was organized—around the tree, of course—residents were so convinced of this belief that they petitioned for the town's post office to be named Center City. In 1877 this post office was granted, and it remained at the site until it closed in 1920.

By the 1880s Center City contained a general store, drug store, hotel, school, two blacksmith shops, several saloons, and several dry goods stores—all built more or less around a central square. Town builders left the center of the square vacant for a future county courthouse because local residents believed their town would become the seat of Mills County when it organized in 1887. To their disappointment, Goldthwaite was named the seat of government. The big oak tree, however, did provide shade for numerous early meetings of the local Justice of the Peace court that served the eastern part of the county. By 1875

Beyond an abandoned store stands the old live oak around which Center City was built. Photograph by the author, 2000.

An abandoned roadside business on U.S. Highway 84 at Center City. Photograph by the author, 2000.

residents had organized the first church for Center City, followed the next year by the first union Sunday school. The two-story wooden church later housed Center City's school as well.

The population of Center City remained stable at approximately one hundred residents from the mid-1880s to the 1910s, but with the mechanization of agriculture and the consolidation of farms, the town declined through most of the twentieth century to become a quiet, dispersed rural community. Although it still had three stores and about seventy-five residents half a century ago, today Center City has only one operating store, two active churches, a handful of occupied residences, and a number of abandoned houses and former businesses.

LOCATION: *Center City is on U.S. Highway 84 at its intersection with Mills County Road 332 at a point that is 9.6 miles east of Goldthwaite and 15.5 miles west of Evant. The cemetery is located on gravel Mills County Road 324 just 0.4 miles east of the slowly dying live oak tree at the center of the old townsite.*

Cherry Spring

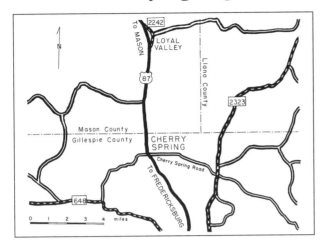

Cherry Spring is a German immigrant community that flourished during the second half of the nineteenth century on the old road leading northwestward from San Antonio through Fredericksburg to Fort Mason. According to oral traditions, when the first Germans arrived in the vicinity, a Mexican family and a black slave family had settled on land near a large spring and a thick growth of wild cherries. These two attractive features inspired the name of the locale.

German farmers and live-stock-raisers began settling in the vicinity during the late 1840s or early 1850s. Well before the Civil War, a considerable community had grown up at Cherry Spring. On 1 July 1858 a post office was granted for the town, which by 1860 had grown to forty-one families—a total of 202 people. The earliest settlers erected log houses, some of which survived into the twentieth century, but the more affluent members of the community built sturdy limestone rock houses, many of which still stand.

Diedrich Rode's three-story stone house at Cherry Spring as it appeared during the mid-1930s. Courtesy of Bartlett Cocke, Sr.

The marker at the Cherry Spring grave of John O. Muesebach, who in the 1840s led German immigrants in founding colonies at New Braunfels and Fredericksburg. Photograph by the author, 2000.

emphasis on marksmanship, were prominent in many German immigrant settlements throughout Texas, and the Cherry Spring group remained active for a number of years. Members gathered at their shooting range on the fourth Sunday afternoon of every month for target-shooting and socializing.

Public education at Cherry Spring began in 1884, when the residents of the community organized a school district. They contributed funds and labor toward the construction of a stone schoolhouse that was completed in 1885. This building replaced the small private school Diedrich Rode had built years before. The building was expanded several times and used well into the twentieth century. Church services continued in the Rode home until 1907, when the faithful built a new stone Lutheran church.

The Cherry Spring neighborhood abounds with small cemeteries, but the most interesting for visitors is the Marshall-Meusebach Cemetery just off the main road through the townsite. The graveyard contains the mortal remains of John O. Meusebach, who came to Texas in 1845 as the leader of the Society for the Protection of German Immigrants in Texas, the organization that promoted the large-scale organized German immigration to the state and also founded the towns of New Braunfels and Fredericksburg.

One of the most influential settlers at Cherry Spring was Diedrich Rode, who personally built the first school in the community. He became a Lutheran lay minister and for many years held religious services in a large open room on the second floor of his three-story rock house. To this day tales are told about the elaborate meals guests ate at long tables in the broad ground-floor hallway of the house after worship.

A number of commercial enterprises sprang up at Cherry Spring, among them Lange's and Marshall's stores, which also housed saloons, and a community dance hall. Adjacent to the dance hall stood lodge number 114 of the Sons of Herman, a German fraternal order. Also nearby was one of the most important social institutions in the town—the Cherry Spring Schuetzen Verein, or shooting society. Such organizations, with their

LOCATION: *Cherry Spring is located east of U.S. Highway 87 about 1.5 miles south of the Gillespie-Mason county line. The town is approximately 15 miles north of Fredericksburg and 23 miles southeast of Mason. The community stretches about two miles along a gravel county road known locally as "Cherry Spring Road" that leads eastward from U.S. Highway 87. The road is marked by a highway department sign for Cherry Spring. Several commercial enterprises have been erected along the highway, but most of them have gone out of business. The Marshall-Meusebach Cemetery is just north of the county road at a point that is 0.5 miles east of U.S. Highway 87. The 1880 Diedrich Rode house and 1907 Christ Evangelical Lutheran Church are 1.4 miles east of the highway. The Cherry Spring School, the earliest part of which was built in 1860, is located at a sharp right bend in the county road 1.6 miles east of the highway. Visitors should note that the Cherry Spring School is now a private residence.*

A long quiet Route 66 gasoline filling station in Conway. Photograph by the author, 2000.

Conway

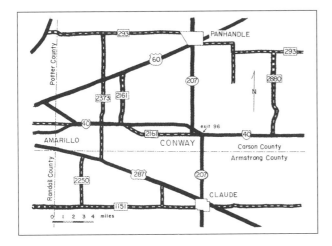

A community that dates back to the days of the cattle ranching kingdom in the Texas Panhandle, Conway received a new lease on life when U.S. Highway 66 was designated a transcontinental highway in 1926. Years later when highway traffic on Route 66 was routed to the new Interstate Highway 40, the community withered away to a remnant of its former self.

Ranchers occupied the area around Conway during the early 1880s. Then in 1888 the livestock-raisers and others organized Carson County, with the town of Panhandle as its seat. Next, they turned their attention to schools; the one-room Lone Star School in 1892 was built five-and-a-half miles east of what later became Conway. Further economic development came with the arrival of the Chicago, Rock Island and Gulf Railway in 1903. Due to a national economic recession, Conway did not become a town until early 1905, when two land promoters purchased 160 acres of ranch land and laid it out into streets and blocks. They named it Conway after former county commissioner H. B. Conway.

Soon the Lone Star School was moved across the prairie to the new townsite; grocery and mercantile stores opened in the new community alongside the railroad. Among the additional business enterprises that sprang up were a blacksmith shop, an agency for farm implements made by the International Harvester Company, a blacksmith shop, grain elevators, and by 1910 Conway even had a Buick automobile dealership. Local residents built

A Volkswagon Beetle that years ago came to rest in front of an abandoned stucco tourist court on Route 66 in Conway. Photograph by the author, 2000.

Then the unexpected occurred again. Route 66 became Interstate Highway 40, and its route was diverted around Conway. Gasoline stations and cafés moved about three-quarters of a mile north to the new four-lane interstate, and Conway began a steady decline. Today there is not one active place of business in old Conway other than the grain elevators. There are only about a dozen residences, half of them abandoned. Disused historic gasoline stations, cafés, and tourist courts line the route of Highway 66 through the townsite, making Conway a fascinating destination for visitors.

LOCATION: *Conway is located 0.6 miles south of exit 96 on Interstate Highway 40 in Carson County where Texas State Highway 207 intersects Farm Road 2161.*

a wood-frame non-denominational church in 1912, and over the years they expanded the school, finally erecting a new structure in 1930.

In the 1920s the consolidation of agriculture began forcing the population to move away from the rural area that supported Conway businesses. With more and more tractors replacing mules for farming, fewer people were required to work a farm. Although the town's rural hinterland lost population, Conway merchants received a trade influx from an unexpected source. The federal government in 1926 designated the east-west highway through their town as part of a new transcontinental route, U.S. Highway 66. The road began in Chicago and ran all the way to the Pacific Ocean at Santa Monica, California. Throughout the 1920s and '30s, increasing numbers of motorists passed through the little Panhandle community. They stopped for gasoline, food, and tourist-court lodging. While other small towns in the area stagnated due to rural depopulation, Conway for over three decades maintained itself from trade brought by travelers on the "Mother Road."

Crews

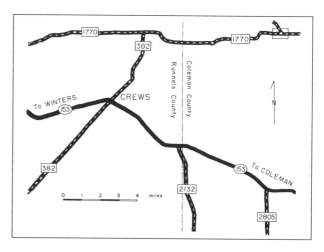

Although it is visually dominated by a large stone gymnasium built for it school by employees of the Works Progress Administration in 1941 during the New Deal, Crews was an agriculturally based town in Runnels County located roughly between Abilene and San Angelo. As happened to many communities in west-central Texas, it withered away when the rural population on which it depended moved to larger cities and towns as agriculture consolidated during the middle years of the twentieth century.

Small numbers of white settlers began arriving in northwestern Runnels County in the early 1860s,

The Works Progress Administration built this cut-stone school gymnasium in 1941. Residents of Crews recently renovated the gym, which now serves as a community center. Photograph by the author, 2000.

but a decade passed before substantial numbers of livestock-raisers began to occupy the area. By 1880 enough people had settled in the valley of the Colorado River and its tributaries to organize formally the county. By 1888 the population in the Crews area was large enough to support a school, and in 1892 two entrepreneurs opened a combination store and post office. They named the place in honor of C. R. Crews, a businessman in Ballinger, the county seat.

During the late nineteenth and early twentieth centuries, farming replaced ranching as the predominate activity in Runnels County. The subsequent increase in rural population led to growth in Crews and other nearby crossroads communities. Expansion in the Crews schools mirrored the general population growth. The first school opened a mile north of Crews in 1888 in a log building with a dirt floor and split-log benches. It was followed two years later by a wood-frame structure. Then in 1905 the school moved closer to the town and grew to two rooms. In 1922 a four-room building took its place. In 1937 the local school consolidated with that of a neighboring community, giving it a total of seven teachers. Finally in 1941— with the assistance of federal government funds—a stone gymnasium, which still stands, was built to

serve schoolchildren in the town and surrounding farms. Crews itself had about 150 residents at the time. During the first half of the twentieth century, the town possessed a substantial number of businesses, including a barbershop, drugstore, confectionery shop, telephone exchange, two cotton gins, four general stores, three blacksmith shops, the offices of several physicians, and three churches. Three principal streets ran through the townsite with residences built along all of them.

With the introduction of tractors and mechanized agriculture, fewer people were needed to do the same fieldwork. Farms increased in size, but the number of families needed to operate them decreased. During the 1930s through 1970s, many rural areas in the state became depopulated. Crews gradually lost its economic base, as did most of Runnels County. From a high of 2,544 farms in 1930, the number of farms in Runnels County dropped to only 941 in 1978. During the same period the county's population decreased from a high of 21,827 in 1930 to a low of 11,872 in 1980, only 4,604 of whom lived in rural areas. The economic reason for the existence of Crews disappeared with the rural population.

Today the Crews townsite consists of a handful of abandoned residences, vacant Baptist and

Exterior of the 1888 Methodist church in Dalby Springs. Photograph by the author, 1999.

Methodist churches, a deserted automobile service station, foundations of extensive schoolbuildings, and a well-maintained cemetery with beautiful ornamental juniper trees. The 1941 school gymnasium is still maintained as a community-center building and has recently undergone a major renovation. The entire site is littered with surface archaeological remains, including bricks, porcelain, enamelware, concrete, tin cans, broken glass, bottles, parts from buggies and automobiles, pieces of furniture, appliance parts, stovepipe, and bits of pressed-metal ceiling.

LOCATION: *Crews is located at the intersection of Texas State Highway 153 with Farm Road 382 in northeastern Runnels County. The site is 11.3 miles east of Winters, 17.3 miles northeast of Ballinger, and 22.3 miles west of Coleman. To reach the Crews Cemetery, drive northeast from the townsite 1.0 miles on Farm Road 382 to its intersection with gravel Runnels County Road 144. Turn east and drive 1.4 miles on the gravel county road. Visitors should take care to avoid snakes, especially around ruins, tombstones, and abandoned buildings.*

Dalby Springs

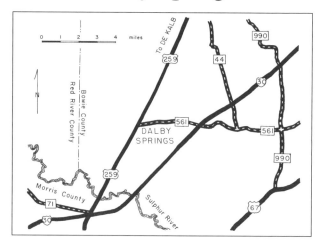

A bustling health resort in the nineteenth century, Dalby Springs many years ago reverted to its former status as a dispersed rural community. Today visitors enjoy viewing its historic church and cemetery and the springs still flow, though few people now bring jugs to fill with the rust-colored mineral water that once made the site famous.

Two brothers-in-law, Warren K. Dalby and Benjamin Booth, came from Arkansas to the Republic of Texas in 1839, settling in virgin forest at the

Detail of the sign at the Dalby Springs United Methodist Church. Photograph by the author, 1999.

A hand pump mounted over one of the mineral-water springs at Dalby Springs. Photograph by the author, 1999.

place that later became known as Dalby Springs. Securing side-by-side tracts of land, they selected a location that in time became the junction of two early roads—one coming northward from Stephenson's Ferry on the Sulphur River and the other running southeast to northwest connecting Jefferson with Clarksville. Little did either man realize that the property they had chosen would be worth far more than ordinary farmland.

In the early 1850s an unknown person discovered a spring of tea-colored mineral water flowing from the bank of a creek that ran across Dalby's property. People who bathed in the water or drank it claimed that it had healing effects. News spread, and other men, women, and children from northeastern Texas began coming to what was soon called Dalby Springs to seek the curative waters. By 1856 a village sprang to life near the springs at the crossroads, and Warren Dalby improved his house into a two-story hotel to accommodate the health-seekers. Booth sold off small tracts of his land to individuals who built small homes there to be near the spring on Dalby's property, and two brothers named Barry opened a general store. The

Civil War in the 1860s, however, slowed development of the community.

The coming of railroads to the region in the 1870s revived Dalby Springs. Horse- and mule-drawn hacks carried passengers the last ten miles over rough roads from the railroad stations that had opened at DeKalb and Bassett. From summer through early autumn, Dalby Springs attracted both health- and pleasure-seekers. Another mineral-water spring was discovered on some of the former Booth property that was then owned by Byron Pirkey, and he opened the area's second hotel at his Pirkey Spring. In the meantime J. W. Farrier acquired the Dalby land around the original spring, which he renamed the Farrier Spring. Investing considerable funds, Farrier developed a fenced fifty-acre camping ground around the spring, improved the original hotel and built another, erected an open-air dance pavilion, constructed baseball fields, and began actively advertising Dalby Springs as a spa. As more people came to the springs during the 1870s and 1880s, the town grew to have not only several hotels, but also boarding houses, a two-teacher school, two cotton gins, a grist mill, a Methodist church, a Masonic lodge, a Grange hall, four general stores, and two practicing physicians. Dr. Louis A. Sager's efforts in promoting the curative properties of the springs during the 1890s helped bring the community of about 250 residents to its apex of development, but with his death in 1897 the town began to dwindle.

As science progressed and people in Texas learned about the existence of microbes and other agents of illness and cure, they ceased coming to Dalby Springs to "take the waters." Because it never had its own railway connections, people had been required to journey there in animal-drawn conveyances over unimproved dirt roads. This was uncomfortable and inconvenient; after heavy rains it could be exceedingly disagreeable. The old-timers died off, and few people came to take their places. The post office closed and the school consolidated with the one in DeKalb, leaving finally just one store, which now has closed. The red-water springs, however, still flow into the creek; cast-iron hand pumps assist locals in bringing the springwater to the surface. Even without the springs, the beautiful 1888 Dalby Springs Methodist Church and adjacent cemetery make the place well worth a visit.

LOCATION: *Dalby Springs is located in southwestern Bowie County on Farm Road 561 at a point that is 0.7 miles east of its intersection with U.S. Highway 259, 10.5 miles southwest of DeKalb, 23.5 miles northeast of Mount Pleasant, and 17.9 miles southwest of New Boston.*

Danevang

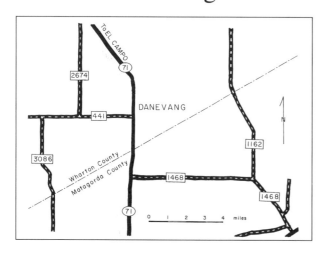

A town founded and inhabited by Danes on the Gulf coastal plain in Wharton County, Danevang has dwindled to a shadow of the community it was during its peak in the 1920s.

The idea for creating Danevang came from leaders in a Danish immigrant organization, the Dansk Folkesamfund, or Danish People's Society. The group sought to establish a colony where Danish ethnic culture and Lutheran faith might flourish in America. Its members visited and investigated potential sites around the country, finally deciding on the coastal plain of Texas as the most promising setting. An agent secured an option for the purchase of several thousand acres of former ranch land south of El Campo from the Texas Land and Cattle Company.

Land sales to Danes began in 1894, and the first settlers arrived in late summer. Most of the Danes came from the north-central United States, where they had lived for several years since immigrating from Denmark, but a handful came directly from

Lifelong Danevang resident Carl Larson raising the Danish flag in observance of the queen of Denmark's birthday. Photograph by the author, 1999.

Danevang settlers P. J. Agerskov Peterson and his wife, Johanna, with their children in their home at the Danish enclave circa 1902. Courtesy of the P. J. Agerskov Peterson Collection, Mr. and Mrs. Verner Peterson, the University of Texas Institute of Texan Cultures at San Antonio.

Europe. After traveling by train to El Campo, eleven miles north of the future townsite, the new arrivals beheld a flat, grass-covered, treeless plain as far as the eye could see. The Danes eventually purchased thirteen thousand acres of former ranch land, which they plowed into farms. They named the center of their colony Danevang, which means "Danish field."

The Danes experienced problem after problem during their first half-dozen years in Texas. Because they knew only north-country agricultural methods, their cold-weather grains and livestock did poorly in near-tropical Wharton County. The level coastal plains flooded with heavy rains, which converted the land into oceans of mud. During the first year the Danes lived mostly on chickens, deer, berries, and sweet potatoes. "I'll have to admit," said one of the women, "that I cried nearly every evening." Gradually the newcomers learned

to raise local crops of cotton and corn, but the weather continued to threaten. The great hurricane of September 1900 that devastated the city of Galveston also struck Danevang, destroying the entire cotton crop. After this disaster, however, the Danes began gradually to improve their agricultural methods, eventually becoming prosperous American farmers.

A church and school were established in 1895, both of which met in a community meeting-hall built that same year. Also in 1895 the new town received a post office and a U.S. weather-reporting station. Over the years, one key to the success of Danevang residents was the Danish tradition of cooperation within the community. Settlers worked together to establish for their town a fire insurance company, a jointly owned cotton gin, and a community-owned telephone exchange. Of most lasting importance has been the Danevang Farmer's Cooperative Society begun in 1920, which still serves the farming community with group-purchasing of livestock feed, farm equipment, and fuel.

The principal reason behind founding Danevang was to preserve Danish culture in the New World, and the community succeeded in achieving this goal for a number of years. Even today it retains a distinct European atmosphere. For decades Danish was the language of home, business, and church. Pastors introduced the use of English in religious services in the 1920s, and English gradually supplanted Danish in most areas of life. Many Danish religious and secular holidays and foods, however, remain prominent in the lives of those who still live in the community.

Although Danevang in 1927 boasted five hundred inhabitants, that number has decreased over the years to about sixty. The community suffered the same effects from consolidation of agriculture during the 1930s through 1960s that prompted decline in scores of other rural Texas communities. Paving of the eleven-mile road northward to county seat El Campo led many Danevang residents to shop at merchants there. Farmers owning only forty, sixty, or a hundred acres found that they simply could not compete. Only by putting together larger farms—some of them totaling thousands of acres—could Danevang farmers survive economically. These changes depopulated the area around the town, so that today Danevang is a dispersed rural community with about thirty occupied residences, a cooperative store with grain storage and cotton gin, a post office, and a tavern. The imposing Ansgar Evangelical Lutheran Church and adjacent cemetery, the latter of which contains many interesting grave-markers in the Danish language, stand to themselves in the midst of agricultural fields located southeast of the built-up part of "town."

LOCATION: *Danevang is located in Wharton County 10.8 miles south of El Campo on Texas State Highway 71.*

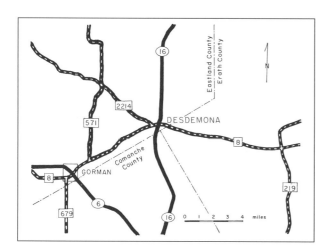

Automobiles, wagons, and buggies crowd the muddy main street of Desdemona after a rain, circa 1920. Courtesy of the Estate of Madie Mitchell Simmons and the University of Texas Institute of Texan Cultures at San Antonio.

Desdemona

Desdemona, a sleepy Eastland County community, witnessed some of the most feverish oil promotion and exploitation in the history of Texas. The petroleum industry reached Desdemona in 1918, and the town was never again the same.

The great oil discovery at Desdemona happened within months of similar discoveries at Ranger, fifteen miles to the northwest. For a while desultory oil exploration had taken place in and around the town, which was known at the time as Hog Town because of nearby Hog Creek. In 1918, however, a gusher blew in at the nearby Duke No. 1 well. Shortly after midnight on 2 September, drillers had lowered a newly sharpened bit into the well—then just over 2,600 feet deep—when a strong and unexpected flow of gas began. The gas ignited from flames in a nearby forge where drillers were sharpening another bit and the fire quickly devoured the entire wooden derrick.

W. N. Koonce, a longtime resident of the neighborhood, recalled, "I happened to wake up and saw that the derrick of the well was on fire, so Ben, one of my boys, and I jumped in the car and started to the well." There they found a gas flame ten feet high coming from the mouth of the well, and they started helping the drillers drag some of their tools away from the burning derrick. Koonce recollected, "We heard a noise down in the well and the driller told us to run; but there was no use of his saying that, for we were already running." He remembered that he had been suffering from rheumatism and "hadn't been able to run for eight or ten years," but on that night when the ground began to shake and rumble with a gusher of oil, "I think I passed everything on the hill."

The discovery at Duke No. 1 opened three years of wild leasing, drilling, and production in the immediate area of Desdemona. From a crossroads community founded in the early 1870s with a school and a few straggling, run-down stores, Desdemona mushroomed into a bustling oil boomtown with over two thousand residents and a multitude of businesses. It even had a primitive airport—a dirt landing strip—with service by early-model airplanes. By January 1919 Desdemona was a new town that included a bank, real-estate office, lumber yard, an array of stores, many rooming houses, restaurants, gambling dens, illegal saloons, and brothels. Because the townsite stood over one of the richest petroleum pools in the state, occasionally a building would be demolished or pushed aside to make room for yet another drilling rig. A

"Casing Crew Alley" in Desdemona during the oil boom, circa 1920. Casing crews provided the steel casing used to line oil wells. Courtesy of the Estate of Madie Mitchell Simmons and the University of Texas Institute of Texan Cultures at San Antonio.

journalist wrote in June 1919 that he could stand on a street corner in Desdemona and count three hundred twenty-nine drilling rigs and that there were scores of others he could not see.

Crime ran rampant in Desdemona during much of its boom, for there had not even been a town government when the oil discoveries were made. When the municipality incorporated, the city officials allegedly became some of the most active members of the criminal element. Many stories are still told about the lawlessness in Desdemona, but one of the most frequently recounted concerns a Greek immigrant laborer for the Magnolia oil company.

While returning to the Magnolia camp from town, the Greek was held up at gunpoint for the seventy dollars in cash that he was carrying. He accepted the loss in a philosophical manner, but two weeks later he found himself being held up by the same men. After this occasion he came into the Magnolia camp furious and cursing the thieves to the extent that his limited English permitted. When his friends asked what had happened, he replied that after taking his dollar the hoodlums had cursed him for carrying so little cash and for troubling them. "They turned me around and they kicked my breeches all the way to the bridge. I tell you I could not stand it."

The boom at Desdemona lasted through 1921, but ended almost as quickly as it began. Wasteful methods of oil production quickly reduced the natural flow of the wells to a minimum, and revenues evaporated. Coupled with decreased production were several fires in 1920 and 1921 that

destroyed entire city blocks. By the end of the boom there was no need to rebuild, for business had gone elsewhere. Since the early 1920s Desdemona has continued to decline as residents have moved on to more promising locales. Many of the surviving buildings were long ago removed and demolished for their materials. By 1938 a local historian wrote with much honesty that "Desdemona is just a village a little larger than it was before the boom." Visitors, however, can find material remains from the oil boom of over eighty years ago everywhere in the town, making it a fascinating place to visit.

LOCATION: *Desdemona is located at the intersection of Texas State Highway 16 and Farm Road 8 in the east-southeast corner of Eastland County. The town is 11.5 miles north of DeLeon, 8.4 miles northeast of Gorman, and 19.9 miles southeast of Eastland.*

Commercial buildings from the "flush times" of oil drilling in Desdemona. Photograph by the author, 2000.

A long empty theater where motion pictures once flickered in Direct. Photograph by the author, 2000.

Direct

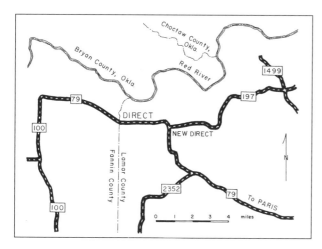

Located less than a mile south of the Red River, Direct for several decades served as a local market center in northwestern Lamar County. Today it is only a shadow of its former self, whereas New Direct—less than two miles to the east—has proved somewhat more successful at clinging to life.

The farming community now known as Direct existed at least as early as 1884, for it was in that year that application was made for its first post office. When the petition went to the Post Office Department in Washington, the name Direct was sent in and approved by the agency. The origin of the name, however, has been debated for decades.

U.S. Congressman Wright Patman, whose district encompassed Direct, in the 1960s entertained audiences with his explanation for the place-name. (Patman's explanation might sound racist to the modern ear.) He related that American Indians on the other side of the Red River were having a powwow when they ran out of alcohol. Because there was a saloon not far away on the Texas side at what would become Direct, one of the participants told the others, "I am going direct to Texas to get some." Patman did not discover this story; it had been published in 1936 by Texas postal historian Fred I. Massengill, and he based it on information he had secured from the local postmaster.

Another explanation for the community name also comes from Lamar County. According to local historian A. W. Neville, a revival preacher came to the Red River valley community and declared that

The collapsing porch of an abandoned home in Direct. Photograph by the author, 2000.

several abandoned residences, a disused wood-frame motion-picture theater, and the sites of former structures marked by uneven ground, foundations, debris, and plantings of yucca, irises, and daffodils.

LOCATION: *Direct is located in Lamar County on Farm Road 79 at a point that is 1.7 miles west of that road's intersection with Farm Road 197 at New Direct, which several highway signs mistakenly identify as Direct. This location is 19.9 miles northwest of the Farm Road 79 intersection with U.S. Highway 82 on the northwest edge of Paris.*

if the local people did not change their evil ways they would go "straight to hell." Whether the story is true or not, the annals of the county do relate that the church at Direct was constructed with the assistance of funds donated by a converted saloon-keeper.

Direct by 1914 claimed a population of 218 and had a considerable business district. Enterprises included a telephone exchange, church, school, four stores, and two blacksmith shops. The town kept about 250 residents until the end of World War II, but after that time its population declined. Like so many other country towns, it suffered from the effects of agricultural consolidation. The creation of New Direct, or East Direct, at a road intersection less than two miles to the east undoubtedly contributed to the decline. By 1983 an estimated seventy residents remained, and in 2000 the author counted only nine occupied dwellings scattered about the townsite.

Present-day visitors to Direct can see an active church and a small auto-salvage yard, as well as

Dryden

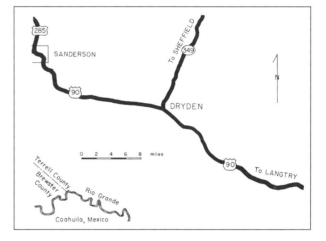

One of many Texas towns established as railroads were built across the state, Dryden was born when the Galveston, Harrisburg and San Antonio Railway crossed Terrell County in 1882.

New modes of transportation provided the lifeblood of Dryden during the decades that its residents lived alongside the railroad and later the highways. The town came into existence after construction on the Galveston, Harrisburg and San Antonio Railway continued westward beyond San Antonio to El Paso, forming one more link in the Southern Pacific Railroad lines connecting New Orleans to Los Angeles. The railroad company established a track-section maintenance-house and railway siding at the community, naming it after its chief engineer, Eugene E. Dryden.

Heavy east-west traffic on U.S. Highway 90 barely slows down through Dryden. Photograph by the author, 2000.

The railway siding instantly made Dryden a cattle-shipping point, and over the years thousands of cattle passed through its pens on the way to market. With cattle-shipping came stores and other businesses to serve the surrounding ranch country, as well as a hotel to provide lodging for railway trainmen. From 1884 to 1895 Dryden served as the headquarters for a large ranching enterprise, the Pecos Land and Cattle Company, and this attracted more people to the remote area. As it was located in arid country, the community had only two sources of water—the railway drilled one well for its steam locomotives and employees; the Pecos Land and Cattle Company drilled another well for use by everyone else.

Beverly Caster Farley, a cowboy for the ranch company, is credited with being the "father" of Dryden. When the Pecos company dissolved in 1895, he acquired eight sections of land, to which he added the section of land encompassing the Dryden townsite in 1912. He built the Dryden Hotel and a mercantile store, and donated the land for the first school. Farley played a major role for ranchers on both sides of the Rio Grande, making arrangements for the shipping of their cattle via the Southern Pacific Railroad to market, mostly in San Antonio. Between 1914 and 1917 he shipped over 55,000 cattle belonging to John Blocker,

who liquidated his ranch across the Rio Grande during the Mexican Revolution. Farley also shipped 40,000 cattle that belonged to Francisco Madero, President of Mexico, who was assassinated in 1913. Concurrent with the revolution in Mexico, two units of the U.S. Army saw duty at Dryden, most of the time patrolling strategically important bridges on the Southern Pacific Railroad line.

The often remote "Sunset Route" of the Southern Pacific Railroad attracted robbers. One of the best-known train hold-ups in West Texas took place near Dryden in the early morning hours of 13 March 1912. Two bandits boarded a westbound Southern Pacific train at Dryden, one man entering a passenger coach and the other climbing aboard the engine. The latter man ordered the engineer at gunpoint to stop at Baxter's Curve, the first bridge west of Dryden. There he ordered the trainmen to uncouple the coaches and pull forward. In the meantime the second thief proceeded to the express car, where he stole money and valuables from the U.S. Mail and from railway express packets. Express-car messenger Dave A. Trousdale managed to club the robber in the head with an ice mallet, killing him on the spot. Trousdale, correctly assuming that the thief was not working alone, waited for the

The hulk of the Dryden school, no longer the scene of classes. Photograph by the author, 2000.

other man, who came to see what had happened to his partner. Trousdale used the thief's gun to shoot his partner in the head. For his courage in the face of two armed bandits, Trousdale received a $500 reward from the railroad and an additional $1,000 reward from Wells, Fargo and Company. Though this incident put the name of Dryden in the newspapers, robberies were exceptions to normal life in this shipping point and ranching supply town.

Twice Dryden's population topped one hundred residents, during the late 1920s and then from the 1940s through the 1960s, but economic changes were its downfall. The surrounding big ranches divided their lands into smaller properties during the twentieth century, thus ending their much-needed support of businesses in Dryden. And once it was improved, the main east-west highway siphoned off most trade to Sanderson, leaving the few stores in Dryden with decreasing numbers of customers. Even increased tourist traffic on the highway could not compensate for the losses. By 1988 Dryden reported only thirteen residents, and today more residences and stores are abandoned than occupied. The former townsite is strewn with vast amounts of surface archaeological remains in the forms of broken glass, crockery, metal, brick, and building fragments.

LOCATION: *Dryden is located on U.S. Highway 90 at its intersection with Texas State Highway 349 in south-central Terrell County. The townsite lies 20.5 miles east of Sanderson, 58.7 miles south of Sheffield,*

Standing open with its contents removed, this toolbox remains from auto repairs that were once made in Dryden. Photograph by the author, 2000.

and 39.4 miles west of Langtry. Visitors examining this site must take care to avoid rattlesnakes.

Electric City

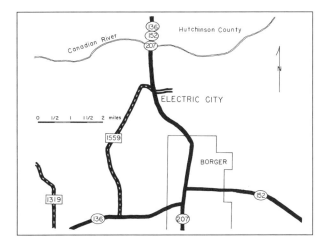

Electric City was one of several boomtowns that sprang up in the wake of oil discoveries in the

Electric City during its heyday in the 1920s oil boom. Courtesy of Patman & Osborn, Austin, Texas.

Texas Panhandle Oil Field during the mid-1920s. Located immediately north of Borger in Hutchinson County, the town hung on for a number of decades, but it lies almost completely abandoned at the beginning of the twenty-first century.

The story of Electric City begins with the discovery of rich oil reserves on 11 January 1926 at the No. 1 Smith oil well, which the Dixon Creek Oil and Refining Company drilled in the Canadian River valley. Soon dozens and dozens of wooden derricks and drilling rigs appeared in the area as an estimated forty-five thousand men and women flooded the new oilfield. In March 1926 town promoter Asa Phillip "Ace" Borger and his partner, John R. Miller, purchased 240 acres of ranch land on the southern bluffs above the river. They divided it into blocks and lots and auctioned them to buyers on 8 March. On the first day their Borger Townsite Company sold between $60,000 and $100,000 in real estate, and within six months it had sold all the 240 acres for more than a million dollars.

The new town, named in Borger's honor, became the center of the Texas Panhandle Oil Field. With a three-mile-long main street, it boasted almost every conceivable place of business, both legal and illicit. Borger, however, could not contain all the people who came to work in the oil field, so other communities sprang up to meet their needs. Electric City was one of these satellite towns.

Between July and November 1926, the Panhandle Light and Power Company built an electric-power generating plant beside Rock Creek on the Canadian River flats about three miles north of Borger. Work proceeded with great haste, for oil-well drillers and operators desperately needed power to operate their equipment. As construction progressed on the electric plant, workers gathered in its vicinity, creating a camp they called Electric City. In time, the outlying community also contained scores of homes for oilfield workers, mercantile stores, grocery stores, rooming houses, dance halls, speakeasy bars, gasoline filling-stations, a drugstore, school, post

Steel house-mover's beams already beneath it, this Electric City home is ready to be moved away. Photograph by the author, 2000.

office, and even a large church. Also scattered throughout Electric City were drilling rigs and, later, pumping jacks, all extracting oil from the ground.

The boom in the Texas Panhandle Oil Field continued for less than a decade, as overproduction depleted the petroleum reserves. The industry around Borger continued employing people through the Great Depression, but not in such numbers as during the boom. Then World War II brought renewed prosperity to the area in the form of many jobs producing synthetic rubber and carbon black, both needed for the war effort. Borger itself reached its population peak after World War II, with 20,911 residents in 1960. Since that time, however, the population has declined in concordance with petroleum production. Lower prices for oil in the 1980s and '90s brought decline to the oilfield, and during this time virtually all the residents of Electric City departed for homes elsewhere. The townsite in 2000 had paved streets but only four occupied residences; over two dozen dwellings stood abandoned. The historic 1920s electric generating-station functions today as a substation for Southwestern Public Service Company. Most of the buildings in Electric City have been relocated or demolished—their sites marked by uneven ground, large elm trees, and foundations.

LOCATION: *Electric City lies just east of the combined Texas Highways 136/152/207. Farm Road 1559 intersects the highway at a point that is 2.0*

miles northwest of the traffic circle on the north side of Borger in Hutchinson County. From the intersection with Farm Road 1559, drive east on unmarked paved streets into the former townsite, which lies on the river flats below the bluffs of the Canadian River valley. Visitors should be wary of rattlesnakes, which are known to inhabit the area.

Eliasville

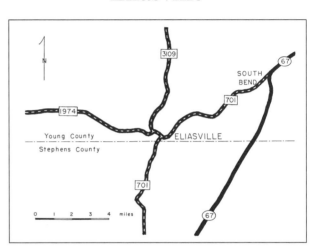

One of the most picturesque ghost towns in Texas, Eliasville lies on a high east bank of the Clear Fork of the Brazos River in southern Young County. For many years the shady banks of the river at Eliasville have attracted people for picnics, revivals, family reunions, and all-night fishing parties.

Eliasville began as a settled community in the 1870s when J. L. Dobbs located his ranch headquarters on the land where the town later sprang up. In 1878 Elias DeLong established a store at the site, and later settlers named the town in his honor. Among the most prominent early residents were brothers William Leonard Donnell and Thomas Franklin Donnell, who began a livestock-raising operation at Eliasville in 1876. In time, they built a stone dam and gristmill on the Clear Fork of the Brazos; these improvements served the community for decades. The brothers also constructed a locally notable cable-suspension footbridge across the river.

In addition to its importance as a local market center and gristmill site, during the 1920s Eliasville experienced an economic boom as a result

The Eliasville dam and gristmill on the Clear Fork of the Brazos. Photograph by the author, 2000.

of mineral extraction. Although there had been earlier exploration, it was 1921 before oilmen found commercial quantities of petroleum in the county. Eliasville was surrounded by production facilities; just south of town companies erected gasoline refineries and a carbon black plant, which were served by a line of the Wichita Falls and Southern Railway that had been built through the town in 1921. This infusion of capital and population gave Eliasville as many as 1,500 residents, who supported such businesses and institutions as a bank, multiple churches, a public-school complex, dental and medical practices, a lumber yard, a boilermaker's shop, a feed store, a hotel, two motion-picture theaters, three gasoline filling-stations, and the gristmill.

As oil production eventually declined, the population of Eliasville likewise decreased. During World War II many Eliasville residents left to work in defense plants in Fort Worth and never returned. As the number of farms declined through consolidation of agriculture, the rural population that had supported Eliasville also departed. The

Gate of the now quiet playground at the Eliasville school. Photograph by the author, 2000.

bank closed in 1947, the Presbyterian and Methodist churches dissolved in 1952 and 1955 respectively, and the school consolidated with the one in Graham in 1965.

From a high population estimated at 1,500 during the oil boom, Eliasville dropped to about 400 people in 1940 and to about 100 today. The townsite has about thirty-five scattered occupied dwellings, well over a dozen homes standing empty, four abandoned downtown commercial buildings, the shell of the gristmill, several closed churches, the embankment of the abandoned railroad line, and ruins, foundations, and disturbed ground marking the sites of former buildings in both the commercial and residential districts.

LOCATION: *Eliasville is located at the intersection of Farm Road 701 and Farm Road 1974 in southern Young County near the Stephens County line.*

Emma

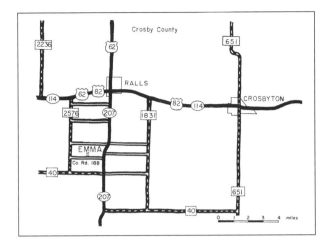

Named for the sweetheart of one of its promoters, Emma served as the seat of Crosby County from 1891 to 1911. At one time the town boasted as many as five hundred residents; today no one lives at the site.

A group of local citizens posed in front of the Crosby County Courthouse at Emma sometime around the turn of the twentieth century. Courtesy of the Panhandle-Plains Historical Museum Research Center.

A sweeping view of the table-flat Texas South Plains from the cemetery at Emma. Photograph by the author, 2000.

Emma was the second town in Crosby County—following Estacado, founded by Quaker settlers. Because of rivalries between the Quakers and non-Quakers, Emma was established in 1890 by the Emma Townsite Company as a non-Quaker community and became the county seat. Founders chose the location because they believed it was near the center of the county, but unfortunately it was bounded on all sides by large ranches. The unwillingness of the ranch owners to sell land to farmers retarded the growth of the community, but even so Emma remained active for over a decade.

At one time Emma boasted a hotel, a substantial wooden courthouse, a bank, churches, and offices of attorneys and physicians. The courthouse stood at the center of a square surrounded by a wooden plank fence with a stile on each side. Black locust trees were planted around the square, and for many years after the abandonment of the town these trees remained as a testament to the hopes of its founders.

The story of the Emma Cemetery, today the last readily visible remains of the town, is told well in a letter written on 4 October 1891. According to Beatrice, the writer, a young man named Levi Jones had gone into the roughly eroded brakes in the eastern part of the county to cut wood and to gather wild plums. As he removed his loaded gun from his wagon, it accidentally discharged, killing him on the spot. Jones ironically had joked earlier that it would be necessary for the residents of Emma to ship in an old man so that they could begin a cemetery, never dreaming that he would be the one to start the graveyard. Beatrice noted in her letter that "it was such a sad, sad funeral. As there was no preacher, his sister read the scripture and prayed the prayer."

Another letter written by a young woman named Margaret to a former schoolmate in 1890 described the home that H. E. Hume built for his wife, Emma, the person after whom the town was named: "One of the nicest homes in Emma was built by Mr. Hume for his bride, Emma. There are three rooms and the front room has a bay window. It would be nice to live in a house as nice as this one, but I am very content with my two rooms and dug-out."

The demise of Emma came about from the competition of two newer towns and the construction of a railway line passing through both of the rivals. The two new settlements were Crosbyton about twelve miles to the northeast and Ralls about five miles to the north, founded in 1908 and 1911 respectively. In 1910–11 the Crosbyton-Southplains Railroad tracks were laid thirty-nine miles eastward from Lubbock through Ralls to Crosbyton, completely bypassing Emma. About the same time an election was held to determine whether the county seat would remain in Emma or move to Crosbyton, which was nearer to the geographical center of the county. Because there was more land available to farmers around the newer town, and so it had a larger voting population, Emma lost the election.

Within only a matter of a few years, most of Emma's residents had moved to either Crosbyton or Ralls. By the 1920s only a gasoline filling station, a country schoolhouse, and two or three residences remained. Today, the cemetery, located about a mile from the actual townsite, is the only visible remnant of Emma.

Encino

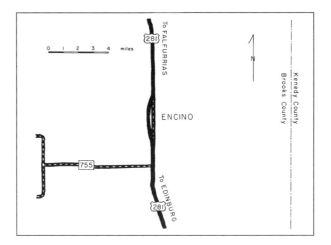

The town of Encino originated as a nineteenth-century Mexican ranch headquarters in present-day southern Brooks County. Today it stands mostly forgotten beside the main north-south highway that connects Falfurrias and the lower Rio Grande valley in South Texas.

In 1832 Lucian Chapa received a grant of land from the Mexican government. The grant's name was *La Encantada y Encinal del Pozo*, which translates to English as "The Enchanted Place and Live Oak in a Hole." Locals report that the place-name originated from a huge live oak tree at the site, around the base of which a depression developed from the abrasion of animals' hooves and also from wind erosion. The

LOCATION: *There are two convenient ways to reach the Emma Cemetery. From U.S. Highway 62/82 in Ralls, drive 4.7 miles south on Texas State Highway 207 to its intersection with graded-dirt Crosby County Road 188. Then drive 0.1 miles west on the county road to a graded-dirt field road leading northward 0.2 miles to the cemetery. Emma can also be reached from U.S. Highway 62/82 by driving south a distance of 4.2 miles on Farm Road 2576 to its intersection with graded-dirt Crosby County Road 188. Turn east and drive 1.2 miles on the county road to the graded-dirt field road leading 0.2 miles northward to the cemetery. These unpaved roads become muddy and are not recommended after wet weather. The most prominent burials in the graveyard are those of Mr. and Mrs. Henry C. "Hank" Smith, who were the first ranchers on the Texas South Plains.*

A former roadside business, overgrown with weeds, on the old highway through Encino. Photograph by the author, 2000.

tree's shade became one of the favored camping places for travelers moving north and south across the brush country between the lower Rio Grande valley and inland Texas.

About the turn of the twentieth century, enough people had settled in the area of the Chapa land grant to begin forming a community that residents nick-named Encino, a shortened form of the grant's name. First serving as a roundup point for local livestock-raisers, Encino became a siding on the Texas and New Orleans Railroad when it came to the area in 1904. This steam railway connection guaranteed that the town would prosper, at least for a time. It was not long before Encino became a market center for the surrounding ranch country.

For the next three decades Encino gradually grew, due to its role of serving people on the cattle ranches. By 1925 it had an estimated fifty residents and reported 100 in 1939. The number grew to a high of 200 by 1941, but dropped during World War II to 125 in 1945. Just after the war the town reported three schools, a church, and several mercantile stores. Improvements to the north-south highway, however, drew business away from the local merchants. The population gradually decreased to about a hundred, where it has remained for about half a century.

At the time of the author's most recent visit in 2000, Encino had just over three dozen occupied residences; an active school, church, post office, and water system; three operating and four abandoned gasoline filling stations-stores; two dozen abandoned dwellings; and five disused, unidentified commercial buildings. Recent construction on U.S. Highway 281 has bypassed the town, so it is most easily viewed from the older business route. The area south and west of the town supports a dispersed rural population, whereas the land immediately east comprises the Encino Division of the King Ranch. Younger versions of the live oak tree that gave Encino its name grow luxuriantly along U.S. Highway 281 north of the townsite.

LOCATION: *Encino is located on off U.S. Highway 281 on U.S. Business Highway 281 in Brooks County, 20.2 miles south of Falfurrias and 41.4 miles north of Edinburg.*

Eskota

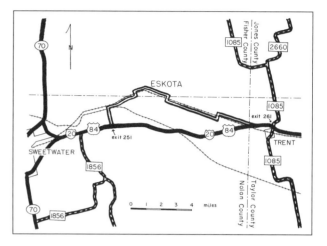

A town that sprang to life along the newly laid rails of the Texas and Pacific Railway through the rolling plains of Fisher County, Eskota prospered during the late nineteenth and early twentieth centuries before subsiding into a dispersed rural community.

In 1881 the Texas and Pacific Railway entered southeastern Fisher County during construction of a railway between Abilene and Sweetwater. As no towns in the region had offered a sufficient money bonus to entice the company to establish it as a division point—the administrative point separating two significant sections of track—the company created a new town to serve that role. Located on the ranch of Dan and Riley Trent on Sweetwater Creek, the railroad town was to be called Trent in their honor. By mistake company crews erected the sign reading Eskota that had been intended for the next stop to the east, and the company never corrected the mistake. Its new division point thus became known as Eskota, a word that may be of either American Indian or Spanish origin and the meaning of which is unclear.

As it was the only place in Fisher County served by any railroad at the time, Eskota prospered during the 1880s and 1890s. Train crews changed places with each other at the division point, and considerable numbers of company men found lodging in a two-story hotel built by W. V. George. By the 1890s trainmen and local residents from surrounding ranches could patronize grocery and dry goods stores, a meat market, a hardware store, and a blacksmith shop. Fisher County school records begin in 1890, and already by this date a school had been operating at

Hand-dug well and prickly pear cactus at the rear of an abandoned home in Eskota. Photograph by the author, 2000.

Eskota. As early as 1892 a real-estate office had begun serving the needs of those interested in investing in either town or ranch properties.

Real-estate speculation likely led to the most notorious unsolved crime in the history of Eskota. According to West Texas historian R. C. Crane's 1941 writings, two unknown men stepped off a Texas and Pacific passenger train from Los Angeles. They left the Eskota station and started walking along the tracks westward toward Sweetwater, ten miles away. Two days later the manager of the Eskota hotel, while riding along nearby Sweetwater Creek looking for some hogs, came onto the body of one of the two men. He found that the man had been shot through the head and spotted his bag nearby—wide open and its contents jumbled. Although the crime was never solved, locals presumed that the corpse belonged to a potential investor, lured to the isolated spot on the pretext of buying a ranch.

Originally the highway between Abilene and Sweetwater paralleled the Texas and Pacific Railway tracks, but when federal highway construc-tion funds became available it was straightened to a more direct southerly route that bypassed Eskota. Already the town was on the wane, as the railroad had moved the division point. Its school was lost to Sweetwater in 1947. The post office closed in 1956. Eventually the only place of business in Eskota was Johnston's Store. Today Eskota contains the still-active railway tracks but no station building, two former commercial buildings that are used for storage, an abandoned residence, and three occupied ranch houses. Almost everywhere are surface archaeological remains in the form of broken glass, ceramics, and scraps of metal, as well as disturbed ground, foundations, and debris from former structures.

LOCATION: *The easiest way to reach Eskota is by taking the old highway, now a county road, that parallels the Texas and Pacific tracks. From east of Eskota, leave Interstate Highway 20 at exit 261 in Trent and take the paved access road westward. This access road, which becomes paved Nolan County*

Road 109, veers to the northwest and runs parallel to the north side of the tracks for 2.8 miles. Then the road crosses over to the south side of the tracks, becomes gravel, and continues as Nolan County Road 109 until it crosses back over to the north side of the railway tracks near the Nolan-Fisher county line. Continue westward along the north side of the tracks on what has become gravel Fisher County Road 170 to the site of Eskota, located at the intersection with Fisher County Road 168, a total distance of 7.4 miles from exit 261 on Interstate Highway 20.

From west of Eskota, leave Interstate Highway 20 at exit 251, marked "Eskota Road," and drive north 1.2 miles on paved Nolan County Road 227 to the intersection with paved Nolan County Road 109. Turn east onto Nolan County Road 109, cross the tracks of the Burlington Northern Santa Fe Railway, and proceed eastward—parallel with and on the south side of the Texas and Pacific Railway tracks— for 2.1 miles to the area of the Nolan-Fisher county line. Here the road crosses over to the north side of the tracks and becomes gravel Fisher County Road 127. Follow the road to the site of Eskota, which is a total distance of 4.9 miles from exit 251 on Interstate Highway 20.

Fairland

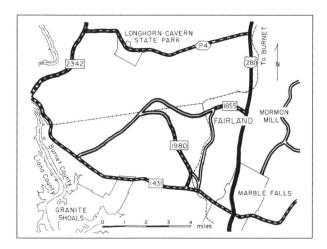

Located in the scenic Backbone Valley south of Burnet in the Hill Country, Fairland in the nineteenth century took its name from the beautiful surrounding landscape. That area of Burnet County remains equally scenic today.

White settlers began entering the Backbone Valley in the early 1850s. Among the first was the R. S. Cates family, who moved into the head of the valley in 1852. The Lewis Thomas family, who settled a little farther down the valley, established a store. Another of the early white occupants of the area was John Harvey, a land surveyor who surveyed much of Burnet County.

In time more and more families moved into the valley, and by the late 1850s residents began feeling the need for a church and school. In 1859 several local citizens, members of the Harvey and Barton families, deeded land at the Fairland community for the construction of a church—the first recorded transfer of land titles for church purposes in Burnet County. Construction began soon thereafter on a meeting house, but the stone walls of the building had only reached the tops of the windows and doors when the Civil War broke out. Work stopped, as many of the men entered Confederate military service. The building project lay uncompleted for the duration of the war.

After the close of the war and the return of most veterans to the community, the still-unfinished walls of the church mocked the Fairland residents for almost five years. There were no funds available to complete the structure, and expensive planks of sawed lumber were needed to complete the roof once the walls were built to their full height. Finally, members of the Crownover family agreed to loan the money necessary to complete the church on the condition that the Methodists would have first claim to its use and that the Methodists would repay the loan. With cash in hand for the materials needed, community members completed the church in 1870. Fairland celebrated the event with a picnic and outdoor barbecue on the day of the church's dedication. Then on 13 July 1872, the Lampasas Circuit of the Methodist Episcopal Church, South designated the meeting place as the Crownover Chapel.

Soon after the completion of the rock church, a school known as the Crownover Chapel School began meeting there, but written records impart little about its operation. It was superseded by a public school in a separate building that operated in Fairland until its consolidation with the Marble Falls schools in the middle of the twentieth century.

Fairland probably never had many more than a hundred residents even during its peak in the late nineteenth and early twentieth centuries. Most of

An old upright piano waits for the next worship service inside the 1870 Crownover Chapel in Fairland. Photograph by the author, 2000.

the people living there engaged in agriculture or livestock-raising, although a few worked as cedar-fence-post cutters as well. By 1940 the population had dwindled to about fifty, and today Fairland has only three or four occupied residences. The interesting cemetery with grave markers dated from the 1870s and the Crownover Chapel are beautifully maintained, however.

LOCATION: *Fairland is located at the western terminus of Farm Road 1855, 1.7 miles west of where that road intersects U.S. Highway 281. This intersection is 8.4 miles south of Burnet and 4.4 miles north of Marble Falls. From the end of paved Farm Road 1855, turn south and drive 0.1 miles on a paved county road to the Fairland Cemetery and Crownover Chapel. Drivers should take care on the farm road because part of it passes through unfenced open range, and livestock may be on the roadway.*

Flomot

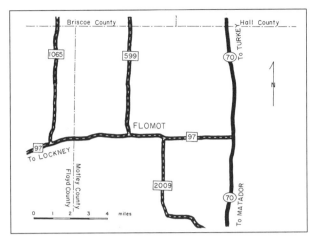

Flomot's unusual name is comprised of the first three letters in the names of Floyd and Motley Counties. For decades the town served as the supply center for an area of farming and ranching along the eastern edge of the *llano estacado* escarpment, also known as the caprock, in the two counties. Today the town gradually is withering away; residents occupy only about a dozen of its thirty-five houses.

Flomot had its beginning when in 1902 Nelson R. Welch became postmaster in his dugout home that was also his ranch headquarters near the Floyd-Motley county line. At the time primarily livestock-raisers occupied the area, but farmers were soon to arrive, as the ranchers began selling off their lands to agriculturists. About that time, Eb Hewitt opened a grocery, dry goods, and hardware store about three miles east of the post office, well inside the Motley County boundary. Carrie Hewitt subsequently became postmaster, and the Hewitts' store, which now housed the post office, became the nucleus around which the town of Flomot grew. Upon the arrival of farmers, Eb Hewitt built the town's first gin to clean seeds and trash from the cotton they raised.

As early as 1893 the South Quitaque one-room school had opened a short distance north of the future site of Flomot. After the new community came into existence, local residents erected a union church about 1906 and moved classes there. Then about 1908 they built a two-story wooden school. Classes continued at Flomot in a series of buildings for the next sixty-six years.

During the first decades of the twentieth century, more and more people moved to Flomot as

55
F

Abandoned businesses in all directions at the center of Flomot. Photograph by the author, 2000.

Former agricultural implement dealership in Flomot. Photograph by the author, 2000.

Decorative welded-steel gateway leading to an overgrown yard and disused Flomot home. Photograph by the author, 2000.

tractor could cultivate the same fields that had required up to ten farm families using only mules for power. The rural area around Flomot began losing population, a situation that has persisted up to the present day. Modern paved highways and automobiles have enabled people in the town and its hinterland to shop in larger towns, causing nearly every commercial enterprise in Flomot to close.

Although the community still has a post office, a community center in a former school, an active Church of Christ, and one working cotton gin, these are the only operating enterprises in the town. Otherwise Flomot consists mostly of abandoned houses, two disused churches, two closed filling stations, two former farm-implement dealerships, six other abandoned commercial buildings, two empty housing units for laborers at the gins, and vast amounts of debris and disturbed ground that mark the sites of former structures.

LOCATION: *Flomot is located in western Motley County at the intersection of Farm Road 97 with Farm Road 599. Many visitors also enjoy the drive 7.3 miles west on Farm Road 97 to the top of the Caprock escarpment for magnificent views across scenic ranch country.*

increasing numbers of farmers purchased former ranch land in the area surrounding the town. These farmers typically raised cotton, and locals operated two gins to process the fiber. By the 1920s Flomot had not only a school, three churches, and two cotton gins, but also a hardware store, a farm-implement dealer, dry goods stores, grocery stores, a dairy, barbershop, gasoline stations, an automobile garage, two cafés, a blacksmith shop, feed mill, meat market, drugstore, and even a small motion-picture theater.

Times were good for farmers around Flomot until 1921, but then agricultural commodity prices fell after the close of World War I. The Great Depression followed in 1929, and prices for cotton dropped even more—to less than the cost of production. Many mortgaged farms had to be given up to financial institutions; some remained in operation only with the help of government subsidies for non-production. One man driving a

Fort Leaton

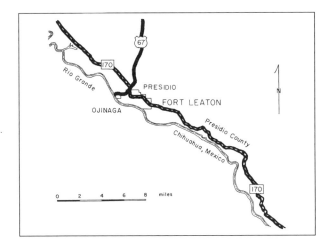

Though the site bears the name of a white man, Ben Leaton, the story of Fort Leaton really belongs to his Mexican wife, Juana Pedrasa y

Fort Leaton as it appeared in the mid-1930s, long before it was restored. Courtesy of Bartlett Cocke, Sr.

Leaton. The adobe building complex—one of the largest earthen structures in Texas—stands on a bluff overlooking the Rio Grande about three miles southeast of Presidio in Presidio County.

Fort Leaton lies at the heart of an area known as *la Junta de los Ríos del Norte y Conchos*. It is the junction, or *junta*, where the Conchos River of Mexico enters the Rio Grande. Above this point the Rio Grande flowed intermittently at the surface, but the contributed waters of the Conchos River converted it into a steadily, if slowly, flowing stream. For centuries this juncture has been a site for human activity and irrigated agriculture. As early as 1684 Spanish priests founded a mission for Native people in the area, then the Spanish added a military fort in 1760.

In 1833 Juana Pedrasa, the twenty-one-year-old daughter of a wealthy family from the Mexican city of Chihuahua, for 5,000 pesos purchased 225 square leagues of land on the Rio Grande near its juncture with the Conchos. Juana, however, remained in Chihuahua. Sometime after American trader Ben Leaton arrived in Chihuahua, probably in 1847 during the U.S.-Mexican War, Juana Pedrasa wed the newcomer. A woman of means,

Pedrasa apparently saw the energetic and at times unscrupulous Leaton as an instrument for increasing her wealth. About the time of their marriage, Leaton purchased from Juan Bustillos a tract of land encompassing an adobe house near Alamito Creek. It seemed that the boundary for this property overlapped the property Pedrasa had purchased in 1833, although Bustillos had purchased his land in 1831 and had occupied it since 1838. This transaction gave Ben and Juana Leaton two deeds to the same piece of land—land they both knew held a strategic location. Ben Leaton expected that the end of war between Mexico and the United States would result in the opening of significant overland trade between the two countries, which is just what happened.

A wagon route known as the Chihuahua Trail had become an increasingly popular trade artery. Hundreds of freight wagons hauled goods between Indianola, Texas, on the Gulf of Mexico, and Chihuahua, Mexico, crossing the Rio Grande at *la Junta*. To Apaches, Comanches, and other tribes, Leaton traded firearms, gunpowder, lead, and alcohol in exchange for livestock, most of which had probably been stolen in Mexico. He then sold

The corral area at Fort Leaton after the Texas Parks and Wildlife Department restored the adobe building complex in the 1970s. Photograph by the author, 2000.

these animals to the freighters, who were always in need of replacement animals to draw their wagons. Ben and Juana, parents of three children, presided over an isolated community of several households of Anglo and Mexican workers. The place was described at the time as the only inhabited town on the American side of the Rio Grande between Del Rio and El Paso. Together the couple owned two-thirds of present-day Presidio County. Their livestock brand indicated both their surnames—PL, for *Pedrasa y Leaton*. The original adobe house, known as Fort Leaton or *El Fortín*, eventually grew to contain forty rooms and a large open compound for livestock.

Ben Leaton died sometime during the first half of 1851. After a customary year of mourning, Juana Pedrasa y Leaton remarried, this time to Edward Hall, an American customs officer and interpreter who was nine years her junior. Although Texas law precluded Juana from inheriting property acquired by her former husband, she could administer the estate, and this she did for more than a decade. In time, Juana and Edward went into debt to one of Ben Leaton's old business partners, John D. Burgess. During the chaotic times of the Civil War—when little civil authority existed in western Texas—Edward Hall refused to pay his debt to John Burgess and was mysteriously killed, possibly by John himself. Whatever the circumstances, doña Juana took her children across the border to live with relatives, while John Burgess occupied El Fortín. The census of 1870 listed him as residing there with his wife and six children, and having real estate valued at $10,000 and personal property worth $6,000. Life obviously was still good at Ben Leaton's old fort, but not good enough to avoid pent-up grievance. On Christmas Day 1875, one of Ben Leaton's sons who had followed John Burgess to Fort Davis, shot him to death there.

The growth of the town of Presidio—founded in 1858 about three miles upstream on the Rio Grande opposite from Ojinaga, Chihuahua—together with the end of overland wagon trade, sealed the fate of Fort Leaton as a community. No longer a strategic location, the town waned to merely serving as the headquarters for a farm and ranch operation before being abandoned totally in the 1920s. During the 1930s the Federal Emergency Relief Administration funded about $6,000 worth of repairs to the historic site, which it was hoped might become a Texas state park. Thirty more years passed, however, before the historic site was formally deeded to the state. Archaeologists excavated the site, determining the outlines of historic walls and other components, and the Texas Parks and Wildlife Department subsequently undertook a complete restoration of Ben and Juana Leaton's fort, which is now open to the public as Fort Leaton State Historical Park.

LOCATION: *Fort Leaton State Historical Park is located 3.2 miles southwest of Presidio in Presidio County on Farm Road 170, which is known locally as "the River Road."*

Fort Parker

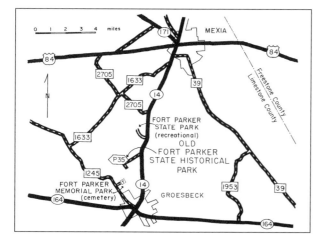

A palisaded wooden fort built by a group of white settlers in 1833 near the head of the Nava-

Reconstructed log cabins with "mudcat" chimneys line one side of the stockade at Old Fort Parker State Historical Park. Photograph by the author, 2000.

sota River in present-day Limestone County, Fort Parker in 1836 was the site of an attack by Comanche and Caddo Indians. The event resulted in the most famous capture of a white settler by Native people, the abduction of Cynthia Ann Parker.

When Baptist Elder Daniel Parker and his congregation came to eastern Texas from Illinois in 1833, most of them settled in what today is Anderson County. At this time Texas remained a province of Mexico. Four of the families chose to move farther west to the headwaters of the Navasota River, where they constructed a wooden stockade fort for protection against possible Indian attacks. The settlers used split cedar logs to erect the rectangular palisade, adding two blockhouses on diagonally opposite corners, the entirety of which was loopholed with openings that served as gun ports. Inside the walls they built several cabins and a corral for livestock. Some of the people left the fort's protection each day to tend animals, haul water from the nearby Parker's Spring, and work in the fields, some of them a mile away.

People in Parker's Fort lived in isolation but comparative security until after the outbreak of the Texas Revolution in late 1835. When Mexican troops headed into the province to quell the revolt in February 1836, the settlers from Parker's Fort fled eastward in a general civilian exodus later referred to as the "Runaway Scrape." After the success of the revolution, these settlers returned in the late spring, finding themselves far behind in their planting and cultivating. Due to this circumstance, many of the men and boys were away in the fields on the morning of 19 May 1836, when a large party of Comanche and Caddo Indians appeared just beyond rifle-shot of the fort.

After a brief parley, the war party forced the gate of the fort. While taking what they wanted from the houses inside, the warriors killed five men, women, and children, but took two women and three children captive. After the attack, the twenty-one settlers who had survived buried the dead and abandoned the site, which was never again occupied as a community. In time the wooden structures rotted, leaving Fort Parker as an archaeological site only.

Four of the five captives were ransomed from the Indians by 1843 and returned to their families, but young Cynthia Ann Parker remained

Cynthia Ann Parker with her infant daughter, Prairie Flower, photographed in Fort Worth, Texas, by A. F. Corning in 1862. Courtesy of the Panhandle-Plains Historical Museum Research Center.

with the Comanches. There she adapted completely to the nomadic Native way of life, became the wife of chief Peta Nocona, and had three children. As her attitude toward her captors changed, Cynthia Ann adopted their language, culture, and manners, living happily among the nomads of the plains for almost twenty-five years. Then on 17 December 1860 a party of Texas Rangers, U.S. Army troops, and volunteers in a fight on the Pease River in western Texas captured her and her infant daughter. Ranger captain Lawrence Sullivan "Sul" Ross saw that a woman in the group possessed blue eyes and was not an Indian. The rangers took Cynthia Ann and her daughter, along with a Comanche boy. Eventually Ross returned her to her family in East Texas. Cynthia Ann, however, never readjusted to life among whites. After the death of her daughter, Prairie Flower, from fever, Cynthia Ann herself passed away in October 1864 at the age of thirty-seven. Contemporary observers felt that she died of a broken heart, longing for her daughter and for the free life she had known on the plains.

Cynthia Ann Parker's son Quanah remained with the Comanches on the Great Plains. After growing to maturity, he led them in their last major war against the U.S. Army in 1874–75. When the military forced the Comanches onto a reservation near Fort Sill, Oklahoma, Quanah realized the futility of further active resistance and led the Comanches in adapting themselves to many aspects of mainstream American life.

During the twentieth century, as Texans became increasingly aware of their past, many people started traveling to visit the site of the former Fort Parker community. In 1922 Parker's descendants and others erected a memorial for the five victims of the 1836 attack at a spot close to their grave in a nearby cemetery named the Fort Parker Memorial Park. Then in 1936, during the Texas Centennial celebration, local residents deeded the site of the former fort to the state. Based on evidence visible at that time, crews reconstructed the timber walls and several of the cabins, and the site was opened as a state park. Then in 1966 state crews removed the deteriorating thirty-year-old construction and rebuilt the fort basically as it had appeared in 1936. Operated as the Old Fort Parker State Historical Park, the site is now administered by

Trees of many species form a canopy over burials in the beautifully landscaped Fort Parker Memorial Park. Photograph by the author, 2000.

Limestone County and the towns of Groesbeck and Mexia, and is open to the public.

LOCATION: *Old Fort Parker State Historical Park is located in central Limestone County just off Texas State Highway 14 on Texas Park Road 35. The entry to the park on Texas State Highway 14 is located 4.0 miles north of Groesbeck and 7.7 miles south of Mexia; the park itself is 1.6 miles from the highway. Just north of the historical park is a recreational facility, Fort Parker State Park, which offers visitors overnight camping and water sports. The beautifully landscaped Fort Parker Memorial Park cemetery, with burials dating from the 1830s, is located just north of Groesbeck. The easiest access to the cemetery is from Farm Road 1245 at a point that is 1.9 miles north from its intersection with Texas State Highway 14 in Groesbeck.*

Frio Town

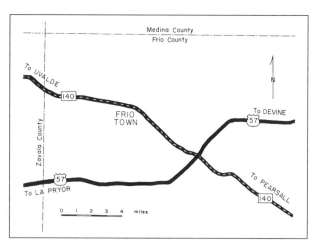

Frio Town, located in ranch country and formerly called the "cowboy capital" of South Texas,

Members of the Long and Slaughter families stand outside a residence in Frio Town, circa 1900. Courtesy of Ruth Higdon and the University of Texas Institute of Texan Cultures at San Antionio.

became the first seat of Frio County in 1871 as Frio City. In 1881 a north-south railway line was built through the county. The newer town of Pearsall sprang up along the rails and became the seat of government, leaving the older town to stagnate and die.

Local government organized in Frio County in 1871. The site chosen for the county seat was near the Presidio Crossing of the Frio River and was known as Frio City. It took its name from the water in the river, as *frio* means "cold" in Spanish. With its central city block reserved for the courthouse, the town fronted the river. In 1871 the commissioners voted to construct a wooden courthouse, followed in 1872 by a stone jail. After the wooden courthouse burned in 1877, the county built a handsome two-story stone replacement. In the meantime, merchants quickly began moving to the townsite—with storekeepers and saloonkeepers in the forefront—making Frio City an important supply center for the ranching country around it. Some sources claim that the town had as many as 1,200 to 1,500 residents, likely an

exaggeration, but Frio City clearly did become the largest community in the county.

Frio City was more than just a focal point for local government and commerce. It also served important social roles for the sparsely settled range country around it. Frances Bramlette Farris made summertime visits to the town in the 1880s, and she relished the balls held there. "Most of our big dances were in the courthouse where there was an enormous hall with a floor as slick as glass," she recalled, adding, "when we were all assembled we could hardly hold our feet till the music began, and the dancing went on until the wee small hours." Vinton L. James as a young man about the same time lived on a ranch between Frio City and Uvalde and recalled, "when there was a dance at either place I attended. . . . We would dance all night, . . . when youth and pretty girls were the inspiration."

In 1880 the San Antonio and Aransas Pass Railway extended its lines through Frio County, but missed Frio City by about sixteen miles. The company established Pearsall near the center of

Overgrown burial plots in the Frio Town Cemetery. Photograph by the author, 2000.

bend in the road that is 16.1 miles northwest of Pearsall and 28.0 miles southeast of Uvalde. This farm road crosses many low washes that fill with running water during rainstorms. Visitors should also watch out for snakes in the cemetery.

Glenrio

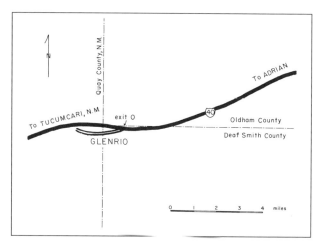

the county, naming it in honor of a company vice-president, and soon merchants and residents from Frio City began moving to the new railroad town. After this general exodus, voters in 1883 chose Pearsall as their new county seat. Frio City became an almost instant ghost town. Its name even reflected the difference; in 1886 Frio City changed its name to Frio Town. It barely clung to life as the location for a rural school, a country store, and a post office, but even these faded away during the mid-twentieth century. Occasional site-seers came to view the gaunt stone walls of the old court-house, but due to vandalism by outsiders the owners of the private ranch encompassing the townsite closed it to the public three decades ago. Today people may visit only the picturesque cemetery alongside a paved farm road.

LOCATION: *The Frio Town Cemetery lies on the south-west side of Farm Road 140 in Frio County at a slight*

Grass grows up through cracks in the four lanes of pavement that once carried the traffic of Route 66 through Glenrio, a ghost town on the Texas-New Mexico state line in northwestern Deaf Smith County. The entire townsite looks like a motion-picture set, and it has indeed served as one on several occasions.

Glenrio began as Rock Island, a siding on the Chicago, Rock Island and Gulf Railway, which connected Amarillo, Texas, with Tucumcari, New Mexico, via Glenrio in 1906. Track construction crews were first to occupy the town of Glenrio. Soon the W. E. Moses Townsite Investment Company of Denver, Colorado, began promoting settlement by farmers on vacant federal lands located on the west side of the state line. "If you want any part of this land," the company advertised, "we can locate you on either forty acres, one hundred and sixty acres, [or] three hundred and twenty acres under the Homestead laws." The railroad had built livestock loading-pens and other shipping facilities at its track siding on the state line. The site seemed well suited to serve as a trading center for the farmers the land promoters wanted to attract.

An abandoned Route 66 service station and café in Glenrio. Photograph by the author, 2000.

In September 1910 Glenrio received its first place of business, a hotel operated by J. W. Kilpatrick. Soon he was joined by other business-people operating grocery and mercantile stores, a restaurant, blacksmith shop, post office, newspaper, barbershop, bakery, feed store, and telephone exchange. Methodists built a church, and an elementary school met for classes in private homes until a school building was erected in 1912. The post office operated on the New Mexico side of the state line, but the railway company placed its depot and steam locomotive water facilities on the Texas side. For several years the railroad brought cars loaded with prospective settlers to the siding at Glenrio. If they chose lands in the area, these new arrivals usually went to Amarillo to buy lumber, livestock, and household items and then shipped them to Glenrio by train. There they loaded the materials onto wagons to haul to their new homesteads.

When the U.S. government in 1926 began numbering major highways, it identified the unpaved east-west road through Glenrio as part of U.S. Highway 66. This transcontinental route connected

Streamline Moderne architecture found expression in this former diner that became a second-hand shop in its later years, located on Route 66 in Glenrio. Photograph by the author, 2000.

Chicago, Illinois, with Santa Monica, California, on the Pacific Ocean. Eventually the highway took the place of the railroad as the principal transportation link for Glenrio. Through the 1930s and 1940s, thousands of motorists passed back and forth through the little community. Glenrio even

Some of the many cars and trucks that ground to a halt on Route 66 at Glenrio. Photograph by the author, 2000.

became a location for filming portions of the motion picture, *The Grapes of Wrath*. All of this helped the town prosper, but Glenrio's location also gave rise to some interesting divisions among its commercial enterprises. Because Texas's gasoline taxes were three to five cents cheaper per gallon, filling stations were on the east side of the state line. The bars, however, were on the New Mexico side, as Deaf Smith County was legally "dry." Glenrio at mid-twentieth century boasted four gasoline stations, three cafés, two curio shops, two bars, two motels, a railway depot, and a post office.

When the new Interstate Highway 40 took the place of U.S. Highway 66, the freeway bypassed Glenrio. As soon as the lifeblood of traffic stopped flowing through the town, most of its residents and all of its businesses went elsewhere. Today not one commercial enterprise operates in the former town, which is filled with abandoned gasoline stations, cafés, motels, and the hulks of cast-off automobiles and trucks that broke down at Glenrio and never went any farther.

LOCATION: *Glenrio is located just south of exit 0 on Interstate Highway 40 at the Texas-New Mexico state line at a point that is 23 miles west of Adrian, Texas, 70 miles west of Amarillo, and 30 miles east of Tucumcari, New Mexico. Three miles west on Inter-* *state Highway 40 is a New Mexico tourist information station and roadside rest area with water and toilet facilities.*

Goodnight

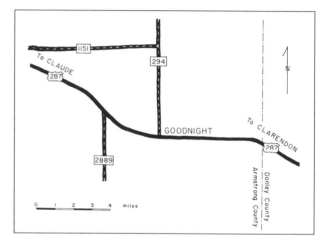

Located on what was originally the Fort Worth and Denver Railway just north of Palo Duro Canyon in Armstrong County, the town of Goodnight took its name from its founder, pioneer rancher Charles Goodnight. It prospered as a local market and educational center well into the twentieth century, but today stands virtually deserted.

Charles Goodnight holds the distinction of having been the first rancher in the Texas Panhandle, where he established a ranch in 1876. Two decades later when he retired from managing the large cattle-raising operation, he purchased a smaller (sixty-section) property astride the future route of the Fort Worth and Denver Railway, which would connect the cities of Fort Worth, Texas, and Denver, Colorado. He erected his two-story ranch house near the edge of Palo Duro Canyon in 1887, just in time to watch the track-laying crews bring in the new convenience of travel by steam railway. The company built a siding and depot named Goodnight. Soon the livestock shipping point became a local market center with a blacksmith, newspaper, post office, and stores.

Charles and his wife, Mary Ann, became interested in promoting education in the new town. In 1898 they donated $30,000, a very large sum at

An open gate leading into the site of a former home in Goodnight. Photograph by the author, 2000.

that time, and 340 acres of land for the creation of Goodnight College. Initially providing only secondary-school-level instruction, the academy in time did become a two-year college. Charles Goodnight first offered the school to the Methodist Church, but that denomination declined the donation. He then turned to the Baptists, who gladly accepted the gift. The school eventually grew to several dormitories, a three-story administration building, and print shop, but only operated until 1917. Competition from other colleges, such as Clarendon College only eighteen miles away, attracted too many potential students from Goodnight College. Its facilities passed to the public schools of Goodnight, which used them until the mid-1950s, when the Goodnight schools were consolidated with the Claude schools.

Goodnight maintained an active market center for decades; the town reached a high population of three hundred in 1940, when it reported nine places of business. Such prosperity, however, would not last. After rural highways were im-proved, businesses in other towns lured away Goodnight's customers. The national consolidation of agriculture also helped reduce the town's rural population. Residents continued to move away

Several decades' worth of household debris surrounding an abandoned home in Goodnight. Photograph by the author, 2000.

Charles Goodnight, a pioneer rancher who later worked to protect America's bison population. He gave his name both to the town of Goodnight and to Goodnight College. Courtesy of the Panhandle-Plains Historical Museum Research Center.

from Goodnight—from two hundred people in 1944, the number dropped to only twenty-five in 1969.

While in its semi-abandoned state, Goodnight unexpectedly became a setting for motion-picture filming. In early spring 1962, advance crews from Paramount Pictures, Inc., began arriving in Armstrong County to film portions of the movie *Hud*, starring Paul Newman and Patricia Neal. Among the areas in which the crews filmed scenes were the near-abandoned town and the nearby Stow Hudson house, which became the buff-colored ranch house in the movie. The motion picture was based on the novel *Horseman, Pass By,* by Texas writer Larry McMurtry. When he reflected on the filming, Goodnight postmaster L. S. Newberry commented in 1966, "After *Hud* was a big suc-

cess as a movie the tourists would flock here, mainly to take a look at the Hud ranch house."

The town of Goodnight continued withering away. When the author last visited the site in 2000, Goodnight and its immediate area had an active community center, ten occupied residences but eight that were abandoned, a collapsing store building that had contained the last post office, and ruins, debris, broken ground, and even ornamental fences at the numerous sites of former structures. Private owners have preserved Charles Goodnight's 1887 ranch house at its original location just south of the town. Goodnight College—its location marked by debris from former academic buildings and by gnarled juniper trees and other ancient ornamental shrubs—lies on the crown of a low hill at the west end of the townsite.

Coeds from a painting class at Goodnight College pose in front of a building in Goodnight around the turn of the twentieth century. Courtesy of the Southwest Collection, Texas Tech University.

LOCATION: *Goodnight lies on U.S. Highway 287 at its intersection with Farm Road 294 in Armstrong County at a point that is 11.3 miles southeast of Claude and 18.2 miles northwest of Clarendon. The graves of Charles and Mary Ann Dyer Goodnight can be seen in the Goodnight Cemetery, which is 0.6 miles east and then 0.5 miles north of the townsite on paved county roads.*

Grapetown

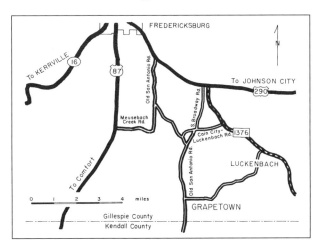

Grapetown was a German immigrant community on the banks of South Grape Creek southeast of Fredericksburg. It is known today primarily for its still-active Grapetown Shooting Club, a marksmanship society.

Settlers bought land along South Grape Creek soon after nearby Fredericksburg was founded by Germans in 1846. Because of its location at the crossing over South Grape Creek on the old Fredericksburg-San Antonio Road, Grapetown became a favored area for settlement. The first known landowner in the vicinity was John Hemphill, who received the deed for his property on 13 May 1848, but soon many others followed. The majority of the arrivals were farmers and livestock-raisers, but a handful of them were professional teamsters who drove wagons between Fredericksburg and the port of Indianola on the Gulf of Mexico.

An example of the typical Grapetown teamster can be seen in Ferdinand Hohenberger. Like most of the freighters, he used oxen before the Civil War but changed to mules afterward because he had discovered that they were faster. Before he switched to mules, it took Hohenberger's oxen a full two months to haul a load of freight to the coast and return with goods and merchandise bound for the interior. In the springtime he would plant his corn and set out on a trip to the coast. He would return in time to find it three feet tall and ready for cultivation. Then he would leave again, coming back to harvest the crop in the summer.

Friedreich Doebbler built the first store at Grapetown in 1860. He called it Doebbler's Inn and placed it where the road crossed the creek. There it served a wide variety of purposes: hostelry for travelers, grocery store, restaurant, post office, livery stable, and community social center. It operated for fifty-five years, finally closing in 1915.

During the early years at Grapetown, children attended school in Fredericksburg, about ten miles away. Their parents placed them with relatives during the school term or boarded them in the town. Then about 1870, members of the Grapetown community built their own log schoolhouse, which they called the Grapetown Line School because the Gillespie-Kendall county line passed through the area from which the pupils came. Then in 1880 a larger school was built from stone, and it remained in use until 1944, when the school consolidated with the

A decorative sign marks the entrance of the Grapetown shooting club. Photograph by the author, 2000.

This historic cottage in Grapetown has been carefully preserved. Photograph by the author, 2000.

Rocky Hill School. The old 1880 schoolbuilding still stands.

For several years the Fredericksburg and Northern Railway operated near Grapetown. The company constructed a railroad line about 1912 to connect Fredericksburg with Kerrville, and it built a small station to serve the residents of Grapetown. It is interesting that the depot was called Bankersmith in honor of Temple D. Smith, the Fredericksburg banker who had spearheaded the movement to construct the line. The railway operated until 1944, at which time it was one of only two railroads in Texas with a tunnel and the only one in the state with a woman president, Mrs. R. F. Spenser.

Throughout its history, one of the most prominent institutions in Grapetown has been the Grapetown Schuetzen Verein, or shooting club. Begun in 1887, the social organization remains active to this day, and its target range, pavilions, and dance hall are the most impressive structures in the old town. Club members still meet every other Sunday afternoon for target practice and competition. Each summer on the weekend with a full moon nearest to the first of August, the Grapetown Schuetzen Verein members participate in a *schuetzenfest*, or marksmanship festival, in competition with the other shooting societies active in Gillespie County. These general and team competitions began in 1893; the first schuetzenfest was held in Grapetown.

Commercial trade in Grapetown began to diminish in the early 1930s. At that time, the rerouting of the highway from Fredericksburg to Comfort and San Antonio completely bypassed Grapetown. This rerouting, combined with the general economic slowdown in the nation, caused the town to decline. From a population of almost 150 at the turn of the twentieth century, the community declined to about seventy residents in 1965. Today it is a rural community with numerous residences scattered on surrounding farms but virtually no one lives at the townsite proper. Several historic structures are preserved on the Schuetzen Verein grounds, including the 1880 Grapetown School.

LOCATION: *To reach Grapetown, drive southwest from Fredericksburg on U.S. Highway 290 a distance of 2.6 miles to the intersection with the paved county-road known as the "Old San Antonio Road." Turn south on the winding Old San Antonio Road and drive 7.4 miles to the grounds of the Grapetown Schuetzen Verein. On this route bear to the left and bypass Meusebach Creek Road at 2.3 miles, bear to the right and bypass Cain City-Luckenbach Road at 4.2 miles, pass South Broadway Road at 4.6 miles, and pass Grapetown Road at 7.0 miles. The Grapetown Cemetery is an additional 0.4 miles south of the Schuetzen Verein grounds on the west side of the Old San Antonio Road.*

Members of the Irish community at Gussettville gathered for this portrait in the Nueces River bottoms after a Sunday Mass at St. Joseph's Church, circa 1910. Courtesy of Allie Burke Young and the University of Texas Institute of Texan Cultures at San Antonio.

Gussettville

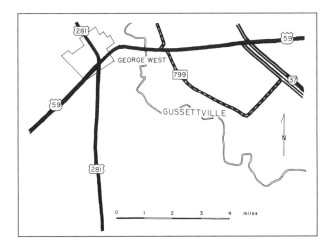

One of the earliest white settlements in Live Oak County in the Nueces River valley, Gussettville grew as a result of Irish immigration promoted by empresario Patrick McGloin. By the 1840s members of the Fox family had settled at the townsite on the high east bank of the Nueces River, and began calling the place Fox Nation. Soon it became a stopping point on a stagecoach route connecting San Antonio to Corpus Christi.

Norwick Gussett, a native of North Carolina who had fought in the Mexican War, settled at Fox Nation. He opened a store in the community and became one of its more prominent citizens, giving the town the name of Gussettville. When the Texas Legislature separated Live Oak County from San Patricio County in 1856, Norwick Gussett actively promoted his town as the seat for the new county, but local voters instead chose the newer town of Oakville. In 1858, however, Gussettville received the third post office granted in Live Oak County.

The 1878 St. Joseph's Church and adjacent cemetery in Gussettville. Photograph by the author, 2000.

with Farm Road 799 in Live Oak County. Then drive 3.0 miles southeast on Farm Road 799 to the townsite. The Farm Road loops around from Gussettville to meet the southbound access road of Interstate Highway 37 at a dead end. The historic church and "new" cemetery lie on the southwest side of the Farm Road and have convenient public access. Summertime visitors may want to wear boots on account of the grass burrs that thrive in the graveyard. The "old" cemetery lies on the northeast side of the Farm Road across the wooden stile over a barbed wire fence and several yards across a privately owned cultivated field. The high, uncut weeds and historic grave markers of the old cemetary are known to provide shelter for rattlesnakes.

During the 1850s and 1860s, Gussettville grew into a substantial community. Not only did it have the only Catholic church in the county, but also a school and stores. The earliest religious services at Gussettville were held under the spreading live oak trees, with a hand-hewn board fastened to a tree trunk serving as an altar. A wooden church soon followed, and in 1878 the current St. Joseph's Church was erected.

Newer towns drew away much of the trade that Gussettville needed to prosper. In 1886 it lost its post office, and then in the second decade of the twentieth century the San Antonio, Uvalde and Gulf Railroad, connecting San Antonio to Corpus Christi on the west side of the Nueces River, bypassed the town by about a mile. Gussettville had remained a viable community, with 126 children attending its public school as recently as 1915, but its isolation from the railroad spelled its doom. Businesses moved away, as did many of the local farmers due to the consolidation of agriculture over the next three decades. Today Gussettville is marked only by its handsome historic St. Joseph's Church, the "new" cemetery in the churchyard, the "old" cemetery located in the middle of a plowed field across the road, and disturbed ground and debris at the sites of former buildings.

LOCATION: *To reach Gussettville, drive 2.8 miles east from George West or 2.9 miles west of Interstate Highway 37 on U.S. Highway 59 to the intersection*

Hackberry

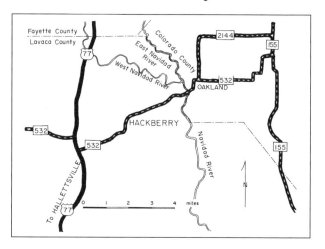

Its one-hundred-twenty-year-old, two-story stone general store building dominates the site of Hackberry to this day. Although the building and the town are vacant now, Hackberry was once a major trading center in the Navidad River valley in northeastern Lavaca County.

The town's genesis came about in 1846 when Ludwig Eduard Neuhaus of Ellerburg, Germany, immigrated to Texas. Settling in what would become Lavaca County, Neuhaus purchased part of a plantation on the west side of the Navidad River near its forks, where he began farming and raising livestock. In 1853 he built a steam-powered sawmill and gristmill, adding cotton gin equipment in 1858. By 1862 Neuhaus secured a post

The two-story stone store that Ludwig Neuhaus erected at Hackberry in 1881. Photograph by the author, 1999.

office, and then in 1865 he opened a general mercantile store. He named the post office Hackberry after the trees growing in front of his house. As more and more people settled in the area, the community gained a saloon, blacksmith and tin shop, two churches, a school, and a number of residences.

Neuhaus had settled directly alongside a major wagon road. The stage and freighting route connected San Felipe and Gonzales, then continued on to San Antonio, and it passed right in front of his house. During the Civil War, hundreds of wagons annually traveled this route from the head of the railroad at Alleyton to Mexico with their loads of cotton. This overland commerce road bypassed the Union's naval blockade of the Texas coast during the war and provided an export outlet for cotton. The growth of a substantial rural population in northeastern Lavaca County in the last third of the nineteenth century made Hackberry into a substantial commercial center that provided for the needs of hundreds of farm families. Because of the trade volume, Ludwig Neuhaus in 1881 built an imposing two-story stone general mercantile building, filling it with everything from fancy soaps to seed potatoes.

Locals boasted that it was the largest store in the entire county, and it may well have been. Most of the merchandise came by rail to Schulenberg, Texas, and then overland by wagon the rest of the way. After Neuhaus retired in 1882, his sons took over the business and ran it until 1902, when most of the Neuhaus family moved to Houston.

With the national consolidation of agriculture during the first half of the twentieth century, the rural population of Lavaca County, which had supported the business in Hackberry, dried up. Fewer and fewer farmers using mechanized equipment were required to cultivate and harvest crops, so the rural population that had previously done such work evaporated. In the last days of the dying town, architects from the Historic American Buildings Survey in Washington, D.C., photographed and made scale drawings of the store and two of the residences at Hackberry, but the town itself had already disappeared. The store closed in 1941, marking the end of Hackberry's commercial activity. Today the impressive store building, historic residences, and hackberry trees are all that remain to mark the site of this once-important marketplace.

LOCATION: *Hackberry is located on Farm Road 532 in northeastern Lavaca County at a point that is 11.3 miles northeast of Hallettsville and 3.5 miles southwest of Oakland.*

Hansford

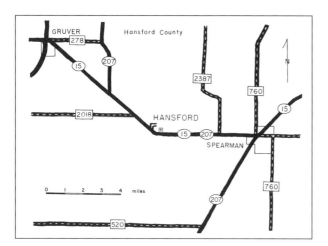

The stone foundation of the 1890s courthouse in Hansford, filled with debris cast off by ranchers and local residents. Photograph by the author, 2000.

Hansford lies in ruins in the northern Texas Panhandle. It was established in 1887 by J. H. "Huff" Wright and Fred Bonfill to serve the surrounding ranch country, and it faced some interesting challenges before the town finally died about sixty years later.

In 1889, two years after the founding of Hansford, citizens of the area organized Hansford County, choosing the new community as its seat of government. Initially county officials had offices in shacks around town, but on 13 May 1890 county commissioners approved the issuance of bonds in the amount of $12,000 for the construction of a native stone courthouse. There was insufficient stone of satisfactory quality in the vicinity, so the commissioners voted an additional $6,000 in bonds to purchase brick. As the structure neared completion in 1891, a tornado demolished it. Lacking funds to rebuild it according to the original plans, the county began work on a one-and-a-half-story courthouse, only to have its roof ripped off by a second tornado. Finally, the structure was completed and opened to public use.

Though never a large town, Hansford generally maintained a population of approximately one hundred residents. Among its places of business over the years were a bank, a barber shop, a drugstore, post office, mercantile stores, a hardware store, a hotel, doctors' offices, a real-estate office, feed store, livery stables, a lumber yard, telephone exchange, church, abstract office, the *Hansford Headlight* newspaper, and blacksmith shops. It had a three-story wooden school, the upper floor of which served as a lodge hall. All supplies were hauled overland by freight wagon, so teamsters enjoyed a strong trade.

Hansford prospered until the North Texas and Santa Fe Railway built a line across the eastern part of the county in the early 1920s. This line connected Shattuck, Oklahoma (and the Santa Fe system), with Spearman, Texas, located a few miles east of Hansford. With their new railroad connections, Spearman merchants could

West Texas residents found an easier way to move their towns across the level plains during the early twentieth century. Courtesy of the Southwest Collection, Texas Tech University.

offer customers far lower prices for goods than could their competitors in Hansford. Soon the businesses in the older town moved to the new, and Hansford began to die. Its post office moved to Spearman in 1920, followed by the county seat in 1926. In this latter year Spearman had a thousand inhabitants, fully ten times that of Hansford in its heyday. By the late 1940s Hansford reported no population whatsoever, and today its ruins are surrounded by scattered rural homes in the valley of Palo Duro Creek.

LOCATION: *Hansford lies on gravel Hansford County Road 18A on the north side of Texas State Highway 15/207 at a point 7.7 miles west of Spearman and 5.6 miles southeast of Gruver. To view the concrete and stone ruins and foundations of buildings, drive 0.2 miles north and then 0.2 miles east on the gravel county road. The ruins stand on private property in the fenced pasture immediately east and south of the L-shaped county road and may be viewed from a distance. The prominent concrete steps once led into a wooden hotel, and the large stone foundations provided the footing for the courthouse. The well-maintained Hansford Cemetery, with burials dating back to the 1880s, lies on the north side of the state highway just east of the townsite. Several historical markers for Hansford stand along the state highway.*

Hueco Tanks

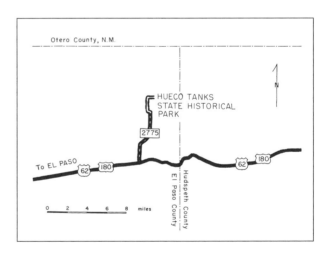

A location occupied by Native people for many years, Hueco Tanks might best be described as an American Indian ghost town in arid El Paso County. The desert-dwellers living at the site depended on water that collected and remained for months at a time in natural cistern-like depressions in the rocks of three prominent hills. *Hueco* is a Spanish word for "hollow."

Hueco Tanks site is located on the western flank of the Hueco Mountains in arid far West Texas. These mountains were formed by the natural injection of molten rock from the interior of the earth into sedimentary layers perhaps thirty million years ago. Over time the softer surrounding

The Hueco Mountains stand above the surrounding desert flats in extreme West Texas. Photograph by the author, 2000.

Erosion of the low-grade granite comprising the Hueco Mountains formed the natural cisterns that gave the place its name, Hueco Tanks. Photograph by the author, 2000.

Figures of dancers painted on the rocks at the Hueco Tanks by prehistoric inhabitants. Photograph by John Davis, 1970, courtesy of the University of Texas Institute of Texan Cultures at San Antonio.

rocks eroded, leaving behind the low-grade granite mountains that stand four hundred feet above the surrounding desert flats. Rainwater from thunderstorms collected in natural depressions in the igneous rock, and this water source has attracted both prehistoric and historic peoples.

The earliest people documented at Hueco Tanks were Folsom-era hunters and gatherers about 10,000 years ago. Archaeological evidence documents visits by other transient Native groups that came to the site to hunt animals and gather edible plants. Sedentary Indians of the Jornada Branch of the Mogollon Culture came to the Hueco Tanks and created a community that thrived there from about A.D. 1150 to about A.D. 1350. Archaeological evidence shows that during this two-hundred-year period, they built and occupied a village comprised of multiple rectangular one-room pit houses. The walls extended upward, and the roofs, supported by pairs of wooden posts, covered the central living areas. The village stood near the north end of the easternmost mountain. There the Indian farmers raised crops in a rich alluvial wash that came down

from the hills on the east. Even to this day plants in the alluvial wash are visibly greener than those in various nearby soils. These inhabitants of Hueco Tanks knew about more than just farming—they ingeniously dammed crannies in the granite hills and built stone diversion dams to increase the flow of rainwater into the natural depressions in order to increase their water supplies. They decorated these same areas with hundreds of figures painted on the rocks.

The village residents at Hueco Tanks departed sometime before A.D. 1400, when many sites in the Southwest were similarly abandoned by sedentary Indians. Once again, only nomadic hunters and gatherers came to the oasis-like site, but they too left their artifacts and their paintings on the stones. After the arrival of Spaniards and their Pueblo Indian allies in El Paso in 1680, both of these groups began making occasional visits to Hueco Tanks. The site gradually became known to travelers, who came in increasing numbers after the 1849 discovery of gold in California. Hundreds of gold-seekers on their way westward passed by Hueco Tanks, which in 1858 became a short-lived stagecoach station on the transcontinental Butterfield Overland Mail.

After the Southern Pacific Railroad came to El Paso in 1881, the importance of Hueco Tanks as a desert watering place decreased. The relative speed and convenience of rail travel eliminated the need for such between-town watering places. Local ranchers occupied the lands surrounding and including Hueco Tanks, and most people forgot their existence. Then, when private real-estate developers in the mid-twentieth century began selling land near the site as rural homesites, historic preservationists and archaeologists prompted El Paso County in 1960 to purchase the Hueco Tanks and insure their protection. Then in 1969 the county sold the property to the state of Texas, which after purchasing additional acreage opened the site in 1970 as the Hueco Tanks State Historical Park.

LOCATION: *The Hueco Tanks State Historical Park is located 32 miles northeast of El Paso in El Paso County, off U.S. Highway 62/82 at the northern terminus of Ranch Road 2775. The park is open for daytime use only. Visitors who plan to leave the park road should wear sturdy shoes or boots, bring protective hats or caps, carry drinking water, and be alert for rattlesnakes, thorny plants, and stinging insects.*

Indian Hot Springs

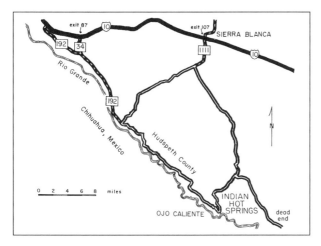

The site of thermal springs used by Native people and also by white settlers, Indian Hot Springs for many years drew health-seekers to its remote desert location on the Rio Grande.

American Indians frequented the area of the hot springs for many years before written history began in Hudspeth County. They carved out depressions near the springs to create what appeared to be "bathtubs" in the rock. Raiding Apaches, who were among the early visitors to the springs, delayed occupation of the region for decades. They even attacked and killed six black members of a U.S. Cavalry detachment at the springs in 1880. After the Apaches were forced onto reservations, both Mexican and white ranchers occupied the Rio Grande valley in the area.

Local residents knew of the springs' curative powers. About 1905, Americans began trekking over the Quitman Mountains or along the banks of the Rio Grande to reach the hot mineral springs. By 1907 locals had opened a primitive lodging with simple food service, as more and more people traveled to the purported healing springs.

Hot water comes to the surface in multiple springs along the river floodplain at the southwest end of the Quitman Mountains. Scientists believe that water from desert storms percolates downward about a thousand meters, where it heats and then discharges upward through the Caballo Fault, forming the springs. Tests in 1976 showed temperatures ranging from 81 degrees Fahrenheit at Soda Spring to 117 degrees Fahrenheit at Stump Spring. Minerals dissolved in the waters include boron, chloride, potassium, sulfate, lithium, sodium, magnesium, calcium, bicarbonate, nitrate, and strontium. Many people who bathed in the waters claimed to be returned to health; some even claimed miraculous cures.

In 1929 a corporation based in El Paso began developing Indian Hot Springs as a European-style spa. It built a twenty-two-room hotel with a dining room and lounge, a number of cabins, and bathhouses over some of the springs. Two physicians and several nurses attended health-seekers. The difficulties of accessing the spa via rough, unpaved roads always made it difficult for people to reach the site, but the Great Depression caused the first of several closures.

Then in 1952, healer Jewel Babb arrived at Indian Hot Springs. She reopened the hotel and assisted many invalids. "We don't have any sick people down here except visitors," she told

The entrance of the privately owned resort at Indian Hot Springs. Photograph by the author, 2000.

Soda Spring, which flows to the surface beside the county road on the north side of Indian Hot Springs. The building houses a pump that forces water from the spring for use elsewhere at the site. Photograph by the author, 2000.

Dallas journalist Frank X. Tolbert, "and they don't stay sick long." Despite this claim, ownership of the spa subsequently passed through the hands of a number of individuals—not the least of whom was Dallas oilman H. L. Hunt. In the 1960s he restored the Indian Hot Springs Hotel and made a number of improvements. Among Hunt's notable guests were boxer Gene Tunney, actor Cameron Mitchell of the *High Chaparral* television series, and U.S. congressman Olin E. Teague. After Hunt's death his heirs sold the spa, which tended to drain its owner's finances, to other individuals. Today it is closed to the public and operates solely as a private retreat at the foot of desert mountains on the Rio Grande located about 125 miles downriver from El Paso.

80
I

LOCATION: *There are two ways to reach Indian Hot Springs from the American side of the Rio Grande. On either of these routes, visitors should carry food, extra water, vehicle repair tools, and one or more spare tires. The easier of two unpaved dirt roads follows the Rio Grande. To take this route, take exit 87 from Interstate Highway 10, and drive south 2.7 miles on paved Farm Road 34 to its intersection with Farm Road 192. Then drive southeast an additional 11.7 miles on paved Farm Road 192 to its terminus. At the end of the pavement continue southeastward on an unmarked graded county road 21.1 miles to the site by way of a winding, scenic route that passes through open range, but is sometimes rough, and crosses multiple drainage paths that may fill with water during rainstorms. At a point that is 14.6 miles from the end of Farm Road 192, the graded county road forks; take the right fork rather than the left fork, which is a steep road up the side of a hill. This route includes multiple rough cattleguard crossings.*

The alternate route to Indian Hot Springs from the American side of the river begins at Sierra Blanca on Interstate Highway 10. This is a considerably rougher route and is recommended only for full-size pickup trucks or for high-clearance vehicles with four-wheel drive. This drive should never be attempted in a motor home or in a vehicle pulling a trailer.

On the second route, drive south from exit 107 on Interstate 10 in Sierra Blanca on paved Ranch Road 1111. Drive 4.9 miles south to the terminus of the paved Ranch Road, where the road forks. Take the

southeastern—not southwestern—fork and continue on the rough to very rough unpaved road an additional 26.3 miles to Indian Hot Springs. The last three miles of this road, which crosses over the mountains, are narrow, very rough, steep, and abound with large, sharp rocks that must be dodged to avoid tire damage. There are sheer drop-offs with no safety barriers. This route, like the first, passes through open range and crosses (and sometimes follows) drainage paths that may fill with water during rainstorms. Drivers will also pass over multiple cattleguard crossings on this route. Visitors might see peccaries, roadrunners, coyotes, and snakes on or near the roadway.

From the Republic of Mexico, a simple suspension footbridge connects Indian Hot Springs with the village of Ojo Caliente on the other side of the Rio Grande.

Ireland

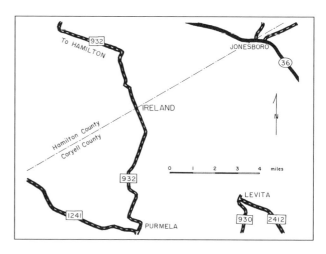

Ireland blossomed as a new railroad town on the Cotton Belt Railway at the Hamilton-Coryell county line in 1911. But the town faded away within three decades as a consequence of changes in agriculture and the discontinuance of railway service.

The townsite now known as Ireland began as a scattered rural community on both sides of the Hamilton-Coryell county line. Taking letters from each county's name, residents formed the name Hamco. Life for the handful of families around Hamco changed in 1911, for in that year the St.

A brick vault and concrete foundations are all that remain of a two-story building that stood on the main street of Ireland. Photograph by the author, 2000.

Louis Southwestern Railway Company, commonly known as the Cotton Belt Railway, built a railroad line thirty-two miles long connecting the county-seat towns of Hamilton and Gatesville. Then just southwest of the Hamilton-Coryell county line, the Mid-Texas Improvement Company laid out the town of Ireland alongside the tracks, usurping the place of the older Hamco. The company named the new town Ireland in honor of former Texas governor John Ireland. When the company auctioned off town lots in November 1911, three special trains carried potential buyers from Waco and elsewhere to the event.

Ireland grew rapidly during its first years. High prices for agricultural commodities in Europe during World War I prompted farmers to break new land for cotton-raising. As more and more agriculturists came to the area between Gatesville and Hamilton, Ireland grew prosperous from their trade. Among its business enterprises were a grain elevator, corn mill, cotton gin, lumber yard, restaurant, drug store, hotel, bank with capital stock of $20,000, saloon, barbershop, three mercantile stores, three churches, a public school, and even a chamber of commerce. The imposing red brick Ireland school, built on top of the county line, stood two stories tall.

Ireland's decline began with the crash of agricultural commodity prices in 1921, followed by the Great Depression eight years later in 1929. The cost of raising crops eventually exceeded their sale price, and family after family found it impossible to live off the land. After selling their properties to others or losing them to financial institutions, the rural residents who had supported Ireland moved elsewhere. Many who remained until the 1940s then left to go work in defense plants during World War II. The hinterland of Ireland was slowly depopulated, and many of the former farms reverted to rangeland. In an essay on Ireland, a Baylor University student recently observed, "Where there were once many families with small farms there are now about six families with large ranches."

Meanwhile, the Cotton Belt Railway had begun making plans to abandon its line through Ireland. It stopped passenger service in 1936 but continued freight service for a while. Then in 1942 the company removed its tracks through Ireland. People continued to move away. One local writer

A brick chimney, rubble, and household debris mark the site of a former home in Ireland. Photograph by the author, 2000.

reported that fourteen houses were moved away from Ireland in just one year. The town that boasted four hundred residents during its heyday could only claim forty inhabitants by the end of World War II.

Today Ireland has about fifteen occupied residences, six disused dwellings, a brick railway station that has been converted to a home, the earthen embankment remaining from the abandoned railway right-of-way, heaps of bricks and concrete foundations from former commercial buildings, the concrete vault from a former bank, two churches, one of which has been converted into a residence, and footings, debris, and disturbed ground that mark the sites of former buildings. A historical marker indicates where the school once stood on the Hamilton-Coryell county line.

LOCATION: *Ireland, which straddles the Hamilton-Coryell county line, is located on Farm Road 932 at a point that is 7.3 miles north of where the road intersects U.S. Highway 84—a total distance of 21.3 miles west-northwest of Gatesville and 15.8 miles southeast of Hamilton.*

Juno

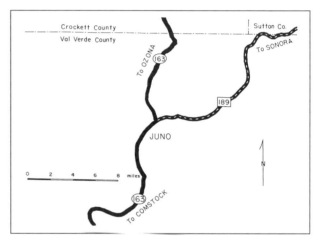

Located on the Devils River in Val Verde County about midway between Ozona and Comstock, Juno prospered for decades as a supply center and stagecoach stop in the arid West Texas ranching country.

Juno's beginnings date to the 1880s, when members of the Edmondson family established a store and Henry Stein opened an eating stand. Both served stagecoach passengers at a stop on the banks of the Devils River. In 1886 Stein secured a post office, submitting the name Juno. Local folklore relates that the only fare Stein offered his dining customers was *frijoles* and beer. When travelers asked what he had to drink he replied, "You know." Mexican residents tended to pronounce the English words "you know" as "juno," which stuck. Stein then suggested it as a place-name on his post office application.

Because of its location on a stagecoach route connecting San Antonio with El Paso, remote Juno saw considerable numbers of people passing back and forth. As livestock-raisers introduced sheep and goats into the region west of the Edwards Plateau, the country around Juno gained

The land around the empty Juno Common School is littered with a few relics of the old town, such as these shattered remnants of a windmill. Photograph by the author, 2000.

Scrub brush and cactus taking over the concrete foundations of a home that long ago disappeared from Juno. Photograph by the author, 2000.

a surprisingly large but scattered rural ranching population. The people who arrived represented Anglo, Mexican, and African-American ethnic groups. Many of these people found Juno was their nearest place to buy the necessities of life and to send their children to school. For years, the segregated school in the town provided separate classrooms and teachers for white and black pupils.

By the beginning of the twentieth century, Juno had grown into a considerable community. It was platted and surveyed as a formal town in 1899—it had two long streets named Main and Flores and lots were laid out to front these two streets. Among the business enterprises found in the town were a hotel, a blacksmith shop that in time became an automobile garage, a land office, mercantile stores, and gasoline filling stations. Sev-

eral doctors and pastors served the town over the years. Because of its location on an important wagon road, the community received telephone service early in the twentieth century. Its growth as a local market center during the twentieth century allowed Juno to claim seventy-five residents from the 1920s through '60s, and the number rose to eighty by 1964. A local booster erected a sign reading, "Pull for Juno or pull out."

Declining and erratic demand for wool and mohair eventually caused most of the residents to "pull out." As ranch after ranch ceased to graze herds of sheep and goats, they released their employees. Most of these people could find no employment other than ranch work in the isolated country, so they had to leave the region in order to earn livelihoods. When Juno lost the dispersed rural population that had supported its businesses, the town withered away. Its post office closed in 1975, the last store soon ceased conducting business, and the school closed in the early 1990s. Today Juno consists of the disused Juno Common School, four abandoned residences, two occupied homes, and numerous foundations and a great deal of debris from former structures. The paved highway follows what was once Juno's Main Street. Much of the townsite is overgrown with chaparral, mesquite, and cactus.

LOCATION: *Juno is located on Texas State Highway 163 in Val Verde County about midway between Ozona and Comstock. It lies 40.7 miles south of Ozona, 48.9 miles southwest of Sonora, and 39.9 miles north of Comstock. At the time of the author's last visit, no filling stations where travelers might purchase gasoline existed at Juno or on any of the roads leading there from Ozona, Sonora, or Comstock. The paved state highway crosses numerous low points that may fill with water during rainstorms.*

Justiceburg

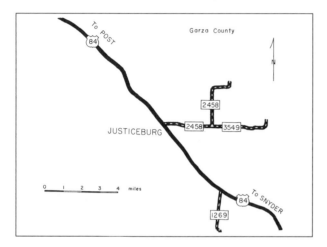

A boarded-up window at the last post office in Justiceburg. Photograph by the author, 2000.

Justiceburg came into existence in the late 1890s as a dispersed ranching community. During the 1910s it became a railroad town alongside the tracks of the Santa Fe Railway. It grew from the trade brought to it by local ranchers, railroad workers, travelers on the highway connecting Post and Snyder, and workers in the oil fields that later developed in the vicinity.

Jefferson Davis Justice became the "father" of Justiceburg. In 1895 the Texas Legislature passed an act that allowed the sale of up to four sections of state-owned public lands to individuals. A section of land measures one mile long on each of two adjacent sides. After some of these lands became available on the Double Mountain Fork of the Brazos River in what would become Garza County, Justice purchased four sections. He moved his family to a one-room shack on the new property and proceeded to develop it as a ranch headquarters. Later he purchased other grazing land in the area.

By 1902 enough ranch families had begun settling around the Double Mountain Fork of the Brazos River to apply for a post office. That post

A tattered American flag marks the gate of an abandoned home in Justiceburg. Photograph by the author, 2000.

office—under the name of Leforrest for Lee and Forrest Tuffing—was granted in 1902 and for a while operated from the Tuffing ranch house. Some of the area's families helped build a one-room school, also located on the Tuffing ranch.

A screen door lies just where it fell in the buffalo grass outside a former store in Justiceburg. Photograph by the author, 2000.

In 1903 local Baptists organized a congregation, which met in the school.

Events took a dramatic turn in 1909. In that year, crews began grading a railway right-of-way from Plainview south toward Lubbock, while other crews began preparing roadbeds and laying rails leading northwestward from Coleman. Jeff Justice knew that the railroad would bring not only convenient communication and transportation, but also a general infusion of investment to the area it crossed. Accordingly, he induced the railroad company to build across his ranch, selling a section of land along the route to the Justiceburg Townsite Company in 1910. The steel rails reached his new town on 17 April 1911, and about the same time the

school, post office, and Baptist church relocated from Leforrest to the new town called Justiceburg in honor of its founder, Jeff D. Justice. Already railroad company crews had begun building an earthen dam on a nearby tributary of the Double Mountain Fork to impound boiler water for the railroad's steam locomotives.

The presence of the railroad insured the growth of Justice's new town, which by 1915 claimed fifty residents. Among its enterprises were a post office, mercantile store, lumberyard, cattle shipping facilities, grocery stores, a confectionery shop, a barber shop, blacksmith shops, automobile repair garages and filling stations, a hotel, land office, and railroad depot, in addition to the relocated church and school. In 1924 a multi-room stucco-brick school replaced its crowded and outdated wooden predecessor. Almost all the town's structures stood on the southwest side of the Santa Fe tracks. Then highway improvements in 1950 re-routed U.S. Highway 84 to the northeast side of the tracks. The post office, store, filling stations, and a church followed it.

The development of oil fields around Justiceburg in the middle of the twentieth century brought new residents to the town just when it was losing population from the consolidation of agriculture. This situation helped maintain a population of about seventy-five from the late 1940s into the early 1990s. Then as petroleum prices dropped, the oil field workers departed and left leaving only a handful of residents. Today Justiceburg stands mostly abandoned, some of its empty homes still containing furniture and the belongings of their former residents.

LOCATION: *Justiceburg straddles U.S. Highway 84 and the tracks of the Santa Fe Railway between Post and Snyder in Garza County. The site is 14.9 miles southeast of Post and 27.6 miles northwest of Snyder. To reach the residential area of Justiceburg, carefully cross the active railroad tracks to a county-maintained gravel road that loops past most of the dwellings and former house sites. The Justiceburg Cemetery is located 0.3 miles east of U.S. Highway 84 on Farm Road 2458 and thence 0.4 miles south on a graded dirt road that becomes very muddy after wet weather.*

Kiomatia

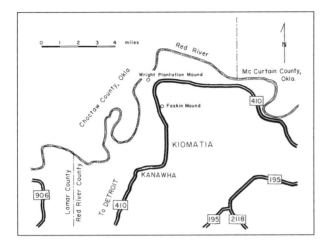

Kiomatia in Red River County has the distinction of being a ghost town twice. First its American Indian residents, who had lived there for centuries, abandoned the site, and then later white settlers created a town and then vacated it.

Prehistoric Caddoan people occupied the area around Kiomatia perhaps as early as the end of the first millennium. They departed the area around 1795. In the floodplain on the south side of the Red River, opposite the mouth of the Kiamichi River, they constructed two complexes of earthen mounds that are believed to have had both religious and administrative roles. Radiating from the Kiomatia mounds were dozens of Caddoan villages. Their residents lived on crops they raised and animals they hunted. The surplus was sent to the people living at the mounds.

The Kiomatia mounds consist of two pairs of earthen mounds located about a mile apart. They may or may not have been occupied at the same time. Each pair consists of a larger mound and a smaller mound about six hundred yards to the northeast. Taking their names from later white occupants, the northwestern pair of mounds is known as the Wright Plantation Mound, and the other is known as the Faskin Mound. The larger

The white farmhouse to the right is built around the 1830s log plantation home erected by Claiborne Wright's sons and slaves. It stands atop one of the prehistoric Caddoan mounds just north of Kiomatia. Photograph by the author, 2000.

The covered entry to the Boulware Store in Kiomatia, the town's last operating place of business. The bars on its windows were flattened by a blacksmith from old buggy wheel rims. Photograph by the author, 2000.

mounds probably served as platforms for ceremonial structures, whereas the smaller mounds may have served funerary roles.

By the time the first white settlers began arriving in this area of the Red River valley about 1816, the mounds had been abandoned for a number of years. Wanting to cultivate the fertile floodplain, the settlers erected homes atop the earthen mounds to escape flooding. Claiborne Wright and his family are considered to be among the first permanent white settlers in the Kiomatia area, known at that time as Pecan Point. In the 1830s his sons and their black slaves erected a dog-trot log cabin atop what became known as the Wright Plantation Mound. The cabin was expanded with later additions, and it remains occupied to this day. Later settlers also constructed a farmhouse atop the Faskin Mound, although the owners removed it in the mid-1970s.

Although today Kiomatia seems out-of-the-way, it once was a hub for river and overland trans-portation. Nineteenth-century planters considered Wright's Landing at Kiomatia to be the head of steam navigation on the Red River, so it became an important shipping point. A military wagon-road stretched southwestward from Fort Smith down through Fort Gibson in present-day Oklahoma to the mouth of Kiamichi River opposite from Kiomatia. In 1844 the Republic of Texas laid out its own wagon-road all the way from the Trinity River in Dallas County to Wright's Landing in order to link up with the Fort Smith-Fort Gibson Road.

One of the Wright sons, Travis George Wright, secured a post office at Kiomatia in 1850, and a settlement began growing around it. By 1880 the Kiomatia community had a population of one hundred, as well as a store, cotton gin, and gristmill. Concurrent with the agricultural prosperity of the World War I era, Kiomatia reached its population peak of 250 in 1914. Shortly afterward, the consolidation of agriculture and the construction of improved roads drained business away from Kiomatia, which in the 1930s declined to forty-six inhabitants. Its post office closed in 1954. Today it has one country store still clinging to life. Visitors might enjoy inspecting the bars on the windows at the store; many years ago a blacksmith forged them from iron buggy tires.

LOCATION: *Kiomatia townsite lies on Farm Road 410 in Red River County at a point that is 2.9 miles north of Kanawah and 18.1 miles north of Detroit. To see the Faskin Mound, drive 2.3 miles north on Farm Road 410 from Kiomatia; the highway right-of-way cuts across the west end of the mound, which is covered with mature trees. To view the Wright Plantation Mound, continue north on Farm Road 410 about 1.1 miles where the roadway turns to the east. The second mound lies 0.3 miles to the east, though it is beneath a white farmhouse—the historic Wright Plantation house. Both mounds are on private property and are not accessible to the public. State and federal laws prohibit the removal of any materials from either site.*

Lagarto

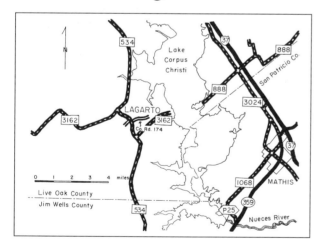

Once known for its college, Lagarto in Live Oak County has succumbed to the South Texas brush that had to be cut away when it was established over a century-and-a-quarter ago.

The area in which Lagarto was born as a town in the mid-nineteenth century had been occupied by Mexican livestock-raisers for decades. At least by 1802 the Spanish rulers of Mexico had made several grants of land along the west side of the Nueces River near what became Lagarto. The most notable of the Mexican ranches was Rancho Ramirez, located on Ramirena Creek. By 1812 it was described as having multiple breeds of livestock, houses, tanneries, pens for animals, and a "considerable clearing for planting." Indian raids, however, decimated these ranchers during the first half of the nineteenth century.

In 1856 a white saddle-tree-maker named John W. Ramsey employed a surveyor to lay out a town on a broad hilltop near Lagarto Creek that overlooked the west side of the Nueces River valley. Ramsey named the place Lagarto for the alligators that had once lived along the creek of the same name. Little more happened at the site for a decade because the Civil War diverted attention and resources away from town-building. After the close of the war, however, James Rather of Corpus Christi opened a store at Lagarto in 1866. From this small start, the community in time became a supply center for the surrounding ranch country. By the mid-1870s it boasted 150 people, three stores, two hotels, a blacksmith shop, and a saddle-maker's shop. A sawmill and gristmill were built before the end of the decade. The first school in the Lagarto area was a private one in the Cornelius C. Cox ranch house, but the local ranchers built a school for the community about 1873.

Continuing to serve as a market center for surrounding ranches, Lagarto grew steadily if slowly. In 1880 the census-taker enumerated 199 residents, among them several dry-goods merchants, a saddler, a blacksmith, a physician, a machinist, several grocers, a wheelwright, a mechanic, a cabinetmaker, a druggist, and several teachers. During the decade of the 1880s, Lagarto had both the *Lagarto Times* and the *Lagarto Echo* newspapers. Churches served the Baptists, Methodists, and a group that simply called themselves "Christians." One writer estimated that Lagarto had many as five hundred residents at the end of the 1880s. This is probably an exaggeration, but the town was indeed substantial. The census-taker counted 266 inhabitants in 1890.

It was Lagarto College that gave the town a reputation outside Live Oak County. Founded in 1884 by local people using their own money, Lagarto

South Texas brush has nearly swallowed an abandoned house near the Lagarto school. Photograph by the author, 2000.

The fate of Lagarto was sealed when it lost the college and then was bypassed by the railroad. As agriculture consolidated and the rural population of Live Oak County decreased during the first half of the twentieth century, Lagarto lost its reason for existence. By 1934 writer Dudley Dobie described Lagarto as having only a post office, a small store, and a country school. By about 1940 all three of these institutions had closed. In 1972 historian Jimmie Ruth Picquet described Lagarto as "hidden by a growth of brush and mesquite trees" so that there was "not enough to enable a visitor to visualize the layout of the business district." The historic 1925 public-school building with its historical marker for Lagarto College, however, does survive, as well as a scattered handful of homes and the ruins of other houses.

LOCATION: *Lagarto is located on Live Oak County Road 174 at its intersection with Farm Road 534. This intersection is 1.0 miles north of where Farm Road 534 intersects Farm Road 3162 in southeastern Live Oak County. A modern residential development located on Lake Corpus Christi immediately southeast of Lagarto has no historical associations with the ghost town, although it has adopted its name.*

College operated continuously until it closed for financial reasons in 1892. Even though the curriculum offered classes comparable to those in a secondary school today, it did give local young people the opportunity to further their education beyond that gained in public schools. To protect their young students from the temptations of drink, Lagarto people convinced the Texas legislature to pass a statute prohibiting the sale of alcohol within two miles of the college.

During the mid-1880s, the San Antonio and Aransas Pass Railway decided to build a line across Live Oak County to connect San Antonio with Corpus Christi. Because certain local ranchers were slow to make their lands available for railway construction, the company chose a route several miles east of Lagarto on the opposite side of the Nueces River. There the company created a new railroad town named Mathis, which in time drew away many of the merchants and residents from the older town.

Lamar

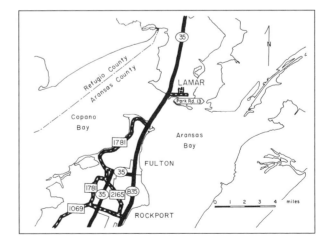

Named for Mirabeau B. Lamar, president of the Republic of Texas, the Aransas County ghost town of Lamar was a minor seaport for a number of years. It competed with other communities on the Gulf coast for maritime trade.

Mirabeau B. Lamar, president of the Republic of Texas, in whose honor the town of Lamar was named. From D.W.C. Baker, *A Texas Scrapbook*, 1875, courtesy of the University of Texas Institute of Texan Cultures at San Antonio.

Peace and quiet prevail under the live oaks that shade the Lamar Cemetery. Photograph by the author, 2000.

Lamar's beginnings can be traced to the days of the Texas Republic. About 1837, land promoter James W. Byrne secured control of over 1,400 acres on the Lamar Peninsula, which partially separates Copano Bay from Aransas Bay. He envisioned the site as becoming a major port serving western Texas, as did other entrepreneurs in similar locations all along the Gulf coast. Within a short time Byrne had the tip of the peninsula laid out as a town and began selling town lots and blocks to other investors and potential residents. Then in 1839 he used his personal connections to President Mirabeau B. Lamar to have the customs house—then located down the bay at the port town of Aransas—relocated to Lamar, where it stayed for several months.

The town of Lamar did make some headway in becoming an important port, but development was not so rapid as Byrne had hoped. He did manage to interest firearm-makers Samuel and James Colt to invest in his land promotion, but

they never visited the site. People did move to Lamar, which by the eve of the Civil War had several docks and warehouses, two stores, two churches, a school, and a post office. During the war the town suffered artillery damage and federal occupation, but its buildings, some of which had been made from a local concrete material, withstood the attacks. After the war, Lamar's boosters found it harder to compete with newly established and better-funded Rockport, which by 1886 had received steam railway connections. Port activities at Lamar subsequently ended and the community isolated at the end of the peninsula languished. The population at Lamar dwindled from 129 in 1880 to a dispersed rural community by the early days of the twentieth century. The Lamar post office finally closed in 1918. By 1930 a local writer characterized it as "the Slumbering City . . . disconnected from the busy world."

Lamar, however, was soon rescued from its status as a ghost town to become a resort. After the

A deserted stucco farmhouse stands open to the West Texas winds in the La Plata townsite. Photograph by the author, 2000.

construction of a highway across Copano Bay in 1931, tourists and sportsmen from Corpus Christi and beyond discovered the Lamar Peninsula. The Civilian Conservation Corps built facilities for the Goose Island State Park on the peninsula, and real-estate developers began promoting the area as a location for retirement homes and weekend retreats. On top of the historic ghost town, today one finds the modern state park and suburban homes. Remnants of historic Lamar, such as its cemetery and Catholic church, have been preserved as monuments to the past.

LOCATION: *Lamar is located at the southern tip of the Lamar Peninsula in Aransas County. The townsite lies beside Texas State Highway 35, northeast across the Copano Bay Causeway from Fulton. To reach the Lamar Cemetery and Catholic church, drive 0.9 miles east on paved Park Road 13 from where it intersects Texas Highway 35 near the north end of the Copano Bay Causeway. At Driftwood Street turn north (left) and drive 0.3 miles to a T intersection with Hagy Drive. Turn southeast (right) on Hagy Drive and continue 0.3 miles to the Lamar Cemetery and Catholic church opposite from the volunteer fire department building. Other nearby popular destinations include the "big tree," a huge live oak tree over 400 inches in circumference, and the beautiful chapel*

located at the 1959 convent of the Schoenstatt Sisters of Mary.

La Plata

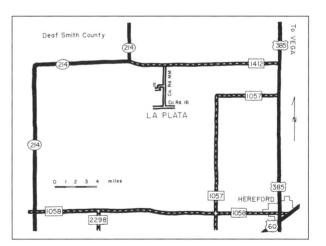

La Plata, the first seat of Deaf Smith County, came to life when that Panhandle county was organized, but lived for less than a decade. It died as a consequence of being bypassed by the railroad.

Rubble in the kitchen of an abandoned La Plata home. Photograph by the author, 2000.

Local citizens organized Deaf Smith County in the summer of 1890. While G. C. Witherspoon rode over the eastern portion of the county gathering the required signatures on a petition, another man canvassed the western half, which at the time was part of the XIT Ranch. Then a delegation carried the signatures to Tascosa, the seat of Oldham County, to which Deaf Smith had been attached for judicial purposes over a decade before. By the time they submitted the petition, it had 180 signatures. In due course an election was held to choose what place would become the county seat.

Two sites vied for that distinction, but neither of them were settled communities. In the election held on 3 October 1890, a place named Ayr competed with one called Grenada. The latter won a poll that pitted the XIT managers and cowboys of Ayr against the small-scale ranchers in the eastern part of the county who supported Grenada. After Grenada won, its promoters learned to their disappointment that a post office could not be granted in that name because there was already one called that elsewhere in the state. Consequently the name "La Plata" was proposed and accepted. A post office was established there on 12 September 1890.

Within half a dozen years La Plata grew to a considerable town. In addition to eighteen residences and its post office, it had a jail; the *La Plata Star* newspaper; hardware, grocery, dry goods, and drug stores; a farm-implement dealer; a hotel; a saloon; a livery stable; a blacksmith shop; a Pres-

byterian church; a public school; and a courthouse that had cost $41,000 to build.

Although it prospered in some years, La Plata saw hard times as well. Dry weather hit the western Panhandle in 1891 through 1894. A local resident later recalled that "it completely forgot to rain in 1892." Then in February 1897 eight inches of snow fell on top of the four inches of sleet that already covered the ground, causing hundreds if not thousands of cattle to starve. The temperatures remained below freezing for three weeks, and the animals were unable to find grazing on the snow- and ice-covered plains. The nearest railroad and source of feed was forty miles away at Amarillo, but it was impractical even to attempt to haul the amounts needed.

The decisive blow hit La Plata in 1898, the year the Santa Fe Railway built a line across the southeastern corner of Deaf Smith County. A new town called Hereford, after the breed of cattle common to the area, sprang up beside the tracks. In an election held on 8 November 1898, voters chose the new railroad town as the seat of the county. Most of the residences and public and commercial buildings of La Plata were moved across the plains to the new site. The former town virtually disappeared, with only a handful of inhabitants remaining. Today it is marked by a granite monument commemorating the town; this monument was erected by local citizens in 1960.

LOCATION: *La Plata is located at the intersection of graded Deaf Smith County Road MM with graded Deaf Smith County Road 16 northwest of Hereford and southwest of Vega. From Hereford, drive north 14.1 miles on U.S. Highway 385 to its intersection with Farm Road 1412. Turn west and drive 11.0 miles on Farm Road 1412 to its intersection with graded Deaf Smith County Road MM. Turn south and drive 4.0 miles to the site at the intersection with graded Deaf Smith County Road 16. From Vega, turn south from Interstate Highway 40 onto U.S. Highway 385 and drive south 14.8 miles to its intersection with Farm Road 1412. Then proceed west 11.0 miles on Farm Road 1412 and then drive south for 4.0 miles on Deaf Smith County Road MM to the site and its historical marker. To reach the La Plata Cemetery, drive north 2.0 miles from the townsite on graded Deaf Smith County Road MM to its intersection with a rough, unpaved field road marked by a sign reading "La Plata Cemetery." Do not take Deaf Smith*

The cotton gin at La Reforma was abandoned long ago. Photograph by the author, 2000.

County Road 17, which heads eastward from this intersection. Turn west onto the rough field road and drive 0.5 miles west, then 0.1 miles south, and then 0.4 miles west along the side of a cultivated field and then through a pasture to the fenced cemetery. The graded county roads and field road become muddy and sometimes impassable after rain or snow.

La Reforma

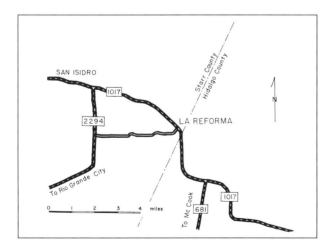

For several decades in the first half of the twentieth century, La Reforma served as a supply center for ranches and, later, farms in northern Starr and Hidalgo counties. It declined due to the consolidation of agriculture and the improvement of roads, a combination that drew its trade and population away to other communities.

Two brothers-in-law, Cayetano Barrera and Arcadio Guerra, established La Reforma as a ranch headquarters in 1898. For a number of years they had operated a family-owned ranch at Los Braziles in Brooks County, where doña Antonia Guerra, Berrera's mother-in-law, had owned property since the 1870s. When Barrera married into the Guerra family, he drove his cattle to Los Braziles from his former home in Meir, Mexico. During the 1890s, South Texas suffered from drought, and it is likely that this situation prompted Barrera to sell his Brooks County holdings in 1898 to Edward C. Lasater, founder of modern Falfurrias.

Whatever the motivation, Cayetano Barrera and his brother-in-law, Arcadio Guerra, moved to northeastern Starr County in 1898 where both men purchased ranch land. Barrera bought 3,089 acres; Guerra purchased a substantial amount of adjoining property. They and their family members set about clearing brush, digging a water well and building a stone tank, and erecting temporary jacales, picket houses with thatch roofs, for their initial shelters. They later built more substantial homes, and their ranch headquarters soon became

The palm trees behind a disused roadside business attest to La Reforma's semi-tropical climate. Photograph by the author, 2000.

the center of a widely scattered ranching community. Though most of the ranches in the area had taken the names of saints, Barrera and Guerra named their ranch *La Reforma*, which translates to "the reformation" in English.

Cayetano Barrera and Arcadio Guerra both recognized the need for schools and education. Barrera built the first school at La Reforma on his ranch, paying the first teacher out of his own pocket. He even boarded children from neighboring ranches, and assigned them chores as part of their education. In 1906 the community became part of a rural school district in Starr County, and at least by 1915 it was being served by its own La Reforma School No. 4, a one-room elementary school. La Reforma retained its own school at least into the mid-1930s, but then it consolidated with the school in nearby San Isidro, where a new facility had been built just a decade earlier.

La Reforma began with an economy based purely on ranching, but in time cultivated agriculture joined livestock-raising as a profitable enterprise in northern Starr County. A cotton gin in the town removed seeds from locally grown cotton before it was shipped out for further processing and sale. During the 1930s La Reforma experienced a minor boom, for workers from two oil fields in the vicinity realized it was a good place to live and buy supplies. At that time the town consisted of several dwellings and three businesses. Mail was delivered from nearby Delmita. The consolidation of agriculture in the mid-twentieth century, however, forced many of the La Reforma farmers to depart because new machines greatly reduced the need for agricultural workers. At the same time, improved roads and the increased use of automobiles allowed local people to shop elsewhere, leaving La Reforma to wither away to a bare skeleton of its former self.

LOCATION: *La Reforma is located on Farm Road 1017 along the northeastern border of Starr County at a point that is 9.8 miles east of La Gloria, 40.2 miles northeast of Rio Grande City, and 37.8 miles northwest of Edinburg.*

Lipscomb

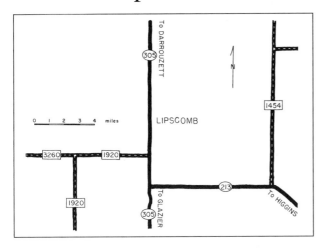

Founded in 1886 and still the seat of Lipscomb County, the unincorporated ranching community of Lipscomb clings to a tenuous life.

Lipscomb once was a town with glowing prospects for the future. Located in a region of the state that was known for its big ranches, Lipscomb was born when James W. Arthur erected a combination store and post office on the south side of Wolf Creek. He named it after Abner Smith Lipscomb, an early Texas jurist. Arthur anticipated the arrival of track-laying crews from the Southern Kansas Railway Company of Texas, a Santa Fe subsidiary that was laying tracks from Kiowa, Kansas, to the town of Panhandle, Texas. Others joined Arthur at the site, but all were disappointed when the railroad instead routed its line across the southeast corner of Lipscomb County, missing the town by over a dozen miles. Quickly a new railroad town named Higgins sprang up alongside the tracks.

Lipscomb County was organized in 1887, and the people who had invested in the town of Lipscomb combined forces with the ranchers in the northern part of the county to protect their interests. They voted Lipscomb the seat of the county, a distinction it has held since that time. For almost a century-and-a-quarter Lipscomb residents have expected prosperity to come to their town, and during its early years they actively promoted its economic development. When a five-inch-thick vein of coal was found beneath the town in 1888, local promoters

The business district of Lipscomb soon after its founding but before the planting of the trees that shade it today. Courtesy of Debby Opdyke.

The operator's seat of a derelict wheat-harvesting combine at Lipscomb. Photograph by the author, 2000.

The back door to a long quiet home in Lipscomb. Photograph by the author, 2000.

announced that coal in paying quantities must lie under the entire community. No investors, however, wanted to speculate on coal reserves located so far from any railroad. Then when the North Texas and Santa Fe Railway expanded westward across the northern part of the county in 1920, Lipscomb residents hoped to lure it southward—but to no avail. The new line only brought a string of additional competing towns along the steel rails—Darrouzett, Follett, and Booker. Even so, the seat of county government remained at Lipscomb.

For most of its history the town maintained a population of between 200 and 250 residents. Lipscomb's places of business early in the twentieth century included general mercantile stores, grocery stores, a post office, real-estate offices, restaurants, two newspapers, saloons, a bank, a drugstore, physicians' offices, a lumber yard with a hardware store, and an office of the stage line that offered daily transportation and express service between the county seat and railroad town of Higgins. For many years, especially during the last five decades of the twentieth century, the county government was the largest single employer in the town. Lipscomb had schools as early as the 1880s; a new brick school was erected in 1923. One of its teachers, Edward Everett Dale, went on to become one of the most prominent historians of the ranching industry and the chair of the history department at the University of Oklahoma.

Because they did not have a volunteer fire department until the 1970s, Lipscomb residents could do little when their buildings caught fire. Over the decades they lost many important structures, a factor that contributed to the decline of the town.

Never able to attract a railroad, Lipscomb remains the smallest town in Lipscomb County. The county government gives the community its reason for survival. When the author last visited Lipscomb in 2000, it had less than thirty occupied residences; fifteen dwellings stood empty. At the time there were no operating grocery stores or gasoline filling stations, but there were two art galleries, a museum that is open on a limited schedule, and an active union church. In recent years the town has drawn several hundred visitors each summer for occasional open-air dances held adjacent to an art gallery located in the 1908 Bank of Lipscomb building on the courthouse square. Lipscomb boasts a tree-shaded, oasis-like setting in the Wolf Creek valley, and provides a welcome break for travelers who have had all the sun and dust they can take in crossing the generally treeless Panhandle.

LOCATION: *Lipscomb is located on Texas Highway 305 at Spur 188 in Lipscomb County at a point that is 12.8 miles south of Darrouzett, 19.6 miles northwest of Higgins, and 15.6 miles north of Glazier.*

Los Olmos

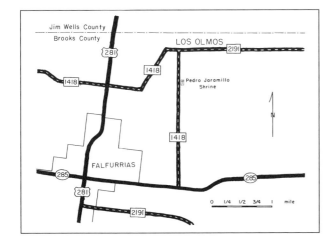

Only a dispersed rural community and scenic cemetery remain from Los Olmos—the oldest white settlement in Brooks County—but the site is still well worth visiting.

The Los Olmos community began as the headquarters of a Mexican ranch. About 1830 Ramón de la Garza received the *El Paisano* land grant from the state of Tamaulipas, Mexico. De la Garza established a ranch on the property, which lay on what would become the overland stagecoach route between Santa Gertrudis and Rio Grande City. By 1880 the community had grown so much that the de la Garza heirs deeded an acre of land to the county for the construction of a public school. In that year the town had not only the

Summertime stillness in the Los Olmos Cemetery. Photograph by the author, 2000.

school, but also a post office and several stores. The post office closed in 1882, but in 1885 another opened in the same community and operated under the name Paisano until 1905. The decade of the 1890s saw Los Olmos at its peak of development. The town had an estimated population of between 240 and 300, five stores, the only public school in the area, and representatives of multiple occupations.

Unbeknownst to most of the Los Olmos residents in the 1890s, things were changing. In 1895, Goliad native and Texas livestock-raiser Edward C. Lasater began making large land purchases in the vicinity. In time he put together the three hundred fifty thousand-acre Falfurrias Ranch. Having acquired the property, Lasater began promoting the construction of a railway to the area. A railroad connection would provide him an economical method of shipping his cattle to market, but, more importantly, a railway would enable him to cut up some of his extensive property for sale to farmers, who would also need easy access to shipping facilities. With Lasater's inducements, in 1904 the San Antonio and Aransas Pass Railway built tracks southward from the town of Alice to Lasater's ranch. There he laid out a town he called Falfurrias and began selling land to farmers, who came mostly from the American Midwest. Lasater prospered in his ventures, and his new town of Falfurrias quickly eclipsed the much older Los Olmos. Although Los Olmos had a population of 148 in 1904, the year the railroad came to Lasater's ranch, it soon diminished to little more than a dispersed rural community.

The most notable resident of Los Olmos was a faith healer named Pedro Jaramillo. A native of Guadalajara, Mexico, in 1881 he moved to a ranch owned by Julia Cuellar de García near Los Olmos Creek. For over a quarter century the healer, known as Don Pedrito, administered curative advice to thousands of ill, injured, and infirm people, his fame spreading far and wide. His natural remedies cost little, for he often prescribed water and other elements to be taken internally or in the form of baths. According to local reports, the Paisano post office at Los Olmos might receive as many as five hundred letters a week addressed to Don Pedrito, all from people seeking his cures for their ailments. The healer served all who came to him until his death in 1907, and his burial place near Los Olmos remains a pilgrimage shrine for believers.

LOCATION: *The historic Los Olmos Cemetery is located on Farm Road 2191 at a point that is 0.1 miles east of the intersection with Farm Road 1418 in Brooks County. To reach this site, drive 1.6 miles east on Texas State Highway 285 from where it intersects U.S. Highway 281 in Falfurrias. When you reach the intersection with Farm Road 1418, turn north onto Farm Road 1418 and drive 2.3 miles to its intersection with Farm Road 2191. At the intersection of Farm Road 1418 and Farm Road 2191, turn east on Farm Road 2191 and drive 0.1 miles to the Los Olmos Cemetery. The shrine to healer Pedro Jaramillo is not located at the cemetery, but beside Farm Road 1418 at a point that is 1.8 miles north of Texas State Highway 285.*

Magnolia

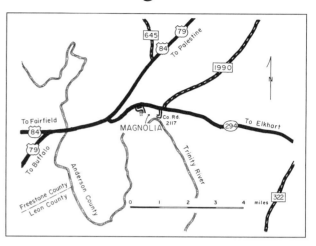

The Anderson County town of Magnolia was considered the head of navigation for larger steamboats on the Trinity River, a position from which it prospered in the 1840s through the 1860s as a shipping point for cotton raised in the area.

Magnolia's beginnings are somewhat unclear, but there is no question that commercial activity began at the site in the 1840s. In 1847 R. W. Davis, a planter located a few miles up-river of what became Magnolia, successfully transported cotton on a flatboat down the Trinity River to its mouth. After a tugboat towed Davis along the coast to Galveston, his cotton caused a considerable stir in the city, for it proved that waterborne commercial transport was feasible for cotton raised in northern areas of East Texas. That same year, one John Shipper secured a license to operate a ferry across the Trinity at Magnolia. A historic handbill, preserved at the Beinecke Library at Yale University, advertised a sale of lots in the town scheduled for 1 September 1840, a date that precedes Davis's and Shipper's activities by about seven years. Although the date on the handbill may be incorrect, it is clear that Magnolia had its beginnings during the decade of the 1840s.

By the 1850s Magnolia had grown into a substantial town with an estimated population of eight hundred inhabitants. It lay on the east bank of a bend in the Trinity River; its docks and warehouses were built near the water, and its residences and businesses occupied higher ground to avoid flood damage. The busy season came in the early spring, when the river ran high and provided enough water for steamboats to travel upstream as

A view from the bluffs down to the eroded riverbanks at the site of the steamboat landing at Magnolia. Photograph by the author, 1999.

far as Magnolia. The *Trinity Advocate* newspaper in Palestine reported on 29 February 1860, that "the Trinity River has been navigable the past ten days. On Saturday the steamboat *Lone Star* arrived at Magnolia. . . . On Tuesday she started for Galveston with eight hundred bales of cotton. Immediately after the steamer left, four flat boats having on board over twelve hundred bales of cotton cast off and started down river." At times during the spring there might be as many as seven steamboats lined up at the Magnolia landing, all unloading goods consigned to East Texas merchants and planters and then loading up with cotton.

The town of Magnolia was laid out with thirty-three commercial and residential blocks. Among its businesses were general mercantile stores, warehouses, saloons, the two-story Haygood Hotel, a post office, a land office, livery stables, a cotton gin, blacksmith shops, carriage shops, a ferry house, and law offices. There was at least one church, which belonged to the Methodists, and a school.

The demand for cotton shipped from Magnolia decreased when the Union navy blockaded the Texas coast during the Civil War. Production suffered at the same time because many of the local white men, who otherwise would have been working in the fields or supervising slaves, had departed to serve in the Confederate army. Even after the close of the war, it took three or four years for East Texas cotton shipments through Magnolia to build up again.

About this time a new competitor arose. After the close of the war, railway construction began anew in Texas. By 1870 the steel rails had penetrated cotton-raising areas in East Texas enough that most planters began choosing to haul their cotton overland to the railroads rather than to the steamboat ports. Planters could avoid worrying about boat schedules, high and low water, and the constant danger of losing cargoes on sinking boats if they used the more expensive but far more convenient steam railroads.

Then in 1879, the tracks of the International and Great Northern Railroad finally came toward

The two graveyards comprising the Magnolia Cemetery—for whites on the left and blacks on the right—still separated by a carefully maintained barbed-wire fence. Photograph by the author, 1999.

Magnolia, but instead the route passed through the Anderson County seat of Palestine. At Magnolia the handful of businessmen and residents packed up to leave. The reason their town existed had evaporated. Soon weeds and grass took over Magnolia. Its name persisted on maps into the twentieth century because of the rural schools for whites and blacks and its ferry, which operated long past the town's death. Even the Magnolia ferry disappeared in 1928, when the Texas Highway Department built a bridge across the Trinity River to take its place.

LOCATION: *The Texas Historical Commission created an aluminum historical marker for the Magnolia ghost town; the marker stands at the south side of Texas State Highway 294 where it intersects Farm Road 1990. This location is 12.5 miles southwest of Palestine, 10.3 miles west of Elkhart, and 26.8 miles east of Fairfield. To reach the townsite, drive south and then west on graded soil-surfaced Anderson County Road 2117 about 0.6 miles to where it dead-ends down a steep slope at the river edge, beside the old Magnolia steamboat landing. This road can become very muddy after rains and is not recommended unless it is dry. The fascinating Magnolia Cemetery, with a modern barbed-wire fence that separates the black graveyard from the white graveyard, is accessible via two gravel*

entrance roads from the south side of Texas State Highway 294 about 0.1 miles west of the historical marker.

Mankins

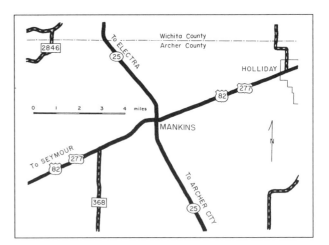

Although it originated as a ranch headquarters in the 1880s, Mankins in Archer County is best known for having been the winter quarters of a carnival show.

Dick S. Dudley's stone-veneer home in Mankins that also served as the headquarters for the Dudley carnival shows. Photograph by the author, 2000.

A truck left over from the Dudley carnival shows, parked in Mankins for the time being. Photograph by the author, 2000.

The initial white settlers in what today is Archer County were livestock-raisers, and to this day ranching remains one of the mainstays of the local economy. In 1886, Sam Lazarus acquired the Archer County property that belonged to the Stone Cattle and Pasture Company. He brought Tom Mankins from Kansas to manage his cattle operation, and erected a ranch house for him. In 1890 the Wichita Valley Railway laid rails across the Lazarus Ranch to connect Wichita Falls with Seymour. The company constructed a spur line to the Lazarus Ranch headquarters, and there the stockman established a supply store. Then in 1908 Charles Mangold of Dallas purchased the ranch.

Mangold erected a store building and a small hotel on the main line of the Wichita Valley Railway, hoping to sell land to farmers and others. Streets and blocks were laid out, the north-south streets given the names of trees, such as Walnut, Pecan, and Elm, whereas east-west streets were numbered. By 1912 enough people had gathered in the vicinity to secure a post office. The first name proposed was Mangold, but because there was already a post office by that name in Texas, it was rejected. The next name proposed was Mankins, in honor of ranch manager Tom Mankins, and the Post Office Department accepted that name.

The town gradually grew as a supply center for the surrounding ranch and farming area, eventually having an elementary and a secondary school, multiple stores, a bank, restaurants, several filling stations and garages, a telephone exchange, both Methodist and Baptist congregations, and a motion-picture theater. Workers from modest oil fields in the area contributed to the population. At one time the school served four hundred children from the town and surrounding rural areas. With such prosperity, however, also came troubles. In March 1938 a tornado struck Mankins. It destroyed the two-story school structure, which the community had to rebuild. The town always suffered from lack of potable groundwater, so for decades the railroad hauled in drinking water.

Throughout West Texas, people tell stories about driving through Mankins and seeing there such exotic animals as zebras and an elephant. This is because Mankins became the winter home for the Dick S. Dudley carnival shows. Originally working as a cowboy, in 1914 Dudley cashed in on his ability as a wild-horse rider. When a traveling wild west show came to Swenson, Texas, its manager offered cash prizes for anyone who could ride his bronco horses. Dudley rode them one after the other, taking all the prize money. He then learned that the owner was having financial troubles, so he offered to buy the whole show. As the owner of the enterprise, Dudley began touring small towns in West Texas, finding that he enjoyed show business.

Dudley was called to military service during World War I. On his return, he and his wife began the carnival business in earnest, eventually providing entertainment to three generations in Texas, New Mexico, Oklahoma, and Kansas. Their traveling show included both circus-type acts and carnival attractions, such as rides and a sideshow featuring a "snake girl." At times employing as many as 250 persons, the carnival spent about four months each winter in Mankins. Then spring after spring into the 1980s, they hit the road about the time the mesquite trees began to leaf.

Despite the yearly influx of carnival people, Mankins suffered the fate of many other former farm and ranch supply centers across the state. The consolidation of agriculture depopulated the rural areas around Mankins that had supported its businesses, while improved highways enabled the people who remained to shop in other larger towns. The Mankins school consolidated with the one in Holliday in 1947; the post office closed in 1958. Today Mankins consists of less than a dozen occupied residences, three disused commercial buildings, the former winter quarters of the Dudley carnival shows, salvage materials from nearby oil fields, the abandoned spur of the Wichita Valley Railway, and disturbed ground, foundations, and debris indicating the sites of former buildings.

LOCATION: *Mankins is located on U.S. Highway 82/277 at its intersection with Texas State Highway 25 in northwestern Archer County. The site is 17.5 miles northwest of Archer City, 6.3 miles southwest of Holliday, and 31.0 miles northeast of Seymour.*

Medicine Mound

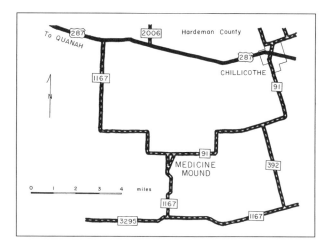

Medicine Mound took its name from the four prominent buttes located just west of the townsite. This Hardeman County town that once boasted five hundred residents served as a market center for the surrounding ranch and farm country.

Before the arrival of white settlers in the 1870s, nomadic Comanche Indians visited the Medicine Mound buttes—four 200- to 250-foot-high landmasses carved by erosion—which overlook the Red River valley to the north and the Pease River valley to the south. It was to such places that the Comanches went for vision quests, healing ceremonies, and burials.

The four buttes that give the Medicine Mound townsite its name. Photograph by the author, 2000.

A deserted commercial building with antique gasoline pumps on the main street of Medicine Mound. Photograph by the author, 2000.

A view of the interesting "cobblestone" construction used in two of the commercial buildings in Medicine Mound. Photograph by the author, 2000.

The area around the buttes was opened to white settlers only after the region's American Indians had been forced onto reservations in Oklahoma in the mid-1870s. Twenty years before that, the State of Texas had given railroad companies legal titles to the land as bonuses for laying track within the state. Thus the land was available for sale as soon as occupation became possible.

Settlers initially founded Medicine Mound in the 1880s, two-and-a-half-miles south of the present site. This first Medicine Mound had a school, church, stores, and a cemetery. When the Kansas City, Mexico and Orient Railway built tracks through Hardeman County in 1909 to connect Sweetwater with the Red River, residents relocated to a siding on the new railroad. The initial settlement soon became known as "Old Mounds" to distinguish it from the new site, which was named Medicine Mound. This name was always singular, even though it took its name from the four mounds.

Convenient access to markets by steam railway insured a good start for the new Medicine Mound. By the 1920s the community was thriving with twenty-two business enterprises and a reported population of five hundred. The community had a newspaper, a hotel, restaurants, multiple grocery and general stores, blacksmiths, three churches, automobile filling stations and garages, a telephone exchange, undertaker's parlor, offices of doctors and attorneys, a post office, grain elevator,

two banks, a two-story school, and four passenger trains arriving daily. A former resident commented to the author, "It's hard to believe they had two banks, but it was a thriving community."

Medicine Mound's future looked bright, but then came the consolidation of agriculture, improvement of rural roads, and a series of fires. As agriculture became mechanized during the twentieth century, fewer and fewer people were needed to do farm work. The rural population that had supported businesses in Medicine Mound melted away. A local resident reported that even though he "had raised eight kids on that quarter section right there . . . you can't do that any more, got to have more land." Improved roads allowed the few residents who remained to shop in larger towns like Chillicothe and Quanah, where selection was better and prices might be lower. Finally, a series of fires in the late 1920s and early 1930s burned down much of Medicine Mound, and many property owners chose to move on than to rebuild. Its school consolidated with the Quanah school in 1955, soon followed by the closure of Medicine Mound's post office, filling station, and cotton gin. The last general store closed down in 1966.

LOCATION: *Medicine Mound is located on Farm Road 1167 at a point that is 8.5 miles southwest of its intersection with U.S. Highway 287. This intersection on U.S. Highway 287 is 6.4 miles east of Quanah and 7.7 miles west of Chillicothe. For an easier route take Farm Road 91 south and west 9.0 miles from U.S. Highway 287 in Chillicothe until it intersects Farm Road 1167 just north of Medicine Mound.*

Minera, Santo Tomás, and Dolores

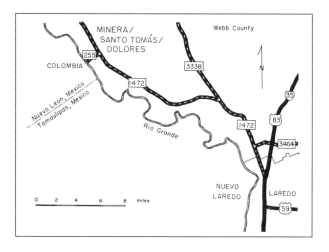

Minera, Santo Tomás, and Dolores were all coal-mining towns along the Rio Grande, located upstream from Laredo in Webb County. Over the years—from the 1880s to the 1920s—each of them in turn merged into the next, as their residents followed the mining operations. The stories of each of these towns blend with the others, illustrating the fluid lives of the people who inhabited such towns.

Underground mining for coal along the Rio Grande began in 1881. Out-of-state lenders backed the first effort, which began on the Texas side of the river about twenty miles upstream from Laredo. There, workers in what was known as the Santo Tomás Coalfield excavated horizontal tunnels in the banks of the river about thirty feet above the water level. After hauling the coal out in carts pushed by hand or pulled by mules, workers dumped it into ox-drawn carts or into steam-powered scows for the trip to Laredo. There the coal fueled locomotives on both the International and Great Northern Railroad and the Texas Mexican Railway in the United States, as well as locomotives on the Mexican National Railroad across the border. Soon a railway line connected the mines

The coal mine on the banks of the Rio Grande in the vicinity of Minera, circa 1890. Courtesy of Charles G. Downing and the University of Texas Institute of Texan Cultures at San Antonio.

with Laredo, greatly facilitating the movement of the product. Webb County coal was considered "cannel" coal, a grade about midway between soft lignite and harder bituminous coal.

Soon a town sprang up on the banks of the Rio Grande adjacent to the mines. In the earliest accounts this place sometimes went by the name of Carbón, but it was usually known as Minera. In time the community grew to about a thousand inhabitants, with an economy based largely on the two mines that were operating by 1895. About this time the Rio Grande Coal and Irrigation Company assumed operation of the mines in the vicinity, which were producing between ninety and a hundred tons daily. These mines, however, had to be closed after high waters on the Rio Grande flooded both the town and the mines in 1912. The company shifted operations away from the banks of the river to higher ground. As the town followed the general movement away from the river, it came to be known as Santo Tomás, after the Santo Tomás Mine. In time the name of the company also changed, becoming the Santo Tomás Coal Company. It sunk more shafts nearby, and the mining camp once again shifted to the new location. The final name of this town was Dolores.

Almost all the residents of Minera, Santo Tomás, and Dolores were Mexican. The community had a number of families, but consisted mostly of young men. Many of them were skilled miners who had come to the Rio Grande coal mines from the interior of Mexico. Yet in spite of the previous mining experience these men had, Anglo engineers usually managed the mines. In 1895, for example, Ohio-born Todd Roy came to Minera to supervise its mines. After his death in 1900 from yellow fever, he was succeeded by his brother, William.

The camps consisted mostly of company-owned, cheaply built wooden and adobe houses that the miners rented. They bought the necessities of life principally in company-owned general stores. Miners received pay ranging from about fifty cents to as high as two dollars a ton for the coal they excavated. That pay generally represented one-fourth to one-third of the price the coal brought on the Laredo market.

Outside events brought an end to coal mining along the Rio Grande. The most important factor was the declining demand for coal to fuel railway steam locomotives. In a trend starting in the

A huge pile of waste earth excavated from the Santo Tomás Mine. Photograph by the author, 2000.

1890s, railroad after railroad abandoned coal in favor of crude oil as locomotive fuel. Within three decades the coal market dried up, except in industrial areas of the eastern United States. The last Texas coal mines along the Rio Grande shut down between 1928 and 1939. Miners departed the old camps and mines, leaving behind debris and huge heaps of the earthen spoil they had excavated in their efforts to extract usable coal. Today these reddish and greyish heaps of eroded waste are the most visible reminders of the Rio Grande coal-mining communities of Minera, Santo Tomás, and Dolores.

LOCATION: *None of the Rio Grande coal-mining camps have public access, but in several areas the huge tips of earthen waste from the mines may be viewed from public roadways. To reach the area of the historic mines, drive northwestward from Interstate Highway 35 in Laredo on Farm Road 1472—identified on local road signs as "Mines Road"—past the intersection with Farm Road 3338 at 7.6 miles. At 17.9 miles from Laredo, visitors looking southwest can see the entry to the privately owned Minas Ranch and a nearby reddish-colored dump of earth from the Dolores Mine. At 18.7 miles Farm Road 255 branches off to the southwest, leading a short distance to the Laredo-Colombia Solidarity Bridge. More large dumps of reddish-colored spoil from the mine lay near the side of the road. Continue northwestward on Farm Road 1472 a short ways, and finally at a total of 19.1 miles from Laredo is the most impressive of the giant piles of waste from the mines, this time grayish in color and originally from the Santo Tomás Mine. Here both sides of the highway are littered with small pieces of shiny black coal from the historic mine. Drivers should note that the first few miles of Farm Road 1472 outside Laredo might have heavy truck traffic.*

Newburg

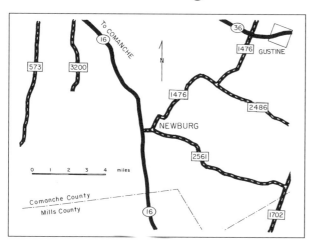

Though it was originally a farming and ranching community in southern Comanche County, Newburg is best remembered for its one highly unusual

A homemade stone and concrete water fountain on the playground outside the now quiet school in Newburg. Photograph by the author, 2000.

feature—radioactive soil. In the 1950s health-seekers visited by the hundreds to sit in Newburg's naturally radioactive dirt.

The families of R. M. Collier and Jesse Mercer settled in 1854 on a creek near what would eventually be Newburg. Over time others gathered in the same area. By July 1872, the settlers organized the first institution at Newburg, the South Leon Baptist Church. The community had forty-eight residents by 1875, and received its first post office in 1884. Later the church moved into a larger structure, which initially doubled as the school. More and more people came to the neighborhood, which by the 1890s had not only the church, school, and post office but also a general store, cotton gin, blacksmith shop, and a gristmill. In 1906 the congregation built a new church structure, which remains in use to this day. The community remained active into the 1920s, when it had its own general store, drugstore, doctor's office, cotton gin, and syrup mill. As recently as 1940 the school had four teachers and over one hundred pupils.

Newburg suffered the same fate as hundreds of other small towns throughout Texas. As its rural population decreased because mechanized agriculture from the 1930s onward required fewer workers, the town lost the economic base that had supported its businesses. At the same time, improved highways made it easier for local people to drive to the nearby towns of Comanche and Brownwood to shop, further strangling Newburg's last businesses. The school consolidated with Comanche schools in the 1950s, and Newburg became little more than a historic school, church, and cemetery surrounded by a dispersed rural community.

Even though Newburg had waned to a remnant of its former self, the townsite became the setting for a remarkable fad during the mid-1950s. In 1953 two strangers approached a local stockman, Jesse Reese, offering to purchase the mineral rights to his ranch just east of town. They said that when they had flown over the property with Geiger counters, the land registered as radioactive. Reese told the men that he was not interested in selling his rights, but after they left he purchased his own Geiger counter. With it he found that the men were right; his property was slightly radioactive. He took dirt samples to Austin and learned that his land had .025 of U238—not

Interior view of one of the 1950s "sitting houses" at Newburg, showing benches and troughs filled with naturally radioactive soil. Photograph by the author, 2000.

enough for commercial uranium mining, but still radioactive enough to register.

During the autumn of 1954, another stranger appeared at Reese's door. This man said he had been taking radiation treatments for rheumatism. He asked if he could try sitting in Reese's dirt as an alternative to his earlier, more expensive treatments. This man was just the first of many, for others followed. Eventually Reese had so many people wanting to sit in his radioactive dirt that he converted a cow shed and then a whole barn to accommodate them. Each person paid one to two dollars an hour for the right to sit in his dirt. Neighbors saw the dozens and then hundreds of cars driving up to Reese's ranch, so they too opened "sitting houses" where health-seekers could take "treatments" by sitting in and even by being partially covered with the radioactive soil. By late summer and fall 1955, national newspapers and magazines were sending journalists to cover the story of Newburg's radioactive dirt. Then the fad passed as quickly as it had begun. By the

next summer the sitting houses were empty, and life had returned to its quiet pace at Newburg.

LOCATION: *Newburg is located at the intersection of Farm Road 1476 with Farm Road 2561 at a point that is 0.5 miles east of Texas State Highway 16 in southern Comanche County. The turn-off for Farm Road 1476 from Texas State Highway 16 is located 10.7 miles south of Comanche and 22.9 miles north of Goldthwaite.*

Newtown

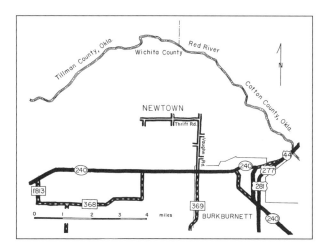

One of a series of Wichita County boomtowns that sprang up in the Burkburnett Northwest Extension Oil Field, Newtown was founded in the summer of 1919. The town served the needs of petroleum workers for three years before it burned in a disastrous fire, never to be rebuilt.

Frenzied oil well drilling began in Burkburnett in the summer of 1918 when a driller struck a large quantity of oil on the S. L. Fowler farm. Scores of drilling crews descended on the area, sinking wells with little regard to safety or proximity to another well, thus insuring rapid depletion of the field. Within a few months production declined, but drillers were already at work to the north and west. In summer 1919 they discovered another huge oil pool about five miles long and two-and-a-half miles wide that curved north and west of the previous oil field. It became known as the Burkburnett Northwest Extension Oil Field. By fall 1919 it was producing a phenomenal one

Looking east on the main street of Newtown during its boom, circa 1920. Courtesy of Patman & Osborn, Austin, Texas.

Children playing in a dirt lot at Newtown, circa 1920. Courtesy of Patman & Osborn, Austin, Texas.

One of the many petroleum fires at Newtown during its heyday. Courtesy of Patman & Osborn, Austin, Texas.

ings, oil-field supply-houses, barbershops, blacksmiths, eating places, saloons, dance halls, brothels, and gambling dens. Everywhere crowded on either side of the road stood wooden oil derricks, each with its own steam boiler and engine to provide power. When it rained, Newtown became an ocean of mud. Whatever the weather, everything smelled of oil.

Fires were common in early-twentieth-century oil fields, and Newtown was no exception. Its great fire happened in 1922. Rains had saturated the ground with water when lightning ruptured a fifty-five-thousand-barrel tank on an elevation slightly above the town. To decrease the chance of an explosion at the tank, workers allowed oil to flow out of the tank down natural rivulets toward Newtown. Then it caught fire. Jack Knight, who witnessed the events, remembered, "That oil, just solid flame, spread out, . . . just enveloped those homes and drilling rigs and

hundred thousand barrels of oil daily, and an estimated sixty-five thousand people flooded into the field seeking work or other income. An unpaved road ran from east to west through this field, and along this road sprang up three boomtowns. Although their identifies sometimes merged and blurred, these three towns, from east to west, were called Waggoner City, Newtown, and Thrift.

Newtown, the central town, probably had the greatest concentration of people and places of business. It was not impressive to see, for all the buildings were temporary constructions, made of canvas, tar paper, sheet metal, and cheap lumber. Nothing was made to last. The business enterprises along Newtown's dirt street included lodg-

Rubble and foundations from a former commercial building in Newtown are barely visible through the weeds. Photograph by the author, 2000.

Pollution created this "moonscape" of soil unable to sustain plants at the heart of what once was Newtown. Photograph by the author, 2000.

earthen mounds at the former sites of open-air oil-storage tanks.

LOCATION: *To visit the site of Newtown, leave the western side of Burkburnett on the paved county road marked "Vaughan Road" from Texas State Highway 240, which is opposite the Texas State Highway 240 intersection with Farm Road 369 south. This intersection is located 1.4 miles west of downtown Burkburnett and 3.5 miles west of exit 12 on Interstate Highway 44. Drive 2.0 miles north on Vaughan Road. At the intersection of Vaughn Road with the paved county road marked "Thrift Road," turn west and drive 1.8 miles to a historical marker for Newtown and Thrift. This road passes from the western edge of Waggoner City to the site of Newtown and then on to the site of Thrift. This historic road formed the main street of all three towns. At a point that is on Thrift Road, 0.9 miles west of Vaughn Road, is a concrete low water crossing that is believed to date from the days of the boom in the Northwest Extension Oil Field. If the story is true, then this concrete crossing would have been the only paved portion of the historic roadway.*

shacks of all kinds, clear down to Main Street and into this creek, and burnt up so many people before they ever knew that there was a fire." He continued, "Women and children was screaming; I never heard such a thing in my life. . . . People just running and them afire and just running and screaming and hollering and there was no place to go."

Production in the Burkburnett Northwest Extension Oil Field was already declining, so no one ever rebuilt Newtown. Today the site is marked by Thrift Road, which eighty years ago was the unpaved east-west street through the heart of the oil field. Scattered alongside this road are chunks of concrete, timbers, rubble, and disturbed ground, all of which mark the sites of former buildings; vast additional amounts of surface archaeological evidence in the form of metal, rubber, glass, and ceramics; and circular

Norse

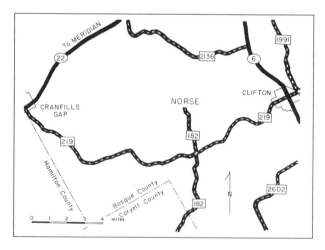

Once the center of a prosperous Norwegian colony, Norse today consists of a historic church and cemetery surrounded by scattered farmsteads. This former Bosque County community is still the best-known Norwegian immigrant settlement in Texas.

The Norse Store and surrounding buildings on a quiet summer day at the turn of the twentieth century. Courtesy of Patman & Osborn, Austin, Texas.

The first Norwegians came to Texas in the 1840s, but the locations they chose—Brownsboro in Henderson County and Prairieville in Kaufman County—proved unhealthy. Malaria fever forced most of the newcomers to seek homes elsewhere. Cleng Peerson, who since the 1820s had brought other Norwegians to the American Midwest, came to Texas and helped the immigrants relocate in Bosque County, which was then on the western frontier. Upon arriving in Bosque County in 1854, the Norwegian settlers declared, "This is so much like Norway that we must settle here." And so they did.

The first of these Norwegians to move to Bosque County was Ole Canuetson, soon followed by many others. In 1855 the Reverend Emil Frederickson led the new Texans in their first worship service, held in the home of a pioneer settler. The Lutheran Norwegians continued to meet in the homes of local residents until they built the still-standing Our Savior's Lutheran Church at Norse in 1878. Since then they have gathered there regularly for services, weddings, and funerals, with burials in the adjacent cemetery. In addition to the church, the town grew to have a school and several shops. A post office was approved in 1880. Local residents even organized their own Norse Mutual Fire Insurance Company in 1884.

Cleng Peerson, already an aged man, remained in Norse. In recognition of his efforts to introduce immigrants to the state, the Texas Legislature granted him 320 acres of land. He remained in Norse until his death in 1865; his grave later became a pilgrimage destination for Norwegian Americans and others.

Economic changes caused Norse to stagnate while other Bosque County communities thrived with their railroads and, later, paved highways. The rural population around Norse diminished as agriculture consolidated. One driver on a tractor could cultivate the same number of acres that before had required the work of ten farmers. Improved highways siphoned business away from Norse to nearby larger towns, such as Clifton and Cranfills Gap. Stores and shops closed in Norse; the post office closed in 1929.

Members of the First Old Norse Band pose with their musical instruments next to a beer wagon. Courtesy of Mrs. Sadie Hoel and the University of Texas Institute of Texan Cultures at San Antonio.

The 1878 Our Savior's Lutheran Church, which a congregation founded at Norse in the 1850s. Photograph by the author, 2000.

Families with their roots in Norse, however, have continued to return to the former town for worship services, social gatherings, and special events. The most notable of these special events was the 1982 visit of King Olav V of Norway. The king visited Norse to lay a wreath on the grave of Cleng Peerson in commemoration of what would have been his 200th birthday. Fifteen hundred people gathered for the special memorial service.

Although the commercial center is gone, Norse still remains as a scattered rural community in the beautiful tree-covered hills of Bosque County. The 1878 church stands as the last remaining public building in what once was the largest Norwegian settlement in Texas, and visitors marvel at the Norwegian-language grave markers in the beautiful cemetery.

LOCATION: *Norse is located at the northern terminus of Farm Road 182 at a point that is 2.8 miles north of where it intersects Farm Road 219. This intersection is located 6.8 miles west of Clifton and 11.8 miles east of Cranfills Gap.*

Noxville

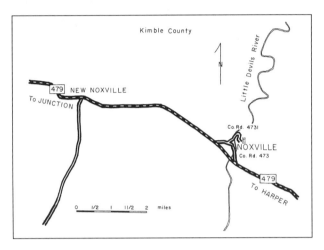

Noxville is now a dispersed ranching community in eastern Kimble County, but in the late nineteenth and early twentieth centuries it was a supply center that served the surrounding livestock-raising area.

By the 1860s the first white settlers had begun establishing ranches in what later became Kimble County. The best-known of these individuals was Creed Taylor, a veteran of the Texas Revolution and the Mexican War, who established a ranch headquarters on the James River in 1869. He and his family had recently been involved in the bloody Sutton-Taylor feud southeast of San Antonio, and they were probably seeking peace farther west. After erecting a two-story stone house, for many years a famous landmark, the Taylor family engaged in cattle-raising and competitive horse-racing well into the twentieth century.

The community of Noxville sprang up on the Little Devils River, a tributary of the James River, about four miles east of Creed Taylor's ranch. Noah Nox, who had come from Illinois, opened a store beside the river in the early 1870s. The families of Munroe McDonald and James H. Parker joined Nox in the neighborhood, which came to be known as Noxville after the storekeeper secured a post office by that name in 1879. By the early 1880s, enough chil-

dren were living in the community that local people erected a stone schoolhouse, which is still standing. Classes met there until 1940, when the Noxville school consolidated with the school at Harper in Gillespie County.

In December 1911 Jason A. Milan became postmaster for Noxville and moved the post office four miles west to a location on the James River. His "New Noxville" had a gasoline filling station and store by the 1920s, but in 1942 the post office closed. It was followed several years later by the filling station and store.

The closings in Noxville—the school in 1940 and the post office in 1942—demonstrated the effects of the general consolidation that had taken place in agriculture during the 1920s and 1930s. Fewer and fewer people were needed to work on increasingly mechanized farms and ranches, so agricultural jobs evaporated, and rural residents moved to larger towns and cities to find employment. Local people continued to vote for county, state, and national elections at the stone school in "Old Noxville" as recently as the 1960s, but now people visit the townsite mainly to attend graveside services in the community cemetery, which remains in use.

LOCATION: *The site of Noxville lies north of Farm Road 479 on rough gravel Kimble County Road 473, which loops through the community. The two ends of the county road intersect Farm Road 479 at two points—6.5 miles and 6.9 miles northwest along Farm Road 479 from its intersection with U.S. Highway 290 in southeastern Kimble County. The gravel county road is rough, at one point fords Little Devils River, and is appropriate only for high-clearance vehicles—not trailers. To reach the historic Noxville Cemetery, turn north onto gravel Kimble County Road 4731, which loops northward from Kimble County Road 473 about 0.6 miles from its eastern end and about 0.4 miles from its western end. This intersection of the two county roads lies at the center of Old Noxville. Proceed generally northward on gravel Kimble County Road 4731 a distance of 0.8 miles, crossing a cattleguard and a gravel ford across the Little Devils River. This sometimes-uneven ford is passable only for high-clearance vehicles, and it should never be attempted after a rain. Proceed a short distance to a fork in the road, take the right fork, and continue to follow the winding gravel road up the side of a hill to the entrance of the cemetery, where the grave of Creed Taylor is*

A stone and wooden barn on a farm at Noxville. Photograph by the author, 2000.

clearly marked. The site of New Noxville is located on Farm Road 479 about 4.2 miles west of the western end of Kimble County Road 473, 11.1 miles west on Farm Road 479 from where it intersects U.S. Highway 290.

Oak Hill

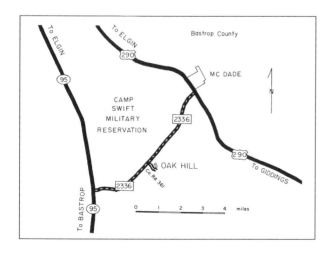

Once a community of farmers and livestock-raisers located roughly between Bastrop and Elgin in Bastrop County, Oak Hill abruptly ceased to exist as a town during World War II. United States military forces moved in to occupy the town and remove its buildings during the hasty construction of the Camp Swift U.S. Army training base.

The site of Oak Hill was originally part of a land grant from the Republic of Texas to Martin Walker for his service as a soldier during the Texas Revolution. A veteran of the 21 April 1836 Battle of San Jacinto, Walker obtained his land and began selling portions of it as early as 1849. Within a dozen years, a number of families had taken up residence on tracts purchased from Walker. At least as early as 1868 the community had established a cemetery among the oak and cedar trees blanketing the area.

About 1872 a school was built at Oak Hill. In time the building served as a meeting-place not only for a local chapter of the Patrons of Husbandry, but also for various religious congregations—Methodist, Episcopal, Presbyterian, and Baptist. In 1880 A. L. Morris purchased land, a

The cemetery is all that remained after Department of War wrecking crews demolished Oak Hill during World War II. Photograph by the author, 1999.

steam engine, boilers, and other equipment to construct a cotton gin and gristmill on Piney Creek near the Oak Hill cemetery. The community continued to grow, adding stores and syrup mills. When Bastrop County created a district-type school system in 1907, Oak Hill became the center of one of the districts. Even though the community had suffered some ill effects from the early movements toward the consolidation of agriculture during the 1920s and '30s, its prospects were still favorable in the early 1940s. Then America entered World War II.

Even though they had never released such information to the public, the U.S. Army had made detailed plans for the creation of a huge military training facility between Bastrop and Elgin. Within days of the Japanese attack on U.S. forces at Pearl Harbor on 7 December 1941, the War Department announced its intention to build Camp Swift on over fifty thousand acres. The projected military encampment included all of the Oak Hill community. Land owners in the town received five months to move out of their homes. Military police began patrolling rural lanes through the community almost immediately. By summer 1942 not one Oak Hill resident remained, and the army proceeded to remove all existing structures except for the cemetery. Some of the buildings were used for target practice by artillery trainees. After the war the government deactivated Camp Swift, returning over half of its acreage to its former owners but keeping a substantial portion as a National Guard training reservation. Part of the former Oak Hill community became privately owned again, while other areas remained government property. With all

Wartime entrance to Camp Swift, the 1942 creation of which spelled the end of Oak Hill. U.S. Army Signal Corps photograph #PICA 27145, courtesy of the Austin History Center, Austin Public Library.

preexisting structures removed and with military construction added in other locations, Oak Hill was far from what its former residents remembered. They never rebuilt the town, and to this day the cemetery is all that remains of a once promising farming community.

LOCATION: *The Oak Hill Cemetery is located just southeast of Farm Road 2336 in Bastrop County. To reach the site from Bastrop, drive north 7.2 miles on Texas State Highway 95 to its intersection with Farm Road 2336. Turn northeast onto Farm Road 2336 and drive 2.9 miles to an intersection with graded Bastrop County Road 361, also called "Oak Hill Cemetery Road." Proceed 0.3 miles southeast on the county road to the cemetery. To reach the site from McDade, drive south 3.9 miles on Farm Road 2336 to Bastrop County Road 361; turn southeast and drive 0.3 miles to the cemetery. Opposite the intersection of Farm Road 2336 and Bastrop County Road 361, behind Gate 3, lies the northwestward continuation of what formerly was known as Oak Hill Road, now a Jeep road through the military reservation. The entry to Camp Swift is located on Texas State Highway 95 just 0.2 miles north of that road's intersection with Farm Road 2336; there visitors can see historical markers that describe the role of Camp Swift as a training center during World War II.*

Ochiltree

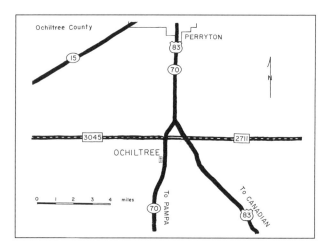

Ochiltree, the first seat of Ochiltree County and once a town of five hundred to six hundred inhabitants, is utterly abandoned. Today only some ruins and a well maintained cemetery survive at the site on the north side of Wolf Creek, south of present-day Perryton.

During the mid-1880s, settlers began to congregate on the banks of Wolf Creek. They lived mostly in dugouts, saying that they lived "in Ochiltree." The surrounding area had sufficient population by 1889 that its citizens petitioned to become organized as a county. In its first election Ochiltree, the one "town" in the proposed county, was chosen as the seat of government. After working from offices housed in private homes and buildings for almost three years, the county commissioners called a bond election in 1891 for the construction of a permanent courthouse to be erected later that year. Lumber for the structure came by freight wagon overland from the nearest railroad at Dodge City, Kansas. The two-story building not only housed county records, offices, and courtrooms, but also served as a community center, auditorium, and church meeting-place. In time the Methodists, Baptists, and a group known simply as "Christians" built their own places of worship.

In its heyday about 1915, Ochiltree boomed at the center of a prosperous region devoted to ranching and agriculture. The town had a waterworks, flour mill, motion-picture theater, two newspapers, an amateur baseball team, modern schools, a national bank, community orchestra, hotel, meat market, mercantile stores, automobile garages, and two mail lines that came by

A real-estate, loans, and insurance office that boomed at the Ochiltree townsite in 1916. Courtesy of G. R. LaMaster.

Beula Bell, Billy Bell, and Charlie Bell at their place on Wolf Creek in Ochiltree County circa 1901. Courtesy of the Panhandle-Plains Historical Museum Research Center.

A present-day fence alongside Texas State Highway 70 bisects the foundations of a former building at Ochiltree. Photograph by the author, 2000.

automobile from Liberal, Kansas, and Glazier, Texas.

One surprisingly popular recreational activity at Ochiltree was automobile racing. In 1915 a circular track was graded around a nearby natural playa lake, and local promoters began advertising as far away as Fort Worth and Wichita Falls for races with total prizes of $2,000. Entrants began arriving two and three days early, coming in cars from such manufacturers as Buick, Hudson, Stutz, and Pierce-Arrow. The first prize of $750 went to Charles and John Ensminger in a Hudson Super Six. The promoters realized a profit and set up additional races, primarily to boost the image of Ochiltree in the surrounding country and also to bring visitors to the town.

In 1919 and 1920, the Panhandle and Santa Fe Railway Company built a line from Shattuck, Oklahoma, to Spearman, Texas, cutting diagonally across Ochiltree County. A new town named Perryton was established beside its tracks about eight miles north of Ochiltree. The merchants in the new town, many of whom emigrated from Ochiltree, were able to offer lower prices to their customers than could merchants in the older town without rail connections; trade shifted almost immediately northward to the railroad. Most of the residences and commercial buildings, which were of wood-frame construction, were transported from the banks of Wolf Creek across the flat plains to the new railroad town. Ochiltree became a ghost town in just a few months—the county seat moved to Perryton in 1919, and in 1921 the post office was also transferred. The site now consists of a historical marker, ruined building foundations, and a cemetery.

LOCATION: *The Ochiltree Cemetery is located 8.3 miles south of Perryton on Texas State Highway 70 at a point that is 2.3 miles south of where Texas State Highway combines with U.S. Highway 83.*

Ogden

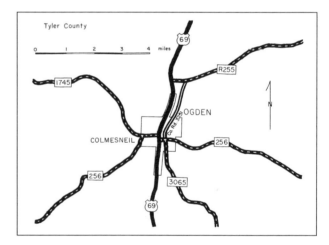

The story of Ogden is really the story of two Tyler County towns: Ogden and Colmesneil. Ogden began as the larger and more promising of the two communities, but is now a dispersed rural community clinging to life on the side of a hill that overlooks the prosperous Colmesneil.

The two towns of Ogden and Colmesneil were born in the early 1880s amid railway construction. The Sabine and East Texas Railway reached Colmesneil in 1882, whereas the Trinity and Sabine Railway reached Ogden about 1884. The two railroad stations stood only about half a mile apart. The existence of these railway lines, which

The road from Colmesneil to Ogden. Photograph by the author, 1999.

would provide easy access to the area's rich resources of pine timber, made Ogden and Colmesneil clear targets for development by timber interests. Soon the Yellow Pine Lumber Company began construction of a huge sawmill east of the Trinity and Sabine depot at Ogden. At the same time, the lumber firm was laying its own steel rails for steam tram lines to haul logs from the forests into its mill. By 1889 Ogden and Colmesneil reported a combined population of 2,200; most people lived on the hill near the sawmill at Ogden. The mill at this time was producing an impressive ninety thousand board feet of lumber daily.

Most of the urban development at Ogden was either around or east of the Trinity and Sabine depot. The town had four hotels—the Ogden, the Yellow Pine, the Tucker, and the Withers—a two-story Masonic lodge, school, several mercantile and grocery stores, a drug store, a millinery shop, and multiple saloons. Even though Ogden was not incorporated, it did have its own jail where officers of the sheriff's department could incarcerate lawbreakers. Residents of Ogden looked down the hill toward the houses and struggling

enterprises of Colmesneil, which lacked Ogden's capital infusions from the big sawmill and its payroll.

Times changed for Ogden on 20 April 1893. That day a fire broke out in the Yellow Pine sawmill; it burned to the ground, taking much of the town with it. Ed Williams howled with pain from blistered feet as he stood on the roof of the Ogden train station, pouring out the water passed up to him in buckets to prevent the roof from catching fire. Others saved their houses and businesses in like manner, but the economic powerhouse of Ogden—the sawmill—was gone. "The smoldering ruins of the Yellow Pine mill give the town a gruesome appearance today," reported the *Galveston News*, adding that, "groups of people stand about discussing the ferocity of yesterday's flames."

Colmesneil had maintained a more balanced economy that was based not only on lumber, but also on farming. While single-industry Ogden withered away, its businesses, churches, and people moved down the hill to Colmesneil. The Beaumont *Journal* observed in 1905, "Colmesneil, which was once a sawmill village, is now a thriving town, maintained by its fruit and truck industry."

Today Ogden is a dispersed, almost haggard-looking semi-rural residential area that stretches up the side of the hill over the foundations and debris that remain from the town's more prosperous past.

LOCATION: *Ogden lies alongside Tyler County Road 3251 on the northern outskirts of Colmesneil. To reach the site of the former town, drive 0.1 miles east on Farm Road 256 from where it intersects U.S. Highway 69 in Colmesneil to the juncture of Farm Road 256, Farm Road 3065, and Tyler County Road 3251. Turn north onto Tyler County Road 3251, also known locally as "North Pitzer Street," which curves up the hill through the townsite of Ogden. The south edge of the old town is 0.3 miles from Farm Road 256 and the north edge is 0.7 miles from Farm Road 256. The townsite contains both modern and historic dwellings; multiple sites of former buildings marked by disturbed ground, debris, ornamental shrubs, and flowering plants; and large amounts of broken glass, ceramics, and pieces of metal.*

Oil Springs

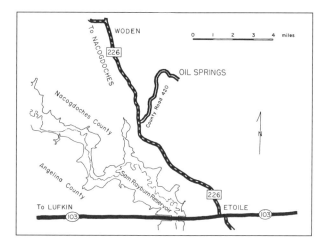

The original spring of water that was found to have traces of petroleum, situated in the forest at Oil Springs. Photograph by the author, 1999.

By 1866 the site of the first commercial oil well in Texas, Oil Springs in Nacogdoches County has been both an oil field camp and an oil field boomtown. Each time it reverted back to unoccupied forest.

Lyne Taliaferro Barret first drilled for oil in 1859, perhaps prompted by Edwin L. Drake's oil-well drilling efforts in Pennsylvania. Barret had come to Texas as a child in 1842; while growing up in Nacogdoches County, he played in the waters at Oil Springs. In these springs, natural petroleum floats to the top. American Indians and early settlers went to these springs, where they could rake the bottom with tree branches to stir up the oil and then skim it off the surface. In 1859 Barret leased 279 acres around the springs and began boring a well into the ground in hopes of striking oil. Then the Civil War intervened and progress halted.

Barret returned to Oil Springs after the war, secured financial backing, formed the Melrose Petroleum Oil Company, and began drilling again. The area around the work site became a camp of tents and shacks. The efforts progressed until the auger drill had gone over a hundred feet deep. Then, as Barret later recalled, "the auger dropped

The two remaining 1880s riveted-steel oil-storage tanks at Oil Springs. They are the oldest steel storage tanks for petroleum in Texas. Photograph by the author, 1999.

through a vein six inches deep, when oil, water, and gas gushed to the top of the well." To his great disappointment, however, Barret discovered that he had no way to market his oil. He did manage to secure more money and backing from Pennsylvania to drill another well several miles away, but it proved to be a dry hole. Barret lost all he had invested, and most people forgot the entire venture.

After the passage of twenty years, a geologist named B. H. Hitchcock decided that it might be economically feasible to drill for oil again in the area of Oil Springs. He and others formed the Petroleum Prospecting Company, which in 1886 began drilling in the vicinity of the springs. Their well struck oil at a depth of seventy feet and yielded 250 to 300 barrels a day. By this time there was no problem finding buyers for the oil. Within three years, forty wells came into production, and a full-fledged boomtown called Oil City sprang forth at Oil Springs. An estimated 150 men worked in the field; their trade and

that of others supported a dozen stores, a barrel-making factory, a small oil-skimming plant, a substantial boarding house, and a saloon. Tents and oil derricks sprang up everywhere. During this boom time Oil Springs saw the fabrication of the first all-steel petroleum storage tanks in Texas, the construction of the first oil pipeline in the state, and the operation of a primitive refinery that is considered to have been the first in Texas. In time production at Oil Springs declined, and with it, the population of Oil City. The springs were again deserted.

Oil Springs had later oil prospecting activity as people attempted to squeeze a few more barrels of petroleum from its wells at times of high energy prices, such as during World War I. The site even merited a siding on a branch line of the Nacogdoches and Southeastern Railroad during the early decades of the twentieth century. Despite the site's connection to the railroads, it was never again home to a substantial population. By the 1960s Oil Springs was abandoned for a second time and soon became overgrown with trees and vines. An effort was made to create a county park at the site, but today it lies totally deserted and increasingly overgrown alongside a dirt road through the East Texas forests.

LOCATION: *Oil Springs lies at the side of a graded county road deep in the forests of Nacogdoches County. The turn-off for this road from Farm Road 226 is marked only by a sign with the county road number and is located 6.7 miles northwest of Etoile and 4.6 miles southeast of Woden. From Farm Road 226, turn east onto Nacogdoches County Road 420 and drive 3.9 miles generally northward and northeastward to the site, which is marked by the two steel oil storage tanks from 1886 and concrete curbing and steel pipe around the flowing spring in the forest. The county road, which consists of a few patches of pavement as well as graded dirt with ruts from logging trucks, is recommended only when it is dry. The woods abound in poison ivy.*

Old D'Hanis

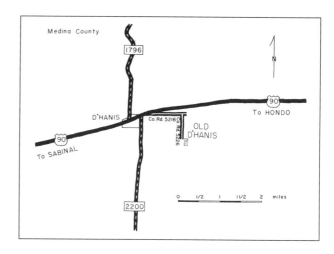

Old D'Hanis in Medina County was one of several colonies of European immigrants brought to Texas by Henri Castro during the 1840s. The community thrived for several decades, but then withered away after the new Galveston, Harrisburg and San Antonio Railway bypassed it in 1881.

Young people out for a ride, posed in front of St. Dominic Church in Old D'Hanis sometime during the early twentieth century. Courtesy of Connie Koch and the University of Texas Institute of Texan Cultures at San Antonio.

The crumbling ruins of St. Dominic Church in Old D'Hanis at the end of the twentieth century. Photograph by the author, 2000.

French-born entrepreneur Henri Castro received a contract from the Republic of Texas in 1842 to bring European immigrants to southwestern Texas, which was on the fringe of settlement at that time. Between 1844 and 1846, Castro and his immigration company founded agricultural settlements of French and German immigrants at Castroville, Quihi, and Vandenburg, all in present-day Medina County. During the winter of 1846–47 surveyor Charles de Montel, Theodore Gentilz, and several others laid out the site for the fourth and last of Castro's colonies. They named this town Dhanis for the immigration company's manager in Antwerp, Guillaume Dhanis. It was not until the twentieth century than an apostrophe was added to change the spelling to D'Hanis.

Immigrants bound for the new settlement landed on the Texas Gulf coast in early 1847. They trekked inland to San Antonio and then on to the new settlement, almost fifty miles beyond the Alamo city. The first group arrived in February; the remainder came by the end of the summer. In all, twenty-nine families immigrated to Dhanis, most of them from the German states of Bavaria and Württenburg. They found their homesite on a high prairie watered by Parker Creek but without trees from which to build their houses. They initially cut lengths of mesquite tree trunks to form pickets, which they placed vertically in shallow trenches to form the walls for thatch-roofed huts. In later years the settlers erected the thick-walled stone cottages that today are often associated with German immigrant communities.

The settlers found their first years at Dhanis more than difficult. They had little money after the expense of traveling from Europe, a lack of food forced many of them to live off the land, an 1848 drought destroyed their crops, and they found themselves unable to communicate with most of the surrounding American and Mexican people. Some of the newcomers had reached the point of abandoning their town when the U.S. Army established Fort Lincoln nearby in July

One of the nineteenth-century immigrant cottages in Old D'Hanis. Photograph by the author, 2000.

Medina County Road 5216 from its intersection with U.S. Highway 90 on the eastern outskirts of D'Hanis. Drive 0.7 miles east on the gravel county road to its intersection with paved Medina County Road 5226; turn south on paved Medina County Road 5226 and drive 0.3 miles through the former townsite to the cemetery and the ruins of St. Dominic Church.

1849. Many of the immigrant men found employment in helping to erect buildings for the military, a job that gave them money wages to support their families in a time of great need. Eventually the immigrants at Dhanis prospered, building for themselves a stone Gothic Revival-style church, establishing schools, and opening stores and shops of craftsmen. Among the enterprises in the town were a grain mill, mercantile stores, saloons, and a stagecoach station.

When the tracks were laid from San Antonio westward toward El Paso for the Galveston, Harrisburg and San Antonio Railway, they passed just north of Dhanis in 1881. Because the immigrant settlers had preferred not to sell their land to the railroad, it bypassed their community. Company engineers laid out a railroad town they called New Dhanis about a mile and a half to the west. The new community, with convenient shipping for its goods, thrived; the initial community, now called Old Dhanis, languished. The 1914 construction of a Catholic church in New Dhanis marked the effective end of Old Dhanis. Today it is a dispersed rural community with a few houses still standing in the historic grid of streets laid out in the winter of 1846–47 by de Montel and Gentilz. The ruins of the Gothic Revival St. Dominic Church and its beautiful cemetery attract hundreds of visitors each year.

LOCATION: *Old Dhanis, spelled D'Hanis since 1936, is located on county roads just east of the new town of D'Hanis in western Medina County. To reach the church and cemetery, drive east on gravel*

Orla

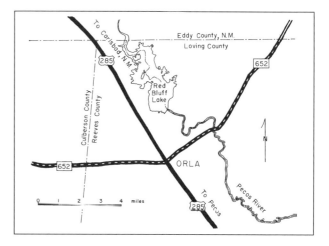

The remote oil-field town of Orla, located west of the Pecos in northern Reeves County, barely clings to life in the West Texas desert.

Orla had several beginnings—not in oil, but in railroads and land promotion. In 1891 the Pecos Valley Railway built tracks northward from Pecos, Texas, to present-day Carlsbad, New Mexico, in order to provide a steam railroad outlet for agricultural crops raised in that portion of the Pecos River valley. Land owners and speculators in the valley also hoped that the rail line would stimulate economic growth and sales of land to farmers from other parts of the country. The railroad created a siding at Orla, which means "border" in Spanish, and erected facilities for livestock-shipping and track maintenance. The hoped-for farmers never came to buy land, for no water was available for irrigation. In fact, there was no drinking water at all. Groundwater at Orla was so alkaline that it was not drinkable, so the railroad had to import all potable water for residents.

A former café and bus station in Orla, its roof blowing away one piece at a time. Photograph by the author, 2000.

Doors standing open to the deserted Orla Baptist Church. Photograph by the author, 2000.

Another effort to promote Orla took place in 1909, when local land owner H. A. Shannon filed a plat to divide the townsite into lots, blocks, and streets alongside the railroad tracks. Again, few people wanted to come to such a remote place with no convenient water source. Orla slowly developed as a small-scale supply center for the surrounding ranch country with a post office, store, livestock holding-pens, and a handful of people.

In 1931 the north-south highway connecting Pecos with Carlsbad was rerouted to its present location about half a mile west of the railroad. Owners of the stores and houses at Orla moved them to the new highway, leaving only the tracks, railway maintenance facilities, and vacant lots

behind. Eventually the railroad company abandoned the line.

Orla, relocated to the highway, continued to be a supply center for the surrounding ranches. Its residents little knew that their community was about to become a boomtown. Since the 1920s oil prospecting had led to petroleum discoveries in the Permian Basin. Occasional wildcat drilling had taken place on the basin's western flanks around Orla, but such experimental drilling had not been productive. Then in October 1947 the Tunstall brothers drilled a valuable well four miles northwest of Orla; the next June Ford Chapman drilled another important well southwest of Orla. Soon drilling rigs dotted the horizon around the little town, which eventually became the center for an area of oil and natural gas production. Orla's population had swelled to an estimated 250 inhabitants by the end of the 1960s, and the town boasted twelve businesses including oil-field supply houses, petroleum trucking firms, cafés, a post office, filling stations, a bus station, water-hauling services, and liquor stores.

Just off the highway in Orla an old-fashioned wooden suitcase rots to pieces amid other debris from the former town. Photograph by the author, 2000.

The population of Orla gradually declined during the 1970s and 1980s as oil production decreased, and then it plummeted with the decline in petroleum prices during the early 1990s. Almost everyone departed. At the time of the author's latest visit in 2000, the only operating businesses in Orla were three remaining oil-field service firms, a post office in a portable building, and one last combination store and filling station. The town had over a dozen abandoned residences, fewer than half a dozen occupied dwellings, and multiple abandoned buildings including filling stations, stores, a church, cafés, and a liquor store. The entire townsite is marked with disturbed ground, foundations, and debris from former buildings, while vast surface archaeological remains such as glass, ceramics, and metal are scattered about. On a clear day visitors to Orla can view Guadalupe Peak, the highest point in Texas, sixty miles away to the west.

LOCATION: *Orla is located at the intersection of U.S. Highway 285 and Ranch Road 652 at a point that* *38.2 miles north of Pecos and 46.3 miles south of Carlsbad, New Mexico.*

Oxford

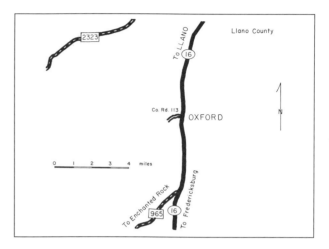

Named for its founder's earlier home at Oxford, Mississippi, the Llano County town of Oxford

A former blacksmith shop looks out on Texas Highway 16 in Oxford. Photograph by the author, 2000.

An abandoned stone house on the outskirts of Oxford. Photograph by the author, 2000.

was established by A. J. Johnson, who moved to the vicinity about 1876. Already there were farmers and livestock-raisers in the area, but Johnson foresaw its growth into a thriving community, and so he hired surveyor Knight Stiff to lay out a formally platted town.

Over the next decade numerous individuals came to the new community south of Llano. The first school was a one-room log structure that was not unlike a similar building that housed the first store. In later years the school held classes in another building and had over one hundred pupils. By the mid-1880s Oxford had not only its school and store, but also a union church, the Grange meeting-hall, a drug store, post office, sawmill, and cotton gin. Although the sawmill made cut lumber available, for several years many residents preferred the economy of building their own log homes. Founder A. J. Johnson donated the land for a cemetery, and it was later enlarged by a gift of adjoining land from C. T.

Moss. A well near the center of the town provided drinking water to the residents and to travelers on the north-south road through Oxford that linked Llano to Fredericksburg.

By 1885 Oxford had seventy-five residents. The population increased to 237 in 1896, a figure never again surpassed there. By 1914 the number had dropped to only thirty. Later in the century improved roads and the proximity of the larger town of Llano sentenced Oxford to dwindle away into oblivion. Today it consists of a few scattered rural dwellings, an abandoned filling station-blacksmith shop, the foundations and ruins of former buildings, and a well maintained cemetery.

LOCATION: *Oxford is 10.5 miles south of Llano and 27.2 miles northeast of Fredericksburg on Texas State Highway 16 at its intersection with Llano County Road 113.*

Penwell

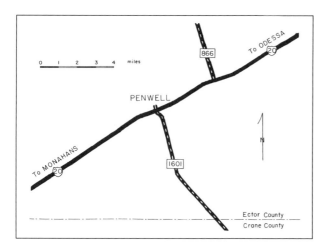

Penwell's unusual name was taken from an oil-well gusher drilled by Robert R. Penn in 1929. A boom-or-bust oil-field town in the Permian Basin region, Penwell was located fifteen miles southwest of Odessa in Ector County.

The Texas and Pacific Railway built a line in 1881 through scrub-brush ranch country that later became Penwell, but the site was not developed at that time. Then in the 1920s the Bankhead Highway, the first east-west highway to cross the state of Texas, was built parallel to the Texas and Pacific tracks through Ector County. It also failed to spur any tangible development at the future site of Penwell. Such a location in semi-arid ranch country without any potable groundwater held little appeal for anyone.

This changed in 1929. Although oil had been found in commercial quantities in other areas of the Permian Basin, none had been discovered in Ector County. Texas oilman Robert R. Penn consulted geologists working in the region, and then he speculated that he might find oil west of Odessa. He chose a site not far from the Texas and Pacific tracks and the Bankhead Highway, both of which assured easy movement of equipment and supplies. His driller, W. A. Black, went to work during the summer of 1929. On 7 October 1929, Black struck oil at a depth of 3,700 feet, the well spraying petroleum over the derrick and the surrounding ranch land. Penn's discovery led to the drilling of dozens of wells, which opened the production of many millions of barrels of oil from beneath Ector County.

The town of Penwell mushroomed alongside the Bankhead Highway and the Texas and Pacific

A GREAT TEXAS GUSHER FIRE THE MOST UNUSUAL PICTURE EVER TAKEN IN AN OIL FIELD SNAPED THE INSTANT THE WELL BURST INTO FLAMES. JACK NOLAN

A remarkable photograph snapped at the moment that an oil-well gusher in Penwell burst into flame on 27 April 1930. Photograph by Jack Nolan, courtesy of Patman & Osborn, Austin, Texas.

Railway tracks to serve the needs of the new oil field. Its rate of growth astounded visitors. A reporter from the Midland *Reporter-Telegram* wrote on 23 February 1930, "W.C. Shull and O.S. Brown, Midland men, bought a lot, erected a sign within an hour and promised to be serving sandwiches in 12 hours and hot 'short orders' in a few hours more." He continued, "A Pyote druggist called that he was sending over a drug store. Within an hour the first truck load of equipment for the building arrived and was unloaded." Penwell became an oil field boomtown almost overnight. In 1930—less than a year after the discovery of oil—locals estimated the population of Penwell and its surrounding oil field at three thousand inhabitants.

A deserted home amid the debris of Penwell. Photograph by the author, 2000.

Where travelers used to stop for coffee and meals in Penwell. Photograph by the author, 2000.

During its heyday Penwell had six lumber yards, several rooming houses, two hotels, a barbershop, three dry goods stores, a school, a drug store, three churches, doctors' offices, filling stations, and a large county-owned community hall, not to mention the saloons, pool halls, dance halls, and bordellos. The *Penwell News* published accounts of local events and promoted the town. The inhabitants of the half a dozen substantial "camps" that petroleum companies built to house their employees helped support businesses in the town.

Penwell's activity, however, mirrored that of the oil field it served. As petroleum output declined, so did the town's population, which dipped to less than a hundred in 1933. Renewed drilling activity in 1938 brought people back; the population jumped to eight hundred to a thousand residents in town. Then in the 1940s an exodus from Penwell began that continues to the present day. Low petroleum prices in the early 1990s led to the virtual abandonment of Penwell. Today the town is known for its huge oil-field salvage yard and a nearby 1960s automobile drag strip. During the author's most recent visit in 2000, Penwell had only seven occupied residences, about the same number of deserted dwellings, multiple abandoned commercial buildings, and vast amounts of surface debris from former buildings and petroleum activity. From more than a mile away, motorists on Interstate Highway 20 can identify Penwell from its scores of multi-colored second-hand oil storage tanks that await recycling.

LOCATION: *Penwell is located off Interstate Highway 20 at exit 101 for Farm Road 1601 in Ector County at a point that is 13.7 miles southwest of Odessa and 20.5 miles northeast of Monahans. The interesting Monahans Sand Hills State Park is located off Interstate Highway 20 at a point that is 15.4 miles southwest of Penwell.*

Pluck

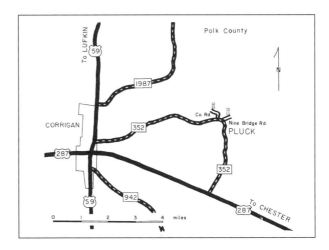

A sawmill town in northern Polk County, Pluck prospered from lumbering during the 1880s and 1890s until the best timber in its area had been cut, after which time the town shrank to little more than a dispersed rural community.

A log barn and abandoned home in Pluck. Photograph by the author, 1999.

Settlement at the town now known as Pluck initially began in the 1850s, when whites and blacks began moving into the undeveloped northern part of Polk County. There they established farms, engaged in small-scale lumbering, and quarried limited amounts of stone. Things changed in 1882, however, when the Trinity and Sabine Railway entered the area. This opened the region to large-scale timber operations because the steam railways could transport lumber to market.

Two New Jersey cousins, D. M. Angle and George Henry Stryker, formed the Angle Lumber Company, secured rights to many thousands of acres of timber in northern Polk County, and, about 1884, began constructing a sawmill. Angle managed the corporate operations from Houston, and Stryker superintended the plant in Polk County. In addition to building the mill, wood-drying kilns, and commissary, the company constructed inexpensive housing for employees, a school, and a church. The company named the place Stryker in honor of the plant manager, and the town secured a post office by that name in 1885. After their firm survived a fire at the mill in 1887, the two cousins installed new equipment at the Stryker mill that enabled it to produce forty-five thousand board feet of lumber daily.

The town boomed so long as its sawmill had timber resources to feed it. By the end of the 1890s, however, that supply of local uncut trees began to run out. The mill's production decreased, and then it stopped operating entirely about 1898. With this closure, most people departed Stryker even though a smaller mill continued to cut local timber into the early 1900s. So many residents left that the post office closed in 1913. Enough people remained in the vicinity, however, that about 1918 a local storekeeper petitioned to reopen the post office. The Post Office Department agreed but stated that it would not approve a post office under the old name of Stryker. Locals had to come up with a new name.

According to Texas postal historian Fred I. Massengill, George H. Deason proposed the name, Pluck, "because, in his opinion, it required 'pluck' to locate here." Long-time local merchant Willie Reinhardt had his own explanation, shared

A cane-squeezing mill used for making molasses, now idle amid the pine trees at Pluck. Photograph by the author, 1999.

closed its doors for the last time. This left only Willie Reinhardt's general store, which operated into the 1960s. Today Pluck has no places of business, but the Baptist church is active, and about half a dozen dwellings are occupied—though approximately the same number of residences stand empty. Two interesting cemeteries are also located at Pluck.

LOCATION: *Pluck is located on a bend in Farm Road 352 at a point that is 2.7 miles north of where it intersects U.S. Highway 287 in Polk County. This intersection is 4.7 miles east of Corrigan and 9.8 miles west of Chester. To reach the Stryker Cemetery for whites, drive 0.5 miles north from the town center on Farm Road 352, then turn east at the Stryker Baptist Church and drive 0.4 miles on a paved county road identified as "Nine Bridge Road." Dominated by a huge magnolia tree, this graveyard contains the 1892 burial of George Henry Stryker. The Pluck Memorial Cemetery for blacks is also near the Stryker Baptist Church. To reach this cemetery, turn north on the county road just west of the church and drive 0.3 miles north from Farm Road 352.*

with Texas journalist Frank X. Tolbert in 1965. According to the story, Reinhardt disagreed with the Post Office Department's refusal to accept the Stryker place-name. He reputedly wrote to officials in Washington, "There's too danged many names in Texas now. Let's just call it Nothing, Texas." According to Reinhardt, officials in Washington replied, "No. But we like your spunk. We'll call it Pluck, Texas, since there is already a Fort Spunky." Whatever the case, the name approved for the reopened post office in 1918 was Pluck, and thus the community changed from Stryker to Pluck.

Pluck managed to hold onto existence as a town for several more decades, its residents working in agriculture, small-scale lumbering, and silica mining at a nearby quarry. Due to the consolidation of agriculture, the local population continued to decrease. In 1953 the reestablished post office

Prairie Hill

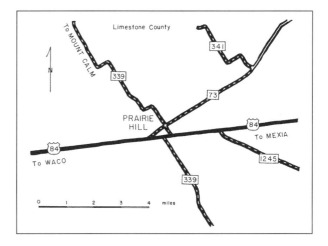

An agricultural center throughout its history, Prairie Hill in Limestone County declined with the mechanization and consolidation of farming during the 1920s through the 1950s.

Sometime during the mid-nineteenth century J. A. Karl and Henry Marcus moved to present-

Overgrown entry of a deserted home in Prairie Hill. Photograph by the author, 1998.

For reasons that are still unclear, Prairie Hill lost its post office in 1906, but another one reopened in 1925. Although the mechanization of agriculture prompted some farming families to leave the Prairie Hill area and seek employment elsewhere, in 1929 the town boasted a bank and 300 residents. The weakening agricultural economy, however, prompted the bank owners to liquidate their business in 1931. Nevertheless, the town claimed 500 inhabitants and ten businesses in 1933, its statistical high point. As the rural population base that had supported Prairie Hill enterprises continued to decrease, the town mirrored the situation—family after family moved away to seek opportunities elsewhere. The opening of an auxiliary landing field south of Prairie Hill for the Army Air Corps at Connally Field in Waco provided jobs for a few local people. Even so the population dropped to 400 by 1945 and to 350 by 1947. The decreasing numbers of pupils forced the high school to close in 1950 and the elementary school to close in 1963; both merged with the schools in nearby Coolidge. In 1969 the last cotton gin ceased operating, and it was followed by the Prairie Grove Milling Company. As the consolidation of agriculture continued, many of the formerly cultivated fields around the town became pasture for cattle.

Although Prairie Grove still has an operating post office, an active Baptist Church, a community water system, and a volunteer fire department, the town is a vestige of its former self. From a high of 500 residents sixty-five years ago, the town retains only a few residents today. On the author's latest visit in 2000, he found three dozen occupied residences and another dozen abandoned. The only operating place of business was a gasoline station half a mile from the center of the townsite on U.S. Highway 84.

day Prairie Hill making them the first white settlers in the vicinity. The immediate area soon became known as Prairie Hill from its location on a rise between Christmas Creek and the Navasota River. By 1884 enough people had settled in the area that one of them petitioned for a post office, which the federal government granted in the name of Prairie Hill. That same year local residents established their first public school to educate their children. The next year Baptists in the neighborhood organized the first church, which still serves the community. During the 1890s Prairie Hill, with a population of two hundred, grew to include several general stores, two hotels, two cotton gins, a gristmill, five churches, a Masonic lodge, and shops of various craftsmen.

Prairie Hill prospered because its businesses received the support of hundreds of rural families that raised cotton and corn on the fields surrounding the town. Residents in the country relied upon the Prairie Hill merchants to provide them with everything they could not raise themselves.

LOCATION: *Prairie Hill is located at the intersection of Farm Road 73 and Farm Road 339 in Limestone County. This intersection is 0.6 miles northeast of where Farm Road 73 intersects U.S. Highway 84, 20.6 miles east of Waco and 18.7 miles west of Mexia. The concrete runways from the historic air corps landing field are nearby, 0.9 miles south of U.S. Highway 84 on the east side of Farm Road 339.*

Pyote

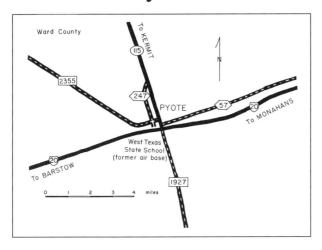

Twice a boomtown and then twice deserted, the Ward County community of Pyote has one of the most interesting town histories in all of West Texas.

Pyote began as a siding and telegraph station constructed when the Texas and Pacific Railway Company laid rails from Fort Worth westward toward El Paso in 1881. Even with access to a steam railway, the site initially known as Pyote Tank did not develop economically for a quarter century.

Then in 1906 local ranch owners sold two hundred acres alongside the railroad to the Pyote Town Development Company. The next year, Cicero Silas Sitton came to the proposed new town and opened its first store. In the meantime the townsite company hosted a three-day barbecue, during which time it began selling town lots to prospective residents and businessmen. In time Pyote grew into a local ranch supply center with a hotel, restaurant, lumber yard, barbershop, school, and post office.

Sources disagree on the origin of the town's unusual name. Some locals say "Pyote" refers to the peyote cactus, which grows in the area. Others say that the name originated from the Chinese laborers who laid rails for the Texas and Pacific Railway in 1881. According to this version of the story, the Asian workers mispronounced the word "coyote" as "pie-oat."

The small town of Pyote was little more than a local supply center and shipping point for ranchers

A pile of rubble that was once a home in Pyote. Photograph by the author, 2000.

Asphalt siding peeling off a deserted home in Pyote. Photograph by the author, 2000.

until 1926. In that year large quantities of oil were discovered in the Hendrick Oil Field, located fifteen miles to the northeast in Winkler County. The ranching community was suddenly the nearest shipping point for what became a major oil field. Pyote mushroomed from no more than 200 inhabitants to an estimated 15,000. At one time in 1928 it had twenty-two branch houses of major oil-field supply firms, six derrick and rig contractors, ten of the largest lumber yards in all of West Texas, an estimated 500 motor trucks and countless teams of horses that hauled supplies to the oil field, and almost unbelievable amounts of freight delivered via the railroad. For a time Pyote had the most freight business of any one station on the entire Texas and Pacific system. The town itself had all of the stores, hotels, boarding houses, cafés, drug stores, barbershops, doctors' offices, two newspapers, and other enterprises necessary to meet the needs of 15,000 residents. Along with the legitimate enterprises came saloons—which were illegal during prohibition but conducted business openly in Pyote—pool halls, gambling dens, and brothels. Then in 1930 the Texas and

Pacific Company constructed a branch railway line to the Winkler County oil fields, and Pyote lost all its former importance. In addition, petroleum production in Winkler County decreased concurrently. Pyote then lost most of its population. The town declined so dramatically that in 1941 city officials met to dissolve the municipal government.

Events overseas brought a second boom to Pyote. Following the Japanese naval attack on U.S. forces at Pearl Harbor, the United States entered World War II. The War Department needed locations for the training of military personnel, and it chose Pyote as the site for a large facility devoted to training crews to fly and operate bomber aircraft. Established in 1942 about a mile south of the town, the Pyote Army Air Field, otherwise known as the "Rattlesnake Bomber Base," trained thousands of crew members for B-17 and then B-29 bombers. At its peak of operation, the base alone had 6,566 residents, including civilians. As the nearest town, Pyote sprang back to life to supply the needs for the military and civilian personnel at the base. Construction work-

Furniture and cabinets are all that still reside in an abandoned home at Pyote. Photograph by the author, 2000.

facilities to house its West Texas State School for juveniles.

With the area's oil fields in decline and no air base to support its economy, residents once again deserted Pyote. Today approximately three dozen of its residences are occupied but five dozen dwellings of all sizes and types stand deserted. The town has about one hundred inhabitants, an active community center, branch classrooms of Odessa College, and the Rattlesnake Bomber Base Museum, which displays World War II memorabilia. During the author's most recent visit in 2000, the town had only one active filling station/store, one operating tavern, and one café open for business. The former downtown commercial strip on the old highway that parallels the railroad tracks through town possessed only one building still standing amid the ruins and foundations of dozens of others.

LOCATION: *Pyote is located off Interstate Highway 20 on Texas State Highway 115 in Ward County, 13.0 miles west of Monahans and 17.0 miles east of Barstow. Some of the historic World War II structures from Pyote Army Air Field can be seen from the access road on the south side of the Interstate Highway, although most of the former base is closed to the public.*

ers and others flooded into Pyote, where businesspeople in the once stagnant downtown found themselves hard-pressed to satisfy the demands of so many newcomers.

After the war Pyote declined a second time, but the gradual decline in military activity at the base cushioned the economic blow. After the large numbers of Air Corps personnel left, the base became a major facility for the storage of and, later, the salvaging of metals from World War II aircraft. In fact, it became the temporary home of the *Enola Gay*, the B-29 bomber that in August 1945 dropped the first atomic bomb on Hiroshima, Japan. During the 1950s thousands of sleek bombers from the war came to Pyote Field to be cut up and melted in scrap dealers' furnaces. In time the base became only a radar station until the Air Force completely abandoned it in 1966. The state of Texas reused a portion of the old radar

Quintana

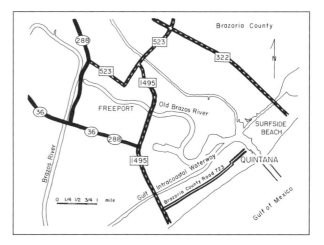

The port town of Quintana on the mouth of the Brazos River has always tantalized its residents

A family of beach-goers walks past the restored home of Captain Henry Seaburn, a nineteenth-century boat-builder from Quintana. Seaburn's home now contains offices and special-events rooms of the Quintana Beach County Park. Photograph by the author, 1999.

with the prospects of future wealth they never seemed to achieve. Today the out-of-the-way fishing village and oceanfront resort shares a narrow strip of land with chemical plants and bulk oil-loading facilities.

Quintana's origins date back to 1821, when Mexico, after winning its independence from Spain, chose the west side of the Brazos River mouth on the Gulf of Mexico as the site for a fortification named in honor of Gen. Andreas Quintana. When Stephen F. Austin first organized the movement of white settlers into Mexican Texas, he secured the site the fort had occupied at the mouth of the Brazos as part of the lands for his colony. For some time he would not let anyone occupy it because he hoped to sell the strategically located property for a profit. Eventually in 1834 merchants Samuel May Williams and Thomas Freeman McKinney established a mercantile business at the site, which was platted as a townsite the next year. Others followed them to the location that was still known as Quintana, gradually building a town of about fifty households by 1860.

Quintana existed because of its geographical location at the river mouth. The town became one of several shipping points for agricultural goods raised in the Brazos valley. After these goods arrived downstream at Quintana's docks and warehouses, they were shipped abroad. Quintana also received imported goods sought by those living inland. A number of the planters from upstream built summer homes atop the sand dunes at Quintana because the oceanfront location offered cooler and purportedly healthier living than the hot, humid inland areas devoid of sea breezes. About a quarter of the people in the town at the time were black slaves, some of whom lived in comparative luxury while serving the planters' families. After the outbreak of the Civil War in 1861, Quintana became one of the destinations for fast vessels that attempted to slip through the Union naval blockade of the Texas coast. Occasionally ships in the blockading squadron exchanged canon fire with Confederate gunners at the river mouth, but no other fighting took place there.

The Reconstruction era began after the Civil War ended, but Quintana languished in economic doldrums. Other nearby Gulf ports, such as Velasco, Galveston, and Houston, outcompeted Quintana for maritime trade even while the entire country was suffering from the Panic of 1873. Then in 1879 the town received a temporary boost from efforts to create jetties at the mouth of the Brazos. The new structures would narrow the mouth of the river where it entered the sea, forcing fresh water into the ocean as quickly as possible and thereby flushing silt out of the channel to keep it deep enough for oceangoing ships. The initial effort failed, but by the 1890s builders had succeeded in improving the harbor mouth. Despite another national depression that began in 1893, the prospects for growth at Quintana looked better than they had at any time during previous years. Among the businesses in the town at the time were mercantile stores, barbers, a meat market, several hotels, a shipbuilding works, ship chandlers, and a customs house, not to mention docks and warehouses. Institutions included various churches and two racially segregated public schools.

In September 1900 a devastating hurricane blew away virtually everything built along the central Gulf coast of Texas, including much of Quintana. With the economy of the region destroyed, only the discovery of nearby sulphur deposits kept Quintana alive. Petrochemical plants were built near the mouth of the Brazos River to process sulphur from the mines near Quintana. The plants, however, boosted the growth of the nearby newer town of Freeport, which had swallowed up the older community of Velasco on the other side of the river

Rainwater-filled concrete foundations of a World War II gun emplacement at the mouth of the Brazos River in Quintana. Photograph by the author, 1999.

mouth. Then in 1929 engineers created a new channel for the extreme lower Brazos, converting the mouth at Quintana, Velasco, and Freeport into a harbor that primarily served the petroleum and petrochemical facilities. The growth of these facilities in time consumed much of the old Quintana townsite. Straightening the harbor entrance in the 1980s entailed further removal of significant riverfront portions of the historic Quintana townsite. A remnant population remained at what was left of the town.

Today Quintana is a fishing and resort village connected to the Texas mainland by a drawbridge over the Gulf Intracoastal Waterway. Visitors driving the streets of the former town will see vacant lots and a few scattered houses. A handful of restaurants operate intermittently, mostly during the summer tourist season. Most visitors come to Quintana because of its well equipped Quintana Beach Park, which is maintained by Brazoria County. At the park, visitors can view two historic Quintana residences—the Seaburn and Coveney houses, which have been renovated—as well as concrete footings that remain from artillery emplacements constructed during World War II for the defense of the Brazos River mouth and its chemical plants. One of Quintana's more unusual distinctions is its popularity as a destination for amateur ornithologists during April bird migrations each year.

LOCATION: *Quintana is located on the west bank of the Brazos River mouth on the Gulf of Mexico, southeast of Freeport in Brazoria County and directly across the river mouth from Surfside Beach. To reach the townsite, drive 1.7 miles southward from Texas State Highway 36 in Freeport on Farm Road 1495, crossing the Gulf Intracoastal Waterway on a drawbridge, to its terminus at a four-way intersection. Turn northeast on paved Brazoria County Road 723 and drive an additional 2.3 miles northeastward to the center of what survives from the former town.*

The log pond that served the 4-C sawmill at Ratcliff. A continuous chain conveyor transported logs from this pond into the three-story mill, where saws cut them into lumber. Photograph by the author, 1999.

Ratcliff

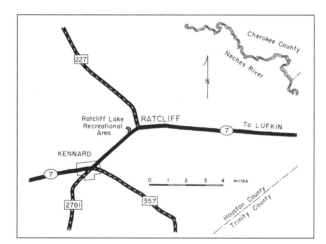

Formerly a town of five thousand inhabitants and the site of the largest sawmill in Texas, Ratcliff today clings to life in the Houston County forests adjacent to a recreational area bearing its name.

A wagon train of settlers from Georgia arrived in the forests of East Texas in 1875. The settlers, devastated by the Civil War and subsequent Reconstruction, had departed their home state to seek opportunities in Texas. Among the emigrants from Georgia was Jesse H. Ratcliff, who built a small

sawmill in 1885. Soon the mill attracted more people; a post office named Ratcliff, stores, a blacksmith, and other enterprises followed.

In 1899 the Central Coal and Coke Company became interested in the land surrounding Ratcliff. Its representatives began buying up forest land in Houston and Trinity counties, eventually acquiring one hundred seventy thousand acres. In 1901 the Eastern Texas Railroad, one of the coal company's subsidiaries, built a line connecting Ratcliff and nearby Kennard with Lufkin to provide an easy means for shipping out lumber and bringing in supplies and equipment.

With thousands of acres of timber land in its hands and the railroad in place, the Central Coal and Coke Company constructed a huge sawmill and planing-mill complex just west of Ratcliff. Loggers cut down trees in the forest and then a steam tram railway carried the logs to a 160-acre mill pond. Continuous chain conveyors hauled the logs from the pond into the three-story sawmill building. The sawmill alone measured 175 feet wide by 386 feet long. There the many saws included a gigantic gang saw with fifty-three circular blades that could cut logs into about fifty 1-x-12-inch boards twenty feet long in one minute.

Brick foundations of the 4-C sawmill have been partially reclaimed by the forest, just outside Ratcliff. Photograph by the author, 1999.

The mill had a phenomenal capacity of three hundred fifty thousand board feet daily. The 4-C company erected a planing mill nearby to process further the rough lumber produced by the sawmill.

The 4-C mill and its five hundred units of worker housing made Ratcliff into a boomtown almost instantly. Its population swelled from a handful to an estimated five thousand, and by 1910 it boasted several stores, a bank, newspaper, school, telephone exchange, restaurants, a drugstore, and a number of saloons. The lumber company provided materials to construct a union church that served Baptists, Methodists, and Presbyterians. The mill compound even had its own commissary store. The store was a major source of income, so the company discouraged employees from patronizing merchants in Ratcliff. At one time it even constructed a twelve-foot-high fence to keep its employees away from the town, but locals dynamited the fence and it eventually came down. Almost everyone "came to town" on Saturdays; as one former resident declared, "You couldn't squeeze your way down the sidewalk."

The 4-C company represented the worst of the absentee-owner "cut over and run" lumbering methods of the late nineteenth and early twentieth centuries. Already by 1914 the managers could see that they had cut down most of the suitable trees in their one hundred seventy thousand acres, and so they had begun shifting equipment and men to a new sawmill near Conroe. In spring or summer 1918 the company shut down the huge 4-C mill at Ratcliff; the town entered an economic slump from which it never recovered.

Ratcliff managed to survive the remainder of the twentieth century by small-scale lumbering and, eventually, by tourism. During the 1930s the federal government purchased ninety-four thousand acres of former 4-C lands and created the Davy Crockett National Forest. The Civilian Conservation Corps then began converting the 160-acre sawmill pond and surrounding lands to the Ratcliff Lake Recreational Area. From that time onward the town of Ratcliff became an outfitting point for sportsmen and families who traveled there to fish and boat on the reservoir. Today the town has about a hundred residents whose homes are scattered throughout the former city blocks that consist mostly of vacant lots.

LOCATION: *Ratcliff is situated alongside Texas State Highway 7 where it intersects Farm Road 227 in Houston County, 3.4 miles east of Kennard, 18.7 miles east of Crockett, and 25.6 miles west of Lufkin. Ruins of the mill foundation and a historical marker for the 4-C mill stand on the south side of Texas State Highway 7 about 0.4 miles west of Ratcliff. The entrance to the Ratcliff Lake Recreational Area is on the north side of Texas State Highway 7 at a point that is 1.0 miles west of the town. Poison ivy abounds in the forest areas around Ratcliff.*

Red River Station

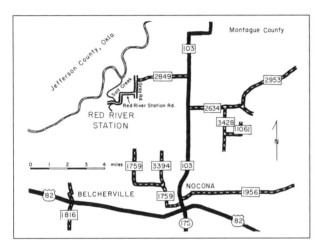

Red River Station was once the major crossing point on the Chisholm Trail over the Red River, but the Montague County town only prospered as long as the cattle drovers brought their herds past the site during the 1860s and 1870s.

The first white settlers probably came to the area now known as Red River Station sometime in the late 1850s and started small farms in the fertile bottom land of the Red River valley. The area where Salt Creek flowed into the Red River formed a natural crossing point that American Indians and herds of bison had used for many years. There the river bent sharply to the north, forcing the current against the south bank, thereby creating a comparatively narrow and constant channel. Texas state militia built an encampment at the site during the Civil War, assuring some measure of protection to nearby settlers and giving the crossing its name, Red River Station. According to one source, as many as fifty families lived in the vicinity by 1865.

The 1867 opening of the Chisholm Trail, the first major cattle trail between Texas and Kansas markets, led to the eventual passage of millions of cattle and mustang horses through Red River Station. Many feeder trails in southern and central Texas came together as a single basic trail in northern Texas to cross the Red River and Indian Territory. The trail then forked into several sub-trails to various railheads in Kansas, including Abilene, Wichita, Newton, and Caldwell. At the river, cattle drovers generally allowed their lead steers to string out and approach the water slowly. After these leaders plunged into the river they headed for the opposite bank, and the rest of the herd followed willingly. If the river happened to be high with floodwater, which typically occurred in springtime, herds might back up several miles waiting until the water level dropped enough to allow safe passage.

Red River Station was the last place in Texas for the drovers to buy supplies before they crossed into Indian Territory. The town capitalized on this circumstance by offering not only groceries and general merchandise, but also hotel accommodations, meals, blacksmith shops for repairs, and saloons to quench the drovers' thirst. Fear of the water prompted some cowboys to abstain from drinking but it prompted some to imbibe more. For the timorous traveler, one-legged Henry Heaton operated a cable ferry just upstream from the town.

Red River Station grew into a respectable town on the river floodplain just west of Salt Creek. Former resident Mrs. Sam King remembered that the town had once supported three saloons, three blacksmith shops, a hotel, livery stable, and several general stores. The cemetery was located on a bluff overlooking Salt Creek and the "flats" where the drovers held their herds prior to crossing. In 1873 the town received a post office in the name of Salt Creek, which changed to Red River Station in 1884. By this time, however, the community's heyday had passed.

Traffic through Red River Station began to wane after 1874, the year that John T. Lytle opened the Western Trail from Texas to the railroad at Dodge City, Kansas, about a hundred miles west of the Chisholm Trail. By 1879 this new route was carrying the great majority of Texas cattle northward. Besides declining business from cattle drovers, Red River Station received a double blow in the 1880s. Early in the decade a tornado destroyed the majority of the buildings in town; in 1887 the Missouri, Kansas and Texas Railway bypassed Red River Station in favor of Nocona

Drovers with a herd of cattle north of the Red River after crossing at Red River Station. Courtesy of the Claude Hensley Collection, Photograph #8687, Archives and Manuscripts Division of the Oklahoma Historical Society.

The flat ground along the east side of Salt Creek at Red River Station has changed little since Chisholm Trail drovers gathered their herds at this site prior to crossing the Red River into Indian Territory. Photograph by the author, 2000.

and Belcherville a few miles to the south. The residents who remained gradually departed, leaving Red River Station completely deserted. Today a modern ranch headquarters occupies the site. Though the town itself is gone, Red River Station still holds the distinction of having witnessed the passage of an estimated five million cattle and one million mustang horses, a movement called "the greatest migration of livestock in world history."

LOCATION: *Red River Station occupies a remote site just south of the Red River in Montague County. The easiest way to reach the former town is to drive 8.0 miles north on Farm Road 103 from Nocona to an intersection with Farm Road 2849. At Farm Road 2849, turn west and drive 3.0 miles to its terminus at a graded Montague County Road known as "Gray Road." Turn south on gravel Gray Road and drive 0.6 miles to its intersection with the graded Montague County Road known as "Red River Station Road." Then drive west, south, and then west on graded Red River Station Road for 1.3 miles to the flats just east of a concrete bridge over Salt Creek. It was on these flats that the drovers held their herds of cattle before crossing the river. Proceed on across the creek in a westerly direction 0.3 miles on Red River Station Road to see a modest ranch headquarters on the south side of the road at the abandoned site of Red River Station. None of these graded county roads are recommended after wet weather.*

Rock Island

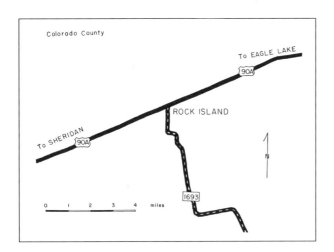

The town of Rock Island was born of a land promotion scheme during the late nineteenth century. The hardworking community prospered for two decades on the Gulf coastal plain before it succumbed to changes in agricultural methods.

The area of Colorado County surrounding Rock Island supported a scattered population by the mid-1890s, but the land was mostly suitable for grazing. In 1887–88 the San Antonio and Aransas Pass Railway Company laid rails to connect Kenedy (south of San Antonio) to Houston. The new railroad crossed Colorado County from west to east and opened considerable areas of the county to more intensive use. In 1895 two enterprising real-estate promoters, C. S. Penfield and Charles Peterson, acquired land along the railroad in the vicinity of Crasco Creek. They cut part of the land into lots and blocks for a townsite and divided the remainder into farms. The two promoters then traveled to Illinois, Iowa, and Missouri, advertising the locale as "a lush tropical paradise" to attract buyers. At the time Midwestern farmers could sell their properties for considerable sums and buy much larger acreages in Texas for the same amount of money. Real-estate salesmen promoted agriculture in Colorado County with such slogans as "Forty acres a living; eighty acres comfort; 160 acres wealth."

Midwestern farmers first began arriving at the new community in 1896; thirty-nine of them came on a specially chartered railway car. Instead of finding a paradise, they found a poorly drained, grass-covered coastal plain and thousands of mosquitoes. Even so, most of the new arrivals stayed where they had invested their money, and in time they succeeded. Soon after the out-of-state farmers arrived the settlement received its first post office, named Crasco for the nearby creek. The family of David A. Black, one of the newcomers, had emigrated from Rock Island, Illinois; they led a movement to change the post office name to Rock Island, which occurred in 1897.

The industrious newcomers in time created prosperous farms and a tidy community. Because almost all the people in the town had come from the Midwest, locals around them knew Rock Island as "the Northern Settlement of the Gulf Coast." Another nickname arose from the all-white population and the town's position alongside the tracks of the San Antonio and Aransas

Vacant brick commercial building at the heart of Rock Island. Photograph by the author, 1999.

Pass—"the White City on the SAP." By 1904 Rock Island had 367 inhabitants, and by 1925 it claimed a total of about five hundred. During its heyday the community had two banks, two hotels, eight dry goods stores, two hardware stores, two furniture stores, a pool hall, barbershop, newspaper, livery stable, two blacksmith shops, two lumber yards, a cabinet shop, tin shop, creamery, ice cream parlor, several churches, high quality schools, real-estate offices, and even a pickle factory. Farmers around Rock Island specialized in fruit and vegetables; for a time some of them found particular success with figs and strawberries.

As agriculture consolidated during the 1920s to 1950s, the accompanying economic and demographic changes sent Rock Island into a dramatic decline. With the increased use of tractors and machines, fewer and fewer people were needed to operate farms. Rural jobs disappeared. As a result, many people who lived and worked on farms around Rock Island had to move elsewhere to find employment. Because the rural population decreased, fewer people were left to shop at the businesses in Rock Island, so the town declined as well. When several fires broke out in the 1960s, the destroyed businesses were never rebuilt. Finally in 1968 the school closed for lack of sufficient pupils.

Today much of Rock Island is unoccupied. At the time of the author's last visit in 1999, it had only two operating places of business and three active churches. About seventy-five residences were occupied, while about thirty-five stood

vacant. The town's square grid of streets still remains, but most of the lots are empty. Uneven ground and crumbling foundations indicate where structures once stood. The downtown business district is lined with several picturesque abandoned commercial buildings. Part of the historic San Antonio and Aransas Pass Railway depot stands empty alongside the abandoned right-of-way.

LOCATION: *Rock Island is located on U.S. Highway 90A in Colorado County at a point that is 15.1 miles west of Eagle Lake and 22.9 miles east of Hallettsville.*

Royalty

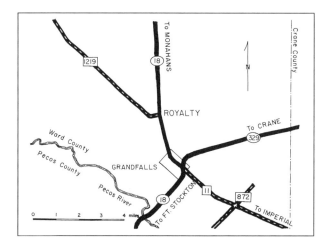

A town named Royalty sprang up in 1928 to meet the needs of workers in a Ward County oil field. At its height the community claimed over a thousand residents and a business district filled with stores, hotels, and eating places. Today it stands virtually deserted in the scrub brush of the Pecos Valley.

Ranchers were the first whites to occupy the Pecos River valley. Pioneer farmers, who sought to irrigate fields with flow from the river, followed them in the 1880s. By the 1890s some of these farmers, many of them immigrants from Scandinavia, had settled a town they called Grandfalls near two natural falls on the river. Four miles north of this town, drillers discovered commercial quantities of oil in October 1928. Grandfalls

The main business district of Royalty during its heyday in the 1930s. Courtesy of John Miller Morris.

A child's bicycle rests amid other debris left by former residents of Royalty. Photograph by the author, 2000.

had no source of potable water because both the Pccos River water and its groundwater were brackish. Instead, residents purchased fresh water at ten cents a barrel from E. H. Clements, who owned fresh-water wells not far from the oil discovery. The wells on Clements's property sparked the development of a new town there for oil workers.

During the summer of 1928, even before the producing oil well came in, Clements decided that petroleum prospecting activity was likely to continue in the area. He laid out a townsite on eighty acres of his land, which included two good water wells. He named his town Royalty, not for any kings or queens, but rather for the royalty payments that petroleum companies paid for oil pumped from land owners' properties. Soon people began purchasing lots in Royalty despite economic problems caused by the stock market crash in October 1929. As more producing oil wells followed the initial success, increasing numbers of people came to the area to work on the rigs and in the services that supported them. A few people settled in Grandfalls but many more chose Royalty, which was considerably closer to the actual production area.

The forlorn interior of Royalty's abandoned post office. Photograph by the author, 2000.

Royalty prospered through the depths of the Great Depression, growing to an estimated population high of 1,200 inhabitants. The north-south main street (the highway between Grandfalls to the south and Monahans to the north) was soon populated with a post office, restaurants, hotels, mercantile stores, a lumber yard, filling stations, groceries, a meat market, machine shops, a motion-picture theater, and, after the end of Prohibition in 1933, saloons and liquor stores. Although Royalty never had an elected municipal government, it did offer electric lighting, natural gas service, and a waterworks. Oil companies constructed camps to house many of their employees near Royalty, so many people lived just outside town but spent their money in town.

By the end of the 1930s oil production had begun declining in the Ward County oil field that had supported Royalty. Even though secondary production methods boosted the flow of oil during the 1950s, the town began to wither away.

Many residents followed the petroleum business to other oil fields. Others simply moved up or down the road to more stable towns of Monahans and Grandfalls. Royalty's population declined to about seventy or eighty inhabitants during the 1970s and '80s, and today all but a handful of people have departed. At the time of the author's most recent visit in 2000, Royalty contained a dozen occupied residences, a dozen vacant dwellings in fair condition, and another half-dozen houses that had collapsed on themselves. The only place of business was an oil-field supply firm. The entire townsite was littered with debris—from a deteriorating motorboat to abandoned household appliances and furniture—left behind by former residents.

LOCATION: *Royalty is located on Texas State Highway 18 at its intersection with Farm Road 1219 in Ward County at a point that is 2.5 miles north of Grandfalls and 15.7 miles south of Monahans. Visitors should watch out for rattlesnakes.*

Ruidosa

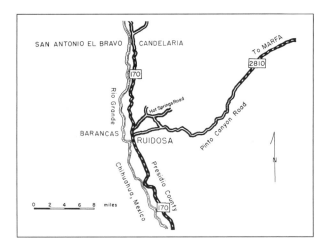

Located on the banks of the Rio Grande thirty-six miles up-river from Presidio in Presidio County, Ruidosa has been a site for irrigated agriculture in the Chihuahuan Desert for many years. It is not known whether the town's unusual Spanish name refers to the sound of the wind or to the noise of water splashing over the nearby rocky ford across the river.

Although indigenous peoples probably raised crops on the floodplain of the Rio Grande much earlier, the first known written records of human habitation at present-day Ruidosa document its use as a penal colony. About 1824 the Mexican government sent a group of convicts, known as the Condemned Regiment, to the area around the rocky river crossing at Ruidosa. The settlement served as a buffer between Mexican ranches farther south and west and the Comanche and Apache territory to the north. The presence of men at the colony served to protect the cattle on these ranches against Indian raids. The men also made the first recorded attempts at irrigated agriculture here. In the early 1850s an American observer described the settlement of about three hundred inhabitants as having "large cultivated fields, which are watered by acequias and yield abundant crops of wheat and corn." Attacks from the Comanches, however, forced the eventual abandonment of the penal colony.

Although some people may have remained in the area, the next known person to develop a substantial system of irrigation at Ruidosa was an

Now quiet, these adobe commercial buildings stand alongside Pinto Canyon Road where it meets the River Road in Ruidosa. Photograph by the author, 2000.

Interior of the 1914 adobe Mission del Sagrado Corazon Catholic Church in Ruidosa. Photograph by the author, 2000.

American, William Russell. In 1872 his primarily Mexican crews excavated canals from nearby creeks to irrigate fields of grain, which Russell contracted to the U.S. Army troops at Fort Davis and Fort Stockton. Oral traditions relate that guards maintained constant surveillance while workers excavated the canals and cultivated the fields. Their caution was well founded, for in 1879 Mescalero Apaches attacked Russell's property, killing four men and wounding three others.

Russell's efforts at Ruidosa prompted a little support from the commissioners of Presidio County. In 1876 they recognized the growing community by adding a precinct to the county at the "settlement known as Rio Doso [*sic*] on the Rio Grande." That same year they funded the construction of a county road from Presidio up the river to Ruidosa. There, Russell—in addition to founding his various farms—had built a gristmill. In a significant recognition of the town's growing status, the county in 1886 funded the survey of a road that would lead northward from Ruidosa to Marfa by way of the Pinto Canyon.

Other people began coming to the area for different reasons. About 1896 or '97 Annie Kingston of Balmorhea, Texas, purchased two sections of land about seven miles northeast of Ruidosa because the land included a hot spring believed to have medicinal properties. Her brother suffered from severe arthritis, and she felt that bathing in the curative waters might relieve his pain. Within four years her brother had recovered enough to walk unassisted. Years later, about 1936 or '37, another member of the Kingston family constructed several plaster-covered adobe cabins and erected a stone bathhouse at the springs, then opened them to the public. Over the years these springs have attracted thousands of health-seekers to the Ruidosa area.

Ruidosa continued to grow, receiving its first county-funded school in 1902. By 1911 the Ruidosa school precinct contained 287 pupils and a total population of 1,722, although only a few of these people lived in the town itself. In the 1950s a long-time resident claimed that Ruidosa once had as many as eight hundred residents, but the numbers were likely much lower. An estimate of one hundred inhabitants in 1914 is realistic. In that year the town had three general stores and a handsome adobe Catholic church with twin towers. Also, 1914 was the first year farmers at Ruidosa raised cotton, which soon became the town's primary cash crop. About 1924 local people constructed a gin to process the cotton. After another five years of growth, Ruidosa in 1929 reported a population of three hundred.

Along with other Texas communities up and down the Rio Grande, Ruidosa began feeling the effects of the Mexican Revolution around 1910. More than a million Mexicans perished in this decade-long civil war. In 1916 U.S. president Woodrow Wilson called upon the Texas National Guard and then regular army troops to protect settlers along the Mexican border. Troops came to Ruidosa in May 1916, building an impressive adobe and stone outpost on the crest of a hill that overlooked both Ruidosa and Barrancas, Chihuahua. The post consisted of barracks, officers' quarters, a mess hall, kitchens, corrals, and hay barns. It even had a generator to power camp

Several cairns mark graves in one of the cemeteries overlooking Ruidosa, the Rio Grande valley, and, in the distance, mountains of Mexico. Photograph by the author, 2000.

of the Rio Grande. The mission was unsuccessful. Then the army abandoned Camp Ruidosa a few weeks later, deeming the post no longer necessary for the protection of American citizens. The camp stood empty unitl about fifteen years later during the Great Depression, when men from the Civilian Conservation Corps lived in the old cavalry outpost while they improved local roads.

In 1933 Ruidosa reported six places of business, but in 1936 its cotton gin closed. Local cotton-raisers found that they could not complete with the large-volume producers elsewhere in the Rio Grande valley and on the Texas South Plains. The end of irrigated agriculture meant the end of Ruidosa. Over the next several decades most of its residents either died or moved elsewhere. By 1954 the post office had closed, and by 1964 the town was reporting no places of business. Today the picturesque but isolated town has one store, one community church, one tavern, and about a dozen occupied residences. Abandoned buildings and the ruins and foundations of former structures are scattered through the townsite. Overlooking the community from their respective hillsides are a striking cemetery with rock cairns piled atop each of the burials and the ruins of the 1916 Camp Ruidosa cavalry post.

lighting and to charge batteries for radio and telephone communications equipment.

Soldiers at Camp Ruidosa were on hand after fighting began across the Rio Grande at Barrancas in October 1917. On this occasion a group of Pancho Villa's soldiers had attacked and routed a small garrison that supported Venustiano Carranza. The Carranza supporters fled for safety across the river. There U.S. troops from Camp Ruidosa detained them for a while before releasing them with orders to cross back over into Mexico. Soldiers from Camp Ruidosa also participated in a 1919 five-day punitive expedition by U.S. troops. The aim was to apprehend the Mexican kidnappers of two army aviators who had been forced down south

LOCATION: *Ruidosa is located 35.8 miles northwest of Presidio on Farm Road 170 at its intersection with graded Presidio County Pinto Canyon Road. Visitors can also reach the town by driving southwest from Marfa on paved Farm Road 2810, which after 32.6 miles changes into the graded Pinto Canyon Road for an additional 19 miles. This last road is recommended for high-clearance vehicles only. Along this route are stone culverts constructed by the Civilian Conservation Corps during the 1930s, as well as the Camp Ruidosa ruins. The hot springs developed decades ago by the Kingston family can be reached by driving 0.5 miles north on Farm Road 170 from the center of Ruidosa to an intersection with graded Presidio County Hot Springs Road. Turn east and drive 7.0 miles up from the Rio Grande valley on the rough graded road, following the signs for "Chinati Hot Springs." This graded road passes the main Ruidosa Cemetery just 0.5 miles up from Farm Road 170.*

Runningwater

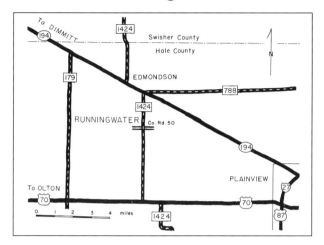

For many years the town of Runningwater served as a ranch supply center and school site on Runningwater Draw in Hale County. Though the small community had once prospered, it began to die after a new route of the Fort Worth and Denver Railway bypassed it in 1928. Today only an abandoned school, foundations and fragments of former buildings, and a cemetery remain to mark its place.

The site of Runningwater was near the earliest ranch headquarters in Hale County. In 1881 J. N. and T. W. Morrison purchased about twenty sections of land near the corners of Hale, Swisher, Castro, and Lamb counties. There they established the headquarters for their Circle Ranch in the well-watered valley of spring-fed Runningwater Draw. In time prominent stock raiser C. C. Slaughter gained an interest in—and then control of—the property.

After the state of Texas began selling land that it owned in western Texas to ranchers and others, a number of small-scale livestock-raisers began acquiring land in Hale County, many of them choosing sites in Runningwater Draw because of its available surface water. One of the buyers was Dennis Rice, who moved to the area with his wife in 1890. Rice planned to start a town and hoped to attract a railroad, thus increasing the value of his property. As part of his strategy, in late 1890 he secured a post office in the name of Wadsworth, initially running the office from his own home. Other local residents suggested that if he changed the name to Runningwater, the name might attract more settlers; in 1891 he had the Post Office Department alter the name. Residents organized the first school that same year.

Then in 1892 Rice organized the Runningwater Townsite and Improvement Company, laid out a proposed town into blocks and lots, and held a three-day barbecue to promote his new community. Little did he know that the next year would bring the Panic of 1893, the worst depression in

The Runningwater School, closed since 1944, now used as a barn by a local livestock-raiser. Photograph by the author, 2000.

Debris from former Runningwater homes, pushed into a gully to retard soil erosion. Photograph by the author, 2000.

150
s

LOCATION: *Runningwater is located on the corner of Farm Road 1424 and graded Hale County Road 50 at a point that is 2.0 miles south of Texas State Highway 194 in Edmondson. Runningwater can also be reached from the intersection of Interstate Highway 27 and U.S. Highway 70 in Plainview. From this intersection, drive 7.6 miles west along U.S. Highway 70 to where it intersects Farm Road 1424. Turn north and drive 4.0 miles on Farm Road 1424 to its intersection with Hale County Road 50 at the Runningwater townsite. To reach the cemetery from the townsite, drive 1.0 miles north on Farm Road 1424, turn east on graded Hale County Road 140, and drive 0.8 miles to the graveyard. None of the local graded roads are recommended after wet weather.*

the history of the United States up to that time, followed by several years of drought. Despite the difficulties, people did begin to come to Runningwater. Eventually the community grew to include a school, three church congregations, two stores, the office of a physician, a gristmill, and a blacksmith shop. Rice attempted for years to open a cheese factory but never attracted the capital he needed. He also tried time and again to bring a railroad to his town, but failed repeatedly.

When the railroad finally came, the year was 1928 and the line bypassed Dennis Rice's town of Runningwater. When the Fort Worth and Denver Railway Company constructed a line to connect Plainview and Dimmitt, it laid the rails two miles northeast of Runningwater. The next year W. W. Edmondson platted a new town on the railroad as near as he could to the older community in order to lure Runningwater residents to the new town, named Edmondson. Despite the onset of the Great Depression, the new community in time prospered. The Runningwater post office moved there in 1935. Over the next years Runningwater withered away—its high school moved to Plainview in 1942 and the elementary classes followed two years later. Today the site of Runningwater is marked only by the 1924 red brick school—now a rancher's barn—and the cemetery. Scattered patches of uneven ground and debris from former buildings characterize the surrounding area, while dead elm trees identify the former sites of business places and houses that have been removed.

Sabine

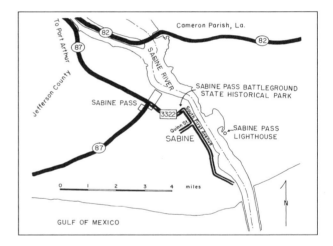

One of the several unsuccessful attempts to create a major port at the mouth of the Sabine River produced the Jefferson County town of Sabine, which barely clings to life as the southernmost settlement on the river.

As early as the 1830s, numerous individuals envisioned the mouth of the Sabine River as a port serving both Texas and Louisiana. In 1839 competing promoters established nearby Sabine City and the City of the Pass, the former having the financial backing of Texas president Sam Houston. City of the Pass was never developed beyond plans, but Sabine City became a modest port for cotton and timber exports from the Sabine

A square-rigged sailing ship anchored just off the mouth of the Sabine River awaits a space at the Sabine dock, circa 1897. From *Sabine Pass in the Texas Coast Country* (circa 1897).

Ocean-going ships and a steam locomotive at the lumber wharf in Sabine, circa 1897. From *Sabine Pass in the Texas Coast Country* (circa 1897).

Porch of a long disused Sabine home, gradually weathering away. Photograph by the author, 1997.

Pass docks asked for too much money to make their property available, Kountze's Sabine Land and Improvement Company in 1896 laid out a new town named Sabine about two miles downstream on the west bank of the river. The company initially erected two hotels and a few houses to accommodate its own engineers and construction crews, who proceeded to build docks, warehouses, and railway facilities. Dredges deepened the anchorages for ocean-going ships; the muck was hauled ashore to increase the new town's elevation. The company's promotional efforts were obviously successful, for in 1900 the town of Sabine had 673 inhabitants in comparison to only 363 in the "old town" of Sabine Pass. At its peak early in the twentieth century, Sabine boasted such enterprises as two hotels, ship chandlers, goods brokers, several mercantile stores, two drugstores, offices of several physicians, a milliner's shop, livery stable, restaurants, a hardware store, boat repair shop, lumberyard, confectionery, tailor, bakery, and "one of the finest liquor stores in the South."

The boom at Sabine did not last. Up the Sabine River an even larger competitor had materialized. Arthur Stillwell had also been developing a port city—his Port Arthur, constructed as the deepwater terminal on the Gulf for his Kansas City Southern Railway. With greater resources available for promotion and construction, Stillwell became the power broker of the lower Sabine River. Ship after ship sailed past the mostly idle docks at Sabine, preferring the larger and more efficient facilities a few miles upstream at Port Arthur. Later, Beaumont and Orange also took a share out of the shipping business, leaving Sabine and Sabine Pass to fade away into little more than fishing camps.

Today Sabine consists of a few scattered houses—some occupied and some vacant—standing in a grid plan of square blocks and streets. Most of the lots are either empty or littered by foundations and other remnants of former structures. The grass- and vine-covered seashore environment is a natural habitat for mosquitoes and rattlesnakes.

LOCATION: *The town of Sabine is located in Jefferson County on the Texas side of the Sabine River near its mouth on the Gulf of Mexico. The site can be reached*

River valley. The U.S. government recognized the significance of the port in 1856 by building a brick lighthouse nearby on the Louisiana side of the Sabine River channel. In 1861 the town's name became Sabine Pass; it survives as a small community under that name to this day though it has encountered its share of difficulties. During the Civil War Union troops burned the town in October 1862 in retaliation for Confederate artillery fire on a federal gunboat. Just below the town, Confederate artillerymen fended off an attempted amphibious landing by five thousand Union troops on 8 September 1863.

In the 1870s, capitalist Augustus Kountze of Omaha, Nebraska, became interested in developing a new port at the mouth of the Sabine River. A number of years passed before he initiated any construction, but he began in earnest in the mid-1890s. Because the owners of the exiting Sabine

easily from the nearby town of Sabine Pass. From the intersection of Texas State Highway 87 and Farm Road 3322 (Dowling Road), follow Farm Road 3322 southeast and then northeast for 1.4 miles. This brings motorists to the Sabine Pass Battleground State Historical Park, site of an 1863 Civil War battle. To continue on to the townsite, proceed one block beyond the entrance of the park to a T intersection with paved South First Avenue. Turn southeast on South First Avenue and drive 0.6 miles to the intersection with paved Quinn Street, in the 4600 block of South First Avenue. Turn southwest onto Quinn Street and drive one block into the heart of the Sabine ghost town. From here, visitors have a clear view across the river to the 1856 Sabine Pass Lighthouse on the Louisiana side. Restrooms, barbecue pits, and sheltered picnic tables are available in the nearby state park.

St. Francisville

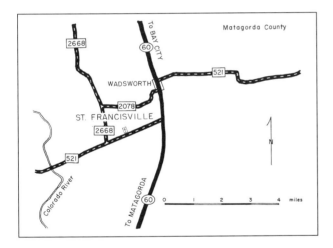

The Matagorda County community of St. Francisville was born during the 1850s, when Texas was a popular destination for Polish immigrants. The town became the center of a community of farmers who had come from the region of Upper Silesia in Prussia.

Polish peasant farmers began immigrating to Texas in 1854 at the encouragement of a priest from their home region who had immigrated two years earlier. The Reverend Leopold B. M. Moczygemba was a Polish Catholic priest who had come to Texas to minister to the spiritual needs of German immigrants in the diocese of Galve-

ston. He observed how his German parishioners had prospered and wrote letters back to his family and friends in Upper Silesia, then part of Prussia, encouraging them to follow him to Texas.

The Polish farmers took his advice and in late 1854 the first of several ships carried the Upper Silesian immigrants from the port of Bremen to Galveston and Indianola on the Texas Gulf coast. Most of the newcomers trekked overland to the San Antonio area where they established a series of Polish colonies, most of which survive to this day. Some of the new arrivals, however, were unable to make it all the way to San Antonio. These immigrants settled along the way, establishing smaller communities of farmers. St. Francisville was one of these Upper Silesian agricultural communities. Families with such names as Petrucha, Gola, Sisky, Waschka, Ryman, and Bonk eventually became successful at farming in the new environment they had found as a sea of grass.

In 1895 the Polish farmers of St. Francisville decided to build a church, hoping that they might secure a priest to serve their community. Mrs. Mary Jadwiga Seerden, a member of the Petrucha family, donated an acre of land for a church and cemetery. The adjoining property was also donated by Mr. and Mrs. Lawrence Butter. The entire community then raised money to hire carpenters from Hitchcock to build their sanctuary. In the meantime they ordered an ornate Gothic Revival altar from woodworkers in Liberty; it eventually arrived by wagon. Bishop N. A. Gallagher from Galveston presided at the first mass. Soon after the farmers built their church, it was destroyed by an 1896 hurricane. Undaunted, the community salvaged the original materials and rebuilt a somewhat smaller structure, which remains at the site to this day.

Even though the farmers at St. Francisville labored willingly to build and then rebuild their church, they were never successful in attracting their own priest. Pastors either visited St. Francisville or conducted services in Liberty, Galveston, and Victoria, because the closest Catholic churches were located in those towns. Later, priests from Bay City visited occasionally to meet the religious needs of the local Polish farmers. As the agricultural community became increasingly dispersed, the priests came less and less often, finally coming only once each year to

Cemetery at St. Francisville and the church the town's Polish immigrant founders built in 1895. Photograph by the author, 1999.

say mass during a special service on All Souls' Day.

Today the 1896 church and its surrounding cemetery are all that remain of St. Francisville. The ladies of the Catholic altar guild from Bay City care for its interior, and men from the surrounding communities maintain the building and grounds. The site is generally deserted except for on All Souls' Day, when descendants of the early immigrant settlers gather to attend mass and a blessing of the graves. As a pastor from Bay City observed, "They consider it a sacred place and keep it up as a kind of token to their forefathers."

LOCATION: *St. Francisville is located on the north side of Farm Road 521 in Matagorda County at a point that is 1.4 miles west of where Farm Road 521 intersects Texas State Highway 80. This intersection is 1.1 miles south of Wadsworth, or 11.9 total miles south of Bay City.*

St. Mary's of Aransas

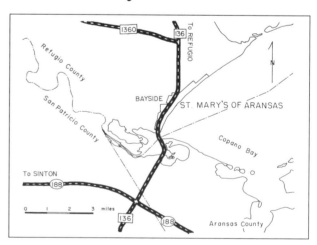

St. Mary's of Aransas was once a shipping port that served the Texas Gulf coast. Today all but a handful of old-timers and history buffs have forgotten the town. The Refugio County town flourished on the northwest side of Copano Bay from

154
s

Looking northeast at present-day Bayside, built over the remains of historic St. Mary's of Aransas. Photograph by the author, 2000.

the 1850s until the 1880s. Today the site of old St. Mary's is overlaid by scattered areas of modern construction from the newer community of Bayside.

Joseph F. Smith, a lawyer and speculator, purchased property on the northwest side of Copano Bay in the 1840s. Then in 1857 he established a town on his property and named it St. Mary's of Aransas. He took the name from Aransas Bay, which at that time included what today is called Copano Bay. From the outset the town was planned as a port to serve San Antonio and western Texas. One of the first structures built was a wooden wharf stretching from the foot of Center Street to about a quarter of a mile into the deep channel, which wound through the bay. St. Mary's was well on its way to becoming a port.

Although the plans for St. Mary's consisted of ninety-one city blocks—each four hundred feet square—arranged in seven tiers of thirteen blocks each, in reality the town stretched about two-and-a-half miles along the bay front. The single wharf served St. Mary's until after the Civil War, when a second wharf was added parallel to the first. The initial wharf, its two warehouses and its palisaded stock pens became the center of business activity

in St. Mary's. Within just a few years the town grew into one of the principal lumber markets for western Texas. Scores of shiploads of cut lumber, much of it from Florida, entered the port, where it was loaded onto wagons for the trip inland.

On the eve of the Civil War, St. Mary's of Aransas was home to an estimated three hundred residents. Among the businesses in the town were two hotels, several boarding houses, a saloon known as the "barrel house," a post office, and numerous other businesses. The mercantile trade served the local community, but most of its market lay farther inland.

Among the popular entertainments of the town's heyday were the formal balls that were held on the decks of lumber ships once they docked. A former resident reminisced that the arrival of the big three-masted schooners was the signal for much activity: "There would be a dance on the deck at every arrival. Sometimes the sailors would furnish the music; most times the fiddling was done by local talent. . . . A dance by moonlight on the decks of these big schooners was something for St. Mary's folk to look forward to." Another of the diversions for which the town became known was gaming in its gambling house, which

A modern visitor reads tombstone inscriptions in the St. Mary's of Aransas Cemetery. Photograph by the author, 2000.

became one of the largest on the Texas coast. It operated until 1886.

St. Mary's was a staunch supporter of secession from the United States in 1861 and of the subsequent Confederate government. Almost all of the town's able-bodied young men volunteered for the southern army, leaving mostly women, children, and older men at home during the Civil War. This was the situation when the port was briefly occupied by Union troops toward the end of the conflict, but the town suffered no appreciable damage other than Union destruction of the wharf warehouses.

The most affluent years for St. Mary's followed the Civil War. The areas inland from the port had begun to develop economically, requiring that more and more goods enter the state through the port. By the mid-1870s, however, the railroads had reached the Texas coastal plain near St. Mary's. All of them passed through other towns, such as Corpus Christi and Rockport, giving those ports an advantage over St. Mary's. The town also suffered from a series of severe tropical storms beginning in 1875. A hurricane in 1886, the same

storm that utterly destroyed the port of Indianola, damaged the St. Mary's wharves to such an extent that the local residents were unable to rebuild them. The town entered a decline that within a quarter century was complete.

Only vestiges of old St. Mary's remain. The extreme southwest end of the former town is marked by the still-standing home that Richard H. Woods built in 1877. That house is now located at the center of the Bayside community. A careful observer proceeding northeastward up the bay front may find scattered remains of late-nineteenth-century concrete houses, their foundations, and the underground cisterns that held rainwater for their residents. About a mile inland from the bay is the beautifully maintained St. Mary's Cemetery, with grave markers dating from the 1860s.

LOCATION: *In order to view portions of old St. Mary's of Aransas, drive up and down the northeastern ends of 1st, 2nd, and 3rd streets of the modern community of Bayside in Refugio County. The old St. Mary's Cemetery is just east of Farm Road 136 about a mile inland from the bay and 1.5 miles north of Bayside. The graveyard is easily identified at a distance by its trees, which stand out above the surrounding treeless cultivated fields.*

Serbin

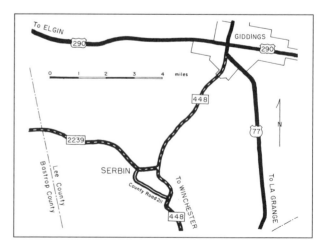

One of only two Wendish ethnic colonies outside of Europe, Serbin is a truly unique Texas commu-

Musicians pose with their instruments during a Lutheran synodical convention held in Serbin sometime around the turn of the twentieth century. Courtesy of the University of Texas Institute of Texan Cultures at San Antonio.

nity. In Europe, the Wends constitute the western-most of all the Slavs. They have lived for centuries in what today is eastern Germany. Though often persecuted for their ethnicity and religious beliefs, the Wends in the Old World even now maintain their own distinctive language and adhere to the Lutheran faith.

Because of the discrimination they experienced in Europe, a party of 588 Wends departed their homeland for Texas in 1854. They traveled to the New World under the guidance of a Lutheran minister, the Reverend John Kilian. The voyage across the Atlantic was a terrible one, for many of the travelers contracted cholera; others caught yellow fever after their arrival in Galveston. Eventually over seventy members of the party perished. After landing on the Texas coast, the immigrants trekked overland to a site in Lee County where most of them settled permanently.

In honor of their homeland—a region called Sorbo Lusatia—the Wends named their new com-munity Serbin. Since that time it has been the center of Wendish settlement and culture in Texas, though most of its sons and daughters have moved to live elsewhere in the state. Soon after the colony was founded, Reverend Kilian established St. Paul's Lutheran Church. The community received its first post office in 1860. The typical businesses of a country town soon appeared, among them general merchandise stores, taverns, blacksmith shops, and the like. In 1870 a second Lutheran congregation, St. Peter's, was founded at Serbin, but it merged with St. Paul's in 1914.

In its heyday about the turn of the twentieth century, the two churches at Serbin counted approximately one thousand baptized members between them. The population began to decline, however, because railways in the area did not come to Serbin. Trade was drawn away from the stores in Serbin to those in towns with railway connections, such as Giddings, Bastrop, and Smithville. This tendency only accelerated in the 1930s through the

Interior of the beautifully embellished and preserved St. Paul Lutheran Church built in Serbin about 1860. Photograph by the author, 1999.

'50s as rural roads were improved and larger towns became easier to access by automobile. The national consolidation of farms into larger units also contributed to the decrease in the Serbin population. Today Serbin is a quiet place with rural homes scattered in all directions around a central church and school. The nineteenth-century stone church—stark and barn-like on the outside—is splendidly embellished inside with designs and colors reminiscent of the old country. Visitors might also wish to see the exhibits at the Texas Wendish Heritage Museum, which is housed in the old school.

LOCATION: *Serbin is located on Lee County Road 211, just off Farm Road 2239 about 1.0 miles west of where that road intersects Farm Road 448 at a point that is 4.8 miles south of Giddings.*

Silver Lake

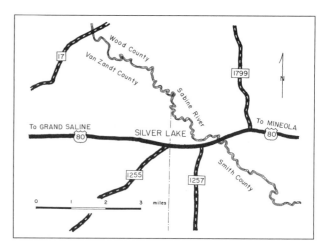

From its position astride two transportation arteries, Silver Lake in Van Zandt County prospered during the late nineteenth and early twentieth centuries, but began to decline for various reasons in the late twentieth century.

Silver Lake was brought to life by the same force that created many other towns throughout Texas—the railroad. Although settlers had come to the vicinity in the 1840s, they did not form a town. In 1873 the Texas and Pacific Railway Company built a line from Marshall in East Texas toward Fort Worth, including a siding in extreme northeastern Van Zandt County near the border of Smith County. The company named the station on this siding Silver Lake after a natural lake nearby.

The origin of the community's name is unclear. Earlier settlers asserted that the name Silver Lake originated during the Texas Revolution. They believed that either Mexicans or Indians hid some silver under the waters of the lake to prevent it from falling into the hands of the Texan army. Other residents averred that the name simply came from the water's silvery appearance on calm days. No one today is sure of the correct source for the name.

As early as 1873 G. W. Rive had opened a store near the Silver Lake depot alongside the Texas and Pacific Railway tracks. Then on 7 May 1874 the railroad company purchased the acreage around the siding, had it surveyed, and on 5 March 1875 filed a town plat at the county courthouse. Soon the company began selling lots to prospective residents, and Silver Lake was on its way to becoming a real town.

This Silver Lake home is gradually collapsing from years of neglect. Photograph by the author, 1999.

The Silver Lake post office opened in 1874; stores and other enterprises soon followed. As it was located in an area known for agrarian radicalism, Silver Lake had lodges for both the Patrons of Husbandry and the Farmers' Alliance. A public school opened by 1890; in 1904 it boasted an enrollment of forty-three. The school operated at Silver Lake until 1952, when it consolidated with the schools in Grand Saline.

In the early twentieth century Silver Lake found itself located on another transportation artery—one of the first major east-west highways across Texas. The 825-mile route connected Waskom at the Louisiana border to El Paso at the New Mexico border. This important auto and truck route, designated as U.S. Highway 80, brought steady business to the gasoline filling stations, garages, and eating places of Silver Lake. Interstate highways, in time began to lure away most traffic, but the historic Highway 80 still passes through town.

The population of Silver Lake varied over the years. It reached a high of eighty in 1914, when the community had stores, a school, and several local businesses. Business began to slow in the 1920s and '30s as the rural population around Silver Lake declined—farmers moved to larger urban areas when the national movement toward consolidated agriculture forced small farms out of business. Then the opening of coal mines in the area brought in new residents during the 1930s, giving Silver Lake a population of fifty in 1940. During the second half of the twentieth century the population gradually declined due to continued agricultural consolidation. Today the community consists of half a dozen abandoned residences, even fewer occupied houses, several disused commercial buildings, and an interesting cemetery. The Baptist church is still active. The sites of former buildings are marked by surface debris and uneven ground as well as still surviving plantings of irises, daffodils, evergreen shrubs, and pecan and fruit trees.

LOCATION: *Silver Lake is located on U.S. Highway 80 at its intersection with Farm Road 1255 in extreme northeastern Van Zandt County. The site is 6.6 miles east of Grand Saline and 5.4 miles west of Mineola.*

South Bend

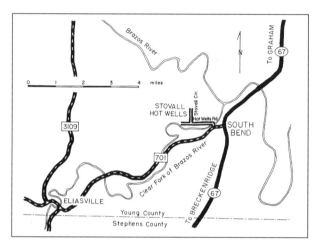

South Bend, a community in southern Young County, is known today for its historic oilfields and for the nearby Stovall Hot Wells health resort.

In the 1850s white settlers began moving onto land near the confluence of the Clear Fork of the Brazos River and the main Brazos River. The settlers did not organize a town in the immediate vicinity until J. N. Smith established a store. The town that consequently formed was called Arkansas. Later arrivals changed to name to South Bend when a post office was granted in the 1890s, taking the designation from a prominent southerly loop in the Brazos River just to the east of town. Located off the beaten path, South Bend merely served as a local market center until the discovery of oil nearby.

During the early twentieth century a number of oil prospectors began drilling exploratory wells in southern Young County, first striking petroleum in 1917. Initial production was weak, but drillers found enough oil to encourage further efforts. The attempts paid off on 4 July 1920, when the McCluskey No. 1 well blew in with a substantial oil flow. Soon an estimated ten thousand people flooded into South Bend and the surrounding area. Overnight the town grew into a supply center for the new oil field. During the next two years South Bend mushroomed—it contained two-story hotels, boarding and rooming houses, a six-teacher school, oil field supply businesses, cafés,

An abandoned three-unit tourist court no longer welcomes visitors to the west side of South Bend. Photograph by the author, 2000.

An advertisement painted on the end of a corrugated sheet-metal tourist court at Stovall Hot Wells, just northwest of South Bend. Photograph by the author, 2000.

grocery stores, general mercantile stores, speakeasy bars, brothels, gambling dens, lumber yards, a small refinery, gasoline stations, automobile garages, a dairy, motion-picture theaters, and at least two churches. Only dirt roads led to the site until the Wichita Falls and Southern Railway laid tracks through the town in 1921, facilitating the delivery of goods and making South Bend an even more important supply center.

Following an inevitable decrease in oil production stemming from unrestricted drilling, South Bend began to decline. The concurrent trend toward the consolidation of agriculture in southern Young County only increased the economic distress in South Bend.

In 1929 an unexpected event changed the course of South Bend's future. In June of that year Eugene C. Stovall struck a gusher of oil and gas. The well he drilled just over a mile northwest of town prooduced about eight thousand barrels of oil and a large volume of natural gas, but then the flow changed. Instead of oil, hot, darkly colored, mineral-rich water began coming from the ground. For Stovall this was a calamity—he wanted oil.

Stovall also owned several farms in Young County. A number of Mexican families worked on his farms, and it was their children who made a surprising discovery. Ignoring their parents' warnings, they played in the murky waters. The oily smelling water did something that other remedies had not done—it cured a skin ailment from which the children had been suffering. Before long other people from the neighborhood came to

A wheelchair left behind by health-seekers in an abandoned building at the Stovall Hot Wells spa near South Bend. Photograph by the author, 2000.

bathe in the waters. Stovall realized that he could charge health-seekers to bathe in his curative waters, so in 1932 he built a bathhouse, hotel, and café at the site. He soon added tourist courts and a campground. He employed masseurs, nurses, and chiropractors to care for his invalid guests, but he also provided a playground, croquet lawn, musical entertainments, and even skeet shooting for visitors who also sought recreation. Stovall Hot Wells prospered into the 1950s, when it began to decline as potential guests learned of new methods of healing, leaving only a few faithful customers and a handful of curiosity seekers to bathe in the hot mineral waters. The spa catered to a diminished clientele until the bathhouse and hotel burned in 1994.

Today South Bend consists of about thirty dispersed residences, six disused commercial buildings, the embankments and other remnants of a vehicular underpass from the 1921 Wichita Falls and Southern Railway tracks, an abandoned motel, a cemetery, and two churches, one of which is still active. At Stovall Hot Wells two historic tourist court buildings, a playground, and auxiliary structures survive, but only ruins of the hotel and bathhouse remain.

LOCATION: *South Bend lies at the intersection of Texas State Highway 67 and Farm Road 701 in southern Young County. The townsite is 9.5 miles south of Graham and 23.9 miles northeast of Breckenridge. To reach the Stovall Hot Wells, drive 0.3 miles west on Farm Road 701 from its intersection with Texas State Highway 67 to an intersection with a paved Young County road marked as "Hot Wells Road." Turn north onto paved Hot Wells Road, crossing the Clear Fork of the Brazos River on a historic concrete bridge, and then follow the road to the west, driving a distance of 1.0 miles to an intersection with a paved Young County road marked as "Stovall Circle." Turn north onto this roughly paved Stovall Circle road and drive 0.6 miles to the site of the historic Stovall Hot Wells spa.*

Stoneham

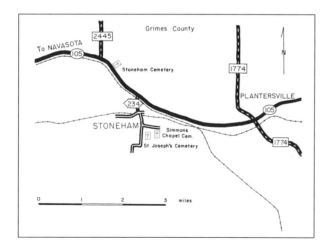

Formerly a multi-racial farming community with an estimated 250 inhabitants in 1900, Stoneham lost population and significance as a result of agricultural consolidation during the twentieth century. Today its three cemeteries give visitors glimpses of the past prosperity once enjoyed by this Grimes County town.

The area around Stoneham was first settled by blacks and whites during the 1830s. For many years the town retained a rural character although it was large enough to support Methodist and Baptist churches as well as a school. In 1879 the Central and Montgomery Railway Company announced plans to construct a railroad line through the neighborhood, so people began relocating to be near the route. John H. Stoneham opened a general mercantile store near the new railroad, and in 1890 he was granted a post office named Stoneham. Then in 1901 the Smith Land and Improvement Company of Beaumont secured acreage alongside the tracks, laid out the present town, and began selling lots.

Stoneham's well established multi-racial community expanded in the 1870s to include recent immigrants from Poland. These European farmers had first felt drawn to the area around New Waverly to the northeast in Walker County, but soon they began moving to land around Stoneham and nearby Plantersville, where a few Germans had already settled. The Europeans organized the still active St. Joseph's Church to serve the religious needs of Catholics in the area.

Around the turn of the twentieth century a second railroad, the International and Great Northern Railroad Compnay, added a line through the Stoneham vicinity, enhancing the town's prospects for the future. Stoneham reached its population peak at this time with an estimated 250 residents. It had several stores, at least three churches, separate schools for white and black children, a blacksmith, drugstore, barbershop, meat market, a physician's office, and an attorney's office.

Modernization in the 1920s through the '50s brought the consolidation of agriculture to Grimes County and to the rest of the country. A few men on tractors could do the work of several farm families using mules or horses to pull implements, so farms grew larger and larger but needed fewer and fewer people to operate them. Many rural inhabitants migrated to cities to find employment. At the same time, improved roads and the increased availability of automobiles drew business away from Stoneham to larger nearby towns. Then in October 1932 disaster struck—the entire Stoneham business district burned to the ground. As

St. Joseph's Catholic Church and graveyard at Stoneham. Most of these graves are of Stoneham's Polish immigrant population. Photograph by the author, 1999.

most of the supporting rural population was already moving away, merchants chose not to rebuild during the worst of the Great Depression. The population dropped to two hundred in 1936 and then to one hundred in 1949. By the 1970s the town reported only twelve residents. The only activity at Stoneham today is on Sunday mornings or during special celebrations, when families from the surrounding farms come into the former town for Methodist or Catholic church services.

LOCATION: *Stoneham is located in Grimes County just south of Texas State Highway 105 at a point that is 3.0 miles west of Plantersville and 11.1 miles east of Navasota. Spur 234 intersects Texas State Highway 105 at this point. Drive south 0.5 miles on paved Spur 234, crossing the Union Pacific Railway tracks and coming to a T intersection with Grimes County Road 304. Turn east and then immediately turn south to drive 0.4 miles across the Burlington Northern-Santa Fe Railway tracks and reach the area of St.*

Hand-crafted 1955 grave marker for Texanner Owens in the black Simmons Chapel (Stonehamville) Cemetery at Stoneham. Photograph by the author, 1999.

Joseph's Church and its Catholic cemetery. The black Simmons Chapel (Stonehamville) Cemetery lies 0.3 miles east on a graded county road. The non-Catholic white Stoneham Cemetery is located on the

Inside the general store at Study Butte during the 1950s. Courtesy of the Peter Koch Collection, Archives of the Big Bend, Bryan Wildenthal Library, Sul Ross State University.

northeast side of Texas State Highway 105 at a point that is 0.8 miles northwest of where that road intersects Spur 234. The cemetery contains several historic burials, including the graves of two veterans of the 1836 Battle of San Jacinto.

Study Butte

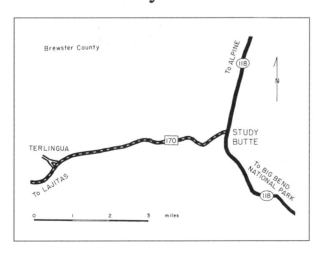

Study Butte—pronounced "Stewdy Butte"—functioned for several decades as a center of quicksilver mining in the Big Bend country of Brewster County. The town took on a new life at the end of the twentieth century when it became a tourist attraction near the western entrance to Big Bend National Park.

Residents named Study Butte after Will Study, the manager of a nearby quicksilver mine owned by the Texas Almaden Mining Company. Quicksilver is the commercial name that mining companies use for the metallic element mercury. Mining of cinnabar—the ore for quicksilver—began on the mountain called Study Butte at the turn of the twentieth century. For years the mineral extraction business formed the economic base of Study Butte. The butte where the mine once operated still dominates the visual landscape of the town.

Cinnabar ore was found at Study Butte in a soda rhyolite intrusion about four hundred feet thick. The igneous rock at the butte was highly cracked. Miners worked to remove the cinnabar, which had filled in the series of fissures in the

Cast-off equipment from cinnabar ore processing rusts beside a dry desert wash at Study Butte. Photograph by the author, 2000.

stone. Although the mine at Study Butte did not contain cinnabar ore as rich as the ore in other areas, such as nearby Terlingua, it was known for its continuous operation over the years. One source estimated that the mine produced more than five hundred tons of mercury. The site of the mine is easily identified by the bare reddish and yellowish heaps of spoil that were extracted from the ground.

The existence of Study Butte depended upon the mine. Most of the supervisory staff there was Anglo and most of the miners were Mexican. The community had a sufficient population by 1917 to receive a post office, and for many years the privately owned Study Butte Store provided local residents with groceries, hardware, and the necessities of life. The town languished during the Great Depression in the 1930s, but then experienced a resurgence because of increased industrial demand for mercury during World War II. After the war ended and the need for mercury decreased, Study Butte withered away—only about five residents remained in the early 1960s. Then in 1966 the mine at Study Butte

Cinnabar processing equipment and structures at the main quicksilver mine on Study Butte. The town of the same name lies in the distance, to the left. Photograph by the author, 2000.

Structures and debris remaining from cinnabar processing at the main quicksilver mine on Study Butte. Photograph by the author, 2000.

reopened for another half-dozen years before finally closing in early 1973. In 1970 the town boasted 115 residents.

Although Study Butte lost its main source of revenue when the cinnabar mine closed for the last time, the town was saved by a different industry—tourism. The increasing popularity of nearby Big Bend National Park has kept Study Butte alive for the past quarter-century with money spent by visitors. The Study Butte Store remains, but motels, modern gasoline stations, a rock shop, and eating places have joined it. The past, however, is never far away. Behind the Study Butte Store, for example, lie the historic graves of Mexican miners and their family members. The graves are covered with rock cairns and topped with weathered wooden crosses. The surrounding area is strewn with the detritus of former mining—ruins of former buildings, abandoned mining equipment, cast-off historic

automobiles, and huge mounds of spoil removed from the mine. There is an otherworldly feel to the area around the mine itself, with the disturbed ground, abandoned buildings, furnaces, and debris that remain from cinnabar extraction and processing.

LOCATION: *Study Butte lies at the intersection of Texas State Highway 118 and Farm Road 170 in southwestern Brewster County. The town is 78.0 miles south of Alpine, 3.0 miles northwest of the entrance to Big Bend National Park, 30.0 miles west of the Panther Junction Visitor Center in the national park, and 16.6 miles east of Lajitas. Just 3.8 miles west of Study Butte is the Terlingua ghost town on Farm Road 170. Visitors to the Study Butte area should be aware of the dangers of open pits, shafts, and other hazards in the areas of any mines or mineral processing. In addition, the Study Butte area is a known habitat of rattlesnakes and tarantulas. Visitors to this desert area are advised to*

Cairns with wooden crosses mark graves in the Mexican cemetery in Study Butte. Photograph by the author, 2000.

wear head coverings and sturdy shoes and to carry plenty of drinking water, as daytime shade temperatures during the summer often exceed 110 degrees Fahrenheit.

Sutherland Springs

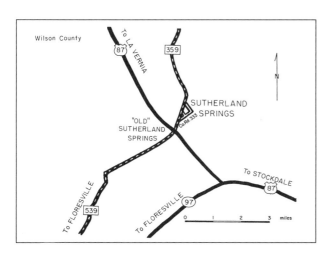

Sutherland Springs, a health resort town southeast of San Antonio, was a popular destination for invalids during the late nineteenth and early twentieth centuries. Today, however, the site lies virtually abandoned.

Dr. John Sutherland, Jr., a veteran of the Texas Revolution, surveyed and received the title to the lands encompassing Sutherland Springs in 1854. He had settled in the area a few years before and operated a stagecoach stop and post office from his home. The site became the provisional seat of government for Wilson County upon its organization in 1860, though the county seat moved to Floresville after the Civil War.

Even during the early days of settlement around the springs, people drank from and bathed in the highly mineralized waters. An 1878 guide to Texas praised the Sutherland Springs, claiming that "they are specially recommended for the relief and cure of those suffering from dropsy, liver complaint, dyspepsia, consumption and all diseases of the kidneys," and that "the white and black sulphur waters are

The Hotel Sutherland at Sutherland Springs during the 1930s, when it had already been closed for several years. Courtesy of the San Antonio Light Collection, the University of Texas Institute of Texan Cultures at San Antonio.

The motion-picture theater in Sutherland Springs, where the lights once flickered to entertain residents and visitors alike. Photograph by the author, 1999.

highly recommended for bathing purposes, and give a delicate smoothness and a rich glow of health to the skin." Lack of good roads, however, made it difficult for people to reach the purportedly curative springs. A town by the name of Sutherland Springs, serving as a local market center, grew up on the west side of Cibolo Creek less

than a mile from the springs, and achieved a population of 150 by 1885.

Then in 1895 the San Antonio and Gulf Shore Railway constructed a line along the east bank of Cibolo Creek, providing easy access to the springs from San Antonio. Within a decade the Sutherland Springs Development Corporation had created a health resort where activities focused on bathing in and drinking water from various springs. One of their promotional brochures declared, "We have more than a score of springs, flowing twelve varieties of mineral waters, the efficiency of which is attested by eminent chemists, physicians and the countless hundreds who have been cured." Health-seekers and tourists both flocked to the springs.

Soon most of the businesses and residents from "Old Sutherland Springs" moved from the west side of Cibolo Creek to the east side into "New Sutherland Springs." The steam railway proved to be the attraction because it promised a secure future for the residents of the "new" town. By the early twentieth century the community boasted a fifty-two-room hotel, electric lighting, a bank, motion-picture theater, drugstore, millinery shop, lumberyard, hardware store, water-bottling plant, school, telephone exchange, churches, a newspaper, Chautauqua grounds, a dancing pavilion, livery stable, bakery, and physicians' offices. The townsite promoters advertised that visitors could bathe in their 275-foot-long pool, "the largest concrete swimming pool in the South."

New Sutherland Springs seemed fated to fail. A series of floods destroyed facilities along Cibolo Creek, and a fire burned down part of the commercial district. More importantly, however, the public proved to be fickle. Improved methods of health care and new fashions in recreation drew visitors elsewhere during the years of the Roaring Twenties, the Great Depression, and World War II. By 1923 the big hotel had closed; its owner demolished it for materials several years later. Most of the residents moved out, many going back to Old Sutherland Springs, which received a modern highway connection to San Antonio in 1925.

Today New Sutherland Springs stands mostly deserted. Concrete sidewalks lead to nowhere in cattle pastures. The old bank, motion-picture theater, and a handful of historic residences still

Abandoned businesses and residences are gradually succumbing to the elements at Tokio. Photograph by the author, 2000.

stand, but the grid of former city streets is mostly lined with overgrown vacant lots. On the west side of the creek and U.S. Highway 87, Old Sutherland Springs still boasts a considerable number of occupied residences, several highway-related businesses, and even a museum that is open to the public a few days each year.

LOCATION: *The still-living Old Sutherland Springs lies on U.S. Highway 87 at its intersection with Farm Road 539 in Wilson County, 7.4 miles northwest of Stockdale, 6.8 miles southeast of La Vernia, and 29.3 miles southeast of San Antonio. To reach the ghost town of New Sutherland Springs, from the intersection of U.S. Highway 87 and Farm Road 539 in Old Sutherland Springs, drive 0.8 miles north on Farm Road 539 until that road intersects Wilson County Road 333. Angle northeast on Wilson County Road 333 for 0.4 miles, driving through the heart of former New Sutherland Springs past a few derelict commercial buildings and the abandoned railroad right-of-way.*

Tokio

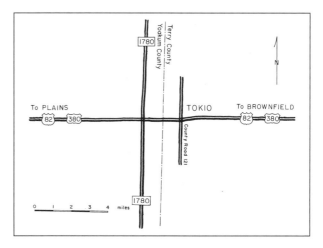

The farming community known as Tokio served for most of the twentieth century as a local market center for farmers on the South Plains west of Brownfield.

Before Tokio became a community in the early twentieth century the site existed as ranch land. During the 1910s the large ranches in the region

The doors leading into the back of a disused automobile garage in Tokio. Photograph by the author, 2000.

began selling acreages of grassland to agriculturists, who wanted to convert the land into farms. By 1912 enough farmers and ranchers had gathered in western Terry County that the area needed a post office, so Mrs. Belle V. Ware applied to the U.S. Post Office Department in Washington, D.C., to open one. The application required her to propose a name, and she selected Tokio. According to Texas postal historian Fred I. Massengill, "Mrs. H.L. Ware, mother of first postmaster here, submitted the name. She had no particular reason only that she liked the name of Tokio, Japan."

Tokio residents erected the first school in 1911. They later replaced the building twice—first because of a fire and second to provide additional classrooms. The school served the community until 1941, when it consolidated with the schools in Brownfield.

Baptists living in the area around Tokio gathered on 20 September 1914 to organize a church to meet community religious needs. They met for services in members' homes until 1929, when they built a 32-×-50-foot church building. The congregation continued adding facilities to their church until late in the twentieth century.

In 1928 the east-west highway between Brownfield and Plains shifted to its present location. Most of the residents and merchants in Tokio moved their buildings to the current site beside the newer road. There the community eventually had a brick school, several stores, automobile and tractor garages, the Baptist church, and—after World War II—a modern supermarket grocery store. The town reported 125 residents during the 1940s but only about sixty in the 1950s through the 1990s.

Tokio suffered from the effects of agricultural consolidation, as did hundreds of other rural towns in Texas. As tractors supplanted horses and mules in field work, fewer and fewer people were needed to plant, cultivate, and harvest the same number of acres. Farms grew larger while the countryside lost its former inhabitants, who had to seek jobs elsewhere in towns and cities. Tokio was no different—the rural population that had supported its businesses, church, and school disappeared, leaving the town with little reason to exist.

Today Tokio stands virtually deserted. During the author's most recent visit in 2000, it consisted of three abandoned residences, two occupied homes, two closed stores, two disused automobile garages, the derelict brick school, and an abandoned church. Well-houses and disturbed ground marked the sites of former buildings, and scattered about the site was a vast amount of surface archaeological remains, including glass, ceramics, and metal.

LOCATION: *Tokio is on U.S. Highway 82/380 at the intersection with Terry County Road 121, 16.5 miles west of Brownfield and 14.8 miles east of Plains.*

Town Bluff

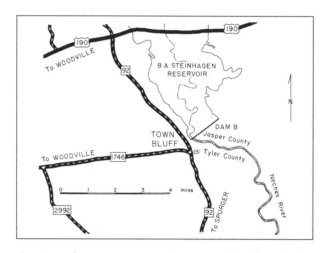

A steamboat port on the west bank of the Neches River, Town Bluff became the shipping point for much of what is now Tyler and Jasper counties. Then Town Bluff lost the election for the seat of Tyler County and the once important port town faded to little more than a small rural community.

Settlers became interested in the spot in 1833, when Wyatt Hanks, a San Augustine merchant, established a ferry across the Neches. With the ferry operating, other settlers soon chose the vicinity for their homes and created a new community. In 1834 Hanks platted a townsite on land he had acquired and began selling lots to both prospective residents and speculators. Among the buyers were John K. Allen and Augustus C. Allen, businessmen who had invested in promising sites across Texas, including the Buffalo Bayou that became the city of Houston. Hanks called his site

Granite monument erected by the state of Texas in 1936 to mark the site of Town Bluff. Photograph by the author, 1999.

Town Bluff because it topped a bluff overlooking the Neches River.

After Texas won its independence in 1836, the congress of the new republic created the Menard District, mainly for judicial administration. Wyatt's town was chosen as the district's temporary capital and it might very well have become its permanent seat of government had not the Texas Supreme Court declared the creation of the district unconstitutional. Then in 1846, when Tyler County was organized, three towns competed for the title of Tyler County seat. Town Bluff was one of the three, but it lost the election to a site on Turkey Creek that was later named Woodville. The town on the Neches bluffs, however, did serve as a temporary county seat for three years. Then, once the county courthouse was completed, most of its residents moved to Woodville with the county offices. In 1853 most of the remaining residents abandoned the site when a legal suit invalidated Hanks's land titles in the Town Bluff area.

Town Bluff survived as little more than a rural community until the mid-1940s, when the U.S. Army Corps of Engineers conducted surveys for a new dam on the Neches River just upstream from the townsite. Actual construction of Dam B began in 1947 and was completed in 1951, when the B. A. Steinhagen Reservoir began to fill. Since that time many new people have moved into the area formerly occupied by Town Bluff—a new community of the same name has sprung up along the highway two to three miles north of the former town.

LOCATION: *The historic Town Bluff townsite lies along Farm Road 92 near where it intersects Farm Road 1746 in eastern Tyler County. The site is located 14.5 miles east of Woodville. Of most interest to visitors is the Town Bluff Cemetery located just east of the Farm Road intersection. A comparatively recent concentration of retirement homes, fishing lodges, and mobile homes is located between two and three miles north of the historic townsite and today is called Town Bluff, but it has no historical ties with the ghost town of the same name.*

Trickham

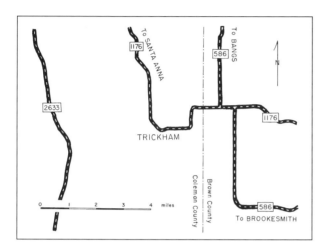

A jumble of abandoned motor vehicles in front of a derelict house in Trickham. Photograph by the author, 2000.

Trickham became a prosperous farming community in Coleman County around the turn of the twentieth century, but the settlement originated in the days of open-range cattle-raising decades earlier.

White settlers first arrived at the Trickham site in the late 1850s, about the time the U.S. Army established nearby Camp Colorado on Mukewater Creek. The army stayed for less than a year before it moved the camp twenty miles north to another site.

Cattleman John S. Chisum opened the first store in the area during the early 1860s. Its main purpose was to provide supplies to his cowboys, who maintained large herds of cattle in the vicinity, but the storekeeper, Bill Franks, also sold merchandise and groceries to other customers. By the late 1860s a considerable number of settlers had come to the Trickham area in the valley of Mukewater Creek. Despite the population growth, they experienced Indian raids for another decade—to this day three graves of unidentified men—purportedly killed by Indians—may be seen at the side of a town street.

According to some sources, the name Trickham came from the humor of storekeeper Bill Franks. He called the Chisum store "Trick-em and

A concrete sidewalk leads past an ornamental juniper to the site of a now vanished home in Trickham. Photograph by the author, 2000.

Skin-em." When an application was prepared for the first post office in 1879, the submitted name was supposedly "Trick-em," which postal officials modified to "Trickham." Postal records fail to confirm this story, but rather indicate that the post office was called Rickham from 1879 to 1888, when it became Trickham.

By the turn of the twentieth century, Trickham had become a substantial agricultural community. Farmers from East Texas had introduced cotton cultivation, which became the prime crop raised by farmers all around Trickham. The community had a two-story wooden schoolhouse where the Masonic lodge met on the upper floor, several mercantile stores, a cotton gin, blacksmith shop, union church, and even a hotel. During these days, as many as sixty children sometimes attended the school.

Trickham was not on the routes of any of the railroads built through Coleman County, and with the improvement of rural roads in the middle of the twentieth century much of its trade was drawn away to larger towns such as Santa Anna, Coleman, and Brownwood. Though it was still home to 125 residents as recent as 1940, today Trickham has no places of business and more houses and buildings that stand empty than occupied.

LOCATION: *Trickham stands on Farm Road 1176 in southeastern Coleman County at a point that is 13.9 miles southeast of Santa Anna and 20.8 miles southwest of Brownwood.*

Wallisville

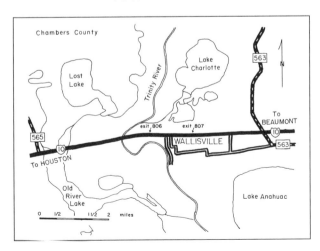

The site of Wallisville has borne many identities— a prehistoric American Indian occupation, a French trading post, a Spanish fort and mission, an 1825 Anglo settlement, a steamboat port, and the first seat of Chambers County. Today Wallisville sleeps alongside Interstate Highway 10 between Houston and Beaumont on the east bank of the Trinity River about four miles above its mouth.

Nearby archaeological evidence documents that Native peoples of the Attakapan cultural group occupied the area. At least as early as 1754 a Frenchman established a trading post near present-day Wallisville. Then the Spanish, fearing further French intrusions into their territory, decided to place both a fort and a Catholic mission on the east bank of the lower Trinity River. In May 1756 soldiers began constructing the Presidio San Augustín de Ahumada and Franciscan missionaries soon followed them in establishing the Mission Nuestra Señora de la Lúz. Soldiers and priests struggled to make the fort and mission successful, but the hot, humid climate, coupled with disinter-

Foundations remaining from the old Chambers County Courthouse at Wallisville. Photograph by the author, 2000.

ested Native charges, made their work difficult. In the meantime, Spain had acquired the Louisiana territory from France, thus eliminating the fear of French intrusion on the lower Trinity. In 1771 authorities abandoned both the fort and the mission. Many years would pass before other whites came to the area.

In 1825 an American settler named Edwin Henry Roberts Wallis settled on a hill just east of the Trinity River, becoming the first known English-speaking resident of the area. His farm and ranch prospered, which drew other people to the neighborhood. His sons employed a surveyor in 1854 to lay out a town on the east bank of the river. Named Wallisville in honor of the family, the town grew slowly but steadily. It profited from its location alongside the river and became an important port in a growing steamboat trade.

Though it never received a railroad connection, Wallisville continued to grow and prosper through the last decades of the nineteenth century, reaching a population of 728 in 1900. By that time the town had a school, a handsome brick courthouse and jail, a hotel, multiple stores, a saddle shop, newspaper, and several churches. As the largest town in Chambers County it became the seat of government in 1858, a distinction it kept for half a century.

Wallisville's location so near the Gulf of Mexico subjected it to danger from tropical storms. The town survived a major storm in 1875, but forty years later a second hurricane caused major damage from which Wallisville never recovered. Wooden houses floated up from their foundations and were battered to pieces by the extreme winds. In 1907 the voters of Chambers County had moved the county seat from Wallisville to Anahuac, so few people remained to rebuild Wallisville after the 1915 hurricane. With no railway to connect the community to the rest of the world, it lost population and then stagnated. The 1886 courthouse, falling to pieces from disrepair, was demolished in 1946 for its brick and other building materials. Only its foundations were left behind, which was true of most of Wallisville.

For decades local rice-growers had experienced the problem of saltwater from Trinity Bay backing up into the lower Trinity River at times of low flow. The U.S. Army Corps of Engineers in 1962 proposed creating a man-made salt-water barrier across the Trinity River at Wallisville. The planned effort included the construction of locks for barge traffic and a dam to create a 19,700-acre freshwater reservoir. Most of what remained in Wallisville would be inundated by the reservoir, so the federal agency purchased the majority of the townsite. Structures were either removed or demolished, leaving only their foundations and archaeological remains. The eastern portion of the town, located on ground higher than the waters of the future reservoir, survived intact and in private hands.

In the meantime, local residents organized the Wallisville Heritage Park in 1979 to preserve surviving historic structures of the old townsite, to document the town's history, and to perpetuate its memory. This group created a new museum and library and also brought various historical structures back to Wallisville, including its 1869 Freedmen's Bureau school.

Outside groups such as the Sierra Club joined local Wallisville residents to battle in court against the plans of the Army Corps of Engineers. After three major project redesigns, the agency completed its Wallisville Lake Project with a "non-impoundment plan" that called for a much smaller reservoir covering only 3,800 acres. Today the townsite is no longer in danger of inundation, and the Wallisville Heritage Park has plans to reconstruct the 1886 courthouse on its original foundations in the heart of the former town.

LOCATION: *From Interstate Highway 10 eastbound out of Houston, take exit 806 and drive 0.9 miles eastward along the two-way south frontage road to the Wallisville Heritage Park. From Interstate Highway 10 westbound into Houston, take exit 807 and drive 0.4 miles westward along the two-way north frontage road to an underpass. Cross under the Interstate to the south side and proceed westward on the two-way south frontage road 0.3 miles to Wallisville Heritage Park. The museum, 1869 school, several relocated historic structures, red brick 1954 Methodist church, and about a dozen scattered historic residences survive at the east side of the Wallisville townsite. East of this area, however, all buildings were removed and only their foundations, some archaeological debris, and remaining ornamental trees and plantings survive. The foundations of the courthouse and jail are accessible in a cleared area just south of the south-*

side frontage road 0.4 miles west of the museum. Visitors to this latter area need to be cautious of both snakes and poison ivy.

Washington-on-the-Brazos

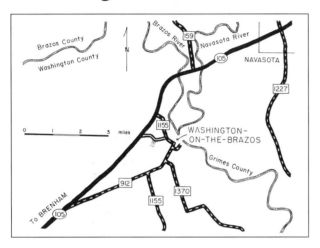

Once one of the most promising towns in all of Texas, Washington-on-the-Brazos has diminished to little more than a rural supply center. Today the Washington County community is one destination for tourists seeking to learn about the history of the Texas Republic.

Whites and blacks from Stephen F. Austin's initial empresario colony began settling the area around what became Washington-on-the-Brazos in 1821. Fertile lands and easy access to transportation arteries attracted settlers to the place; the future townsite lay only a mile from the confluence of the Brazos and Navasota rivers, which was where the La Bahia Road crossed the Brazos. Sometime in 1822 Andrew Robinson began operating a ferry at the La Bahia crossing. Then in 1833 John W. Hall, Robinson's son-in-law, laid out a town. He and others formed the Washington Town Company in 1835, naming the site after Washington, Georgia, the home of one of Hall's partners. Attracted by the site's position on the river and the overland La Bahia Road, merchants and tradesmen began settling around the new town.

Washington-on-the-Brazos entered the annals of Texas in 1836. It was here in a rented, unfinished building, that elected delegates from across

Texas met between 1 and 17 March 1836 to draft the Texas Declaration of Independence from Mexico, to write the constitution for the Republic of Texas, and to create an interim government for the republic. Then with the army of Mexican President Lopez de Santa Anna approaching from the southwest, the delegates evacuated the town. After Texas won its independence a month later, the town of Washington experienced an influx of new settlers.

After the revolution, Washington-on-the-Brazos also grew and began to attract more and more businesses. Among the new enterprises were a brickyard, sawmills, and a post office. By 1839 Washington had 150 residents. Its importance grew even more when the capital of the Republic of Texas moved there in 1842, where it remained until Texas entered the United States in 1845. During the 1840s Washington had several newspapers and was the site of the Republic of Texas Congress, courts, foreign embassies, and Barrington, the home of the Republic's last president, Dr. Anson Jones.

In 1842 the steamboat *Mustang* first brought the possibilities of steam navigation to Washington-on-the-Brazos, which became an important shipping point for cotton grown within its territory. At times as many as three steamboats were reported to be tied up at the Washington landing. In its heyday in 1856, Washington had 750 residents and four churches, two newspapers, two

An old commercial building that has been quiet for many years in Washington-on-the-Brazos. Photograph by the author, 1999.

Tourists at Washington-on-the-Brazos State Historical Park walk toward the reconstruction of the building in which delegates drafted the Texas Declaration of Independence in 1836. Photograph by the author, 1999.

hotels, multiple fraternal lodges, a market house, and a commercial district comprised of two- and three-story buildings. Businesspeople of Washington grew convinced that the future of their town lay with steamboats, so they declined an opportunity to pay an $11,000 bonus to attract the Houston and Texas Central Railway Company that was building a line along the opposite side of the Brazos River. Consequently the company routed its steel rails to Hempstead in 1858 and to Navasota in 1859, bypassing the older town. As the railroad network expanded across the country, the railroads became a more popular method of transportation than steamboats, which soon ceased to operate on the Brazos River. Washington-on-the-Brazos began to dwindle away.

By 1889 most of Washington had become cultivated cotton fields. The town shrank to a mere local market center, known only for events of its early history. A writer in 1915 observed, "Today there is nothing left but a few old buildings fast tottering to the end, and one store, which supplies the wants of the adjacent farmers." In 1916 the state of Texas began acquiring the site of the historic town, including a handful of the remaining old buildings, to create the Washington-on-the-Brazos State Historical Park. Today the park, its interpretive center, the Barrington Living History Farm, and the Star of the Republic Museum attract thousands of visitors from around the world. Tourists can also visit a few more buildings and the cemetery, which are not part of the park.

LOCATION: *Washington-on-the Brazos is located on Farm Road 1155 at a point that is 1.4 miles south of its intersection with Texas State Highway 105 in extreme northeastern Washington County. Inside the Washington-on-the-Brazos State Historical Park, visitors can visit part of the townsite, a new interpretive center, a reconstruction of the building where the Texas Declaration of Independence was drafted and signed, the Barrington Living History Farm, and the interesting Star of the Republic Museum. Historic twentieth-century buildings from the town still stand just outside the park. To reach the historic Washington Cemetery, drive northwest from the center of the townsite 0.3 miles on Farm Road 1155 to its intersection with a gravel Washington County road marked as "Washington Cemetery Road." Turn and drive west 0.4 miles on the gravel county road to the cemetery. The historic black graveyard lies closest to the road. Behind it at the southwest corner lies the overgrown mid-nineteenth-century white cemetery. Many burials there are from the 1840s through 1860s; most of the tombstones are covered with vines and other vegetation. The overgrown white cemetery abounds in poison ivy and provides a habitat for snakes.*

1852—an estimated three hundred people from Alabama, both planters and slaves, made the trip. Not all of the them arrived, however. Four planters and forty slaves lost their lives to yellow fever when the party passed through New Orleans.

By the mid-1850s the farmers at Waverly had recreated the plantation system that most of them had known in Alabama. For the young whites there were separate male and female departments of the Waverly Institute. No blacks at the time were allowed to attend schools or even learn to read and write. Members of the white community attended Methodist, Presbyterian, and Episcopal churches. A post office opened in 1855, and the town was incorporated in 1858. When Texas seceded from the Union in 1861, a number of young men from Waverly volunteered for Confederate military service.

Waverly

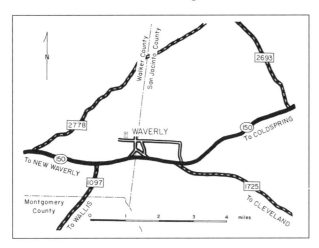

An enclave of Alabama planters and their black slaves became a center of cotton production in Walker County before the Civil War. This town, known as Waverly, suffered when railroad construction bypassed it after the war. Part of the dying town was converted to a residential subdivision after World War II.

The first white settler at what later became Waverly was James W. Winters, who immigrated from Alabama in 1835. Other farmers soon began settling in the area. The largest party came in

The 1904 sanctuary that still serves the Waverly Presbyterian Church congregation, organized at Waverly in 1860. Photograph by the author, 1999.

The 1868 grave of J. M. Powell in the cemetery at Waverly, one of the most beautiful graveyards in Texas. Photograph by the author, 1999.

Waverly might have survived as a town despite its labor shortages, but its leaders made decisions that led to its death. In 1870 the Houston and Great Northern Railroad was building a line northward from Houston and had surveyed a proposed route through Waverly. Because they feared the railway would bring "tramps and ignorance" to the town, several of the landowners refused to sell rights-of-way to the railroad. Company officials decided that they would instead route their tracks eight miles to the west, where they constructed a siding called Waverly. There the railroad town of New Waverly sprang up, and within a matter of months, many families from Waverly relocated to the new town. The old town was further demoralized when San Jacinto County was formed from part of Walker County in 1870, for the new county line split Waverly in half. Strangled on its residents' own sense of self importance, Waverly died out to little more than dispersed rural community. It did, however, possess a handsome historic Presbyterian church and one of the most beautiful nineteenth-century cemeteries in all of Texas. After World War II, the old town was partially revived in the form of a residential subdivision called Old Waverly, built on the east side of the Waverly townsite.

With the end of the war came the emancipation of the black workers who had been enslaved on the plantations around Waverly. Because Confederate money and bonds had become worthless, the white planters lacked the money to pay their former slaves, but managed to convince some of them to stay and work for shares of the crops they raised. Even so there were not enough workers. The planters then made arrangements to bring Polish peasant farmers from Europe to Texas. The planters provided their passage to America, and then the Poles repaid the cost of their passage from the wages they received. These Polish immigrants were the first of many who settled in eastern Texas during the 1870s through 1890s.

LOCATION: *Waverly is located on county roads north of Texas State Highway 150 between New Waverly and Coldspring and is bisected by the Walker-San Jacinto county line. The townsite is accessed via a paved loop of county road, a former curve of Texas State Highway 150 that was eliminated from the state highway by a pavement realignment. The turn-offs for the two ends of the county road are located 7.8 miles and 8.4 miles east of New Waverly, 14.9 miles and 15.5 miles west of Coldspring. From the west end of the loop, drive 0.2 miles, and from the east end of the loop, drive 0.5 miles to a distinct bend in the road, where a paved county road leads straight north. Turn north onto this county road and drive 0.2 miles to a four-way intersection with other unmarked county roads. At the four-way intersection, turn west onto another paved county road and drive 0.3 miles to the Waverly Cemetery. The historic Presbyterian Church is 0.3 miles east of the four-way intersection on a paved county road, across the Walker-San Jacinto county line.*

Wiess's Bluff

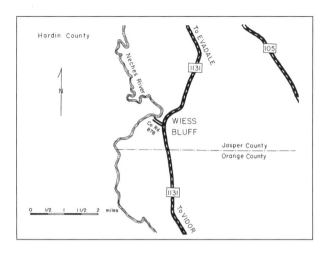

If any place conjures up visions of the Texas steamboating past, that place must be Wiess's Bluff on the Neches River in Jasper County. The townsite lies on the high bank of a gentle bend in the river. The site is now occupied by a scattering of rural homes, but once it was the hub for steamboat navigation on the Neches River.

Wiess's Bluff in 1840 became the new home for Simon Wiess, a German born in 1800 in Lublin, Poland. Spending his early adulthood as a seaman on the Mediterranean, the Atlantic, the Caribbean, and the Gulf of Mexico, he landed in Galveston in 1833 and spent the rest of his life in the United States. After attempting to run mercantile businesses in Nacogdoches and Grigsby's Bluff (now Port Neches), Wiess relocated to his bluff on the east bank of the Neches. This bend marked the head of year-round steamboat navigation, as the river water was deep enough to float steamboats all months of the year. During high water in the springtime vessels could run considerably higher than Wiess's Bluff, but for the rest of the year Wiess's store was as far as they could go without becoming stranded in shallow water.

The high bank of the Trinity River at Wiess's Bluff, site of a nineteenth-century steamboat landing and Simon Wiess's warehouses. Photograph by the author, 1999.

Early springtime narcissus blooms in the yard of an abandoned house at Wiess's Bluff. Photograph by the author, 1999.

external factors to send Wiess's Bluff down an economic decline. After the war, lumbering became more important in the Wiess's Bluff area, but the town profited little from this venture—logs were merely rolled into the river at the bluff to float downstream to processing. Then in 1883 the Sabine and East Texas Railway entered the area, followed in the 1890s by the Gulf, Beaumont and Kansas City Railway. Steam railroads effectively put steamboats out of business on the Neches River and rendered most industries in Wiess's Bluff useless. As the community declined, it lost its post office in 1908. Today Wiess's Bluff is an incredibly beautiful setting for the few scattered rural homes and historic structures that remain.

LOCATION: *Wiess's Bluff is located on the east side of the Neches River on Farm Road 1131 in extreme southwestern Jasper County. A historical marker for the town stands at the west side of Farm Road 1131 at a point that is 7.7 miles south of Evadale and 12.0 miles north of Vidor. The town itself lies 0.4 miles south of the historical marker. At that point, the farm road intersects gravel Jasper County Road 878, also marked as "Wiess Bluff Road." The accessible remains of Wiess's Bluff lie along this county road. There is no public access to the river at Wiess's Bluff.*

Simon Wiess and his family prospered mainly from his wisdom in settling at the strategic head of low-water navigation on the Neches. Most of the year, planters had to haul their cotton, hides, and other products to Wiess's warehouses. From there goods were shipped downstream to the coast and thence on to markets in New Orleans or Galveston. Not only did Wiess export cotton, corn, hides, pelts, tobacco, and other products, but he imported all the necessities of life for farmers and planters living in the area. The community Wiess had encouraged at his landing received a post office in 1858. Wiess also speculated in land and operated a small-scale sawmill. His various enterprises allowed him and his family a comfortable living.

The town that grew up around Wiess's store and warehouses prospered during the 1850s but suffered in the 1860s due to the Civil War and subsequent Reconstruction. The townsite served as a depot for the Confederate military but it was miles from any fighting. The economic problems caused by the war and its aftermath combined with other

Wizard Wells

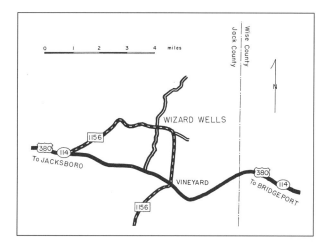

A small agricultural market center in east-central Jack County, Wizard Wells became famous in the

The historic mineral-water well at Wizard Wells, in front of a 1920s-style rock-faced tourist court and historic iris plants. Photograph by the author, 2000.

late nineteenth and early twentieth centuries for its mineral water wells. People came from miles around to bathe in and drink this water that reportedly cured illnesses.

White and black settlers began coming to the valley of Bean's Creek during the 1850s. There they found the land suited to both farming and livestock-raising, and over the years more people arrived. Among them was George Washington Vineyard, who in 1880 dug a well for his home. He found water so laden with minerals that it was barely drinkable. Vineyard, however, used the water for bathing purposes, and in so doing he made a remarkable discovery. Though he had suffered from ulcers on his legs and sores on his eyes, Vineyard found himself cured by his baths in the mineral-rich water.

Word of Vineyard's cure soon spread through northern Texas, and people began appearing at his well, asking permission to bathe in his water. He realized that the water must have some value, so he platted a town named Vineyard around the well and began selling lots. Over time the community grew and served not only the health-seekers, but also the local farmers and livestock-raisers, who came there to buy the necessities of life. At one time the town had three restaurants, three hotels, two bathhouses, a school, a few saloons, Baptist and Methodist churches, a blacksmith shop, general stores, a barbershop, post office, and newspaper.

In 1898 the Rock Island Railroad Company built a line two miles south of the town, creating a competing railroad town named Sebree. While the newer town drew away some of the supply-center business from Vineyard, it also made it easier for invalids to travel to the wells for mineral-water baths. A regular horse-drawn hack service transported people between the two towns.

In 1915 one of the bathhouse operators petitioned the Texas Legislature to make two name changes. At his request, the legislators replaced the name of Vineyard with the more intriguing Wizard Wells. At the same time they also changed the name of Sebree to Vineyard. Locals distinguished between the two communities as "Old Vineyard" and "New Vineyard."

Wizard Wells never competed with the far more developed Mineral Wells in Palo Pinto County, but it did draw its own clientele. The town declined, however, due to advances in technology and medicine. Its general trade diminished as a consequence of agricultural consolidation during the 1920s to 1950s. Because farmers using tractors could do far more agricultural work than laborers using horses and mules, fewer people were needed to do the same work on farms. As the rural population left to find work in urban areas, businesses in Wizard Wells lost their customer base and had to close. The other mainstay of the local economy, the mineral-water springs, suffered at the same time because of changed perceptions of healing. Americans learned in the early twentieth century about microbes and their role in causing illness. Physicians stopped prescribing mineral-water baths, as new medications could give their patients similar results. Consequently fewer and fewer people came to the springs seeking cures. The population continued to decline, and Wizard Wells lost both its school and its post office in the 1950s. Formerly

A historic mobile home that came to rest in Wizard Wells. Photograph by the author, 2000.

home to a hundred or more people, the community today has perhaps a quarter of that number. One last bathhouse still stands, but it has not served health-seekers on a regular basis since the 1970s.

LOCATION: *Wizard Wells is located on a northward loop in Farm Road 1156 in Jack County at a point that is 2.4 miles north of Vineyard and 13.0 miles east of Jacksboro.*

Bibliography

Abbe, Donald R. "Borger: The First Oil Boom Town in the Panhandle." In *Panhandle Petroleum*, edited by Bobby D. Weaver. Canyon, Tex.: Panhandle-Plains Historical Society, 1982.

Abernethy, F. E. "The Deserted Village." *East Texas Historical Journal* 39, no. 2 (2001): 3–9.

Adams, Samuel. "Pieces of the Past: Artifacts Displayed, History Exchanged at Old Fort Parker." *Waco Tribune-Herald*, 20 July 1992, sec. B, pp. 1–2.

Addington, Charles, II. "Profile of a Dream: Justiceburg, Texas." *Texas Historian* 44, no. 5 (May 1984): 9–12.

"Aguilares Still 'Live,' Named for Ranch Family." *The Laredo (Tex.) Times*, 8 November 1981, centennial edition, sec. HH, p. 4.

Alcott, R. S. "Old Quintana." Typescript. 12 September 1955. "Quintana" vertical file, Brazoria County Historical Museum, Angleton, Tex.

Alexander, Thomas E. *The Stars Were Big and Bright: The United States Army Air Forces and Texas During World War II*. Austin: Eakin Press, 2000.

Alford, Shirley. "Ben Ficklin's Existence Brief, Doomed by Flood." *San Angelo (Tex.) Standard-Times*, 25 April 1976, sec. E, p. 7.

Alloway, David. *El Camino del Rio, the River Road: FM 170 from Study Butte to Presidio and Through Big Bend Ranch State Park*. Austin: Texas Parks and Wildlife Department, 1995.

Anderson, Brian. "Theater Planned at Historic Site: Outdoor Drama Would Tell History of Old Fort Parker." *Waco Tribune-Herald*, 17 August 1998, sec. C, pp. 1, 3.

Anderson, Dubb. "Small Communities or Towns around Hutchinson Co." Typescript. March 1976. Historical files, Borger Chamber of Commerce, Borger, Tex.

Angelle, Denny. "Forgotten Graves Ignite Memories of Another Era." *Port Arthur (Tex.) News*, 12 April 1981, sec. D, p. 1.

Applegate, Howard G., and C. Wayne Hanselka. *La Junta de los Rio del Norte y Conchos*. Southwestern Studies, no. 41. El Paso: Texas Western Press, 1974.

Archer County Family History Committee. *Archer County Family History: Shortgrass Saga*. [Archer City, Tex.]: Archer County Family History Committee, 1986.

Armstrong County Historical Association. *A Collection of Memories: A History of Armstrong County 1876–1965*. Hereford, Tex.: Pioneer Publishers, 1965.

Armstrong, Larry. "Quintana." *The Junior Historian* 21, no. 4 (January 1961): 20–22.

Arrillaga, Pauline. "Tiny Encino Gets the Job Done: Ranching Community Pulls Together to Keep Its Only School Open." *Harllingen (Tex.) Valley Morning Star*, 18 August 1996, sec. C, p. 1.

Austerman, Wayne R. "Siege at Hueco Tanks." *Password* 37, no. 1 (Spring 1992): 27–37.

Austin, Rose, and Mrs. S. C. Autry. *Early History of San Angelo: Tom Green County*. San Angelo, Tex.: Fort Concho Museum, [ca. 1950].

Babb, Jewel. *Border Healing Woman: The Story of Jewel Babb*. Edited by Pat Ellis Taylor. Austin: University of Texas Press, 1981.

Bailey, Clyde, and Mabel Bailey. *Vignettes of Coryell County*. Gatesville, Tex.: Gatesville Printing Company, 1976.

Baker, T. Lindsay. *Building the Lone Star: An Illustrated Guide to Historic Sites*. College Station: Texas A&M University Press, 1986.

———. *The First Polish Americans: Silesian Settlements in Texas*. College Station: Texas A&M University Press, 1979.

———. "Glenrio in Two States." *Cleburne (Tex.) Eagle News*, 26 February 1988, p. 6.

———. "Going to See Enola Gay." *Cleburne (Tex.) Eagle News*, 13 March 1997, p. 6.

———. *The Polish Texans*. San Antonio: University of Texas Institute of Texan Cultures, 1982.

Banta, John. "Center City Offers One a Look into Yesterday." *Waco Times-Herald*, 1 August 1973, sec. A, pp. 1–2.

———. "Focus on Prairie Hill: Oil Discovery Helped Spread Town's Name." *Waco Tribune-Herald*, 2 January 1980, sec. A, p. 3.

———. "Historical Marker Dedicated: Ft. Parker Restoration to Begin 'in Near Future,' Director Says." *Waco News-Tribune*, 21 March 1966, sec. A, pp. 1, 9.

———. "No Bonanzas Struck, But It Was Gold Fever." *Waco Tribune-Herald*, 4 October 1978, sec. A, p. 12.

———. "Norwegian Journalist Visits Peerson's Grave at Norse." *Waco News-Tribune*, 24 November 1962, pp. 1, 5.

———. "Program Planned: Norse Lutherans to Observe Church Centennial Sunday." *Waco Tribune-Herald*, 7 January 1967, sec. A, p. 6.

Barkley, Mary Starr. *A History of Central Texas*. Austin: Austin Printing Company, 1970.

Barrick, Rick. "Local Landmarks: Quintana Fort Guarded River Mouth." *Clute (Tex.) Brazosport Facts*, 4 July 1980, Weekend/Plus Section, p. 6.

Bartholomew, Dana. "Penwell's Newest Postmaster 'Rattles' Way through Workday." *Odessa (Tex.) American*, 3 December 1995, sec. B, pp. 1–2.

Bartholomew, Ed. *800 Texas Ghost Towns*. Fort Davis, Tex.: Frontier Book Publishers, 1971.

———. *The Encyclopedia of Texas Ghost Towns*. Fort Davis, Tex.: Frontier Book Publishers, 1982.

Baskin, Robert E. "Norse Colony 100 Years Old." *Dallas Morning News*, 10 January 1954, sec. III, p. 1.

Baylor County Historical Society. *Salt Pork to Sirloin: The History of Baylor County from 1878 to Present*. 2 vols. Quanah, Tex.: Nortex Offset Publications, 1972; Wichita Falls, Tex.: Nortex Press, 1977.

Beane, Wilhelmina. "Old Washington Sleeps in Its Memories of a Glamorous Day: The Cradle of Texas Independence." *Houston Post*, 2 April 1936, pp. 3–4.

Bell, Wayne, Marsha Jackson, and Lawrence Aten. "Orcoquisac Archeological District." Typescript nomination to the National Register of Historic Places. 1971. Office of National Register Programs, Texas Historical Commission, Austin.

"Belmont." *Gonzales (Tex.) Weekly Inquirer*, 19 July 1923, sec. F, pp. 6–7.

"Belmont Begins Life as Road's Stage-coach Stopover." In *Welcome to Gonzales: Official Visitors' & Newcomers' Guide*. N.p., [ca. 1990].

"Ben Ficklin Flood (Tom Green County)" vertical file. Tom Green County Library, San Angelo, Tex.

"Ben Ficklin (Tom Green County)" vertical file. Tom Green County Library, San Angelo, Tex.

Benningfield, Damond. "Ode to the Road." *Texas Highways* 44, no. 9 (September 1977): 16–23.

Benton, Minnie King. *Boomtown: A Portrait of Burkburnett*. Quanah, Tex.: Nortex Offset Publications, 1972.

"Best of Best Rests Quietly in Old Oil Town's Colorful Past." *Austin American-Statesman*, 19 July 1987, sec. B, p. 10.

Beverley, Bob. "Two Texas County Seats That Disappeared." *The Cattleman* 37, no. 11 (April 1951): 29, 78, 80.

Beverley, Mary Frances. "Rattlesnake Bomber Base: Hangar, Museum and Memories Survive on the Site of a Former West Texas Bombardier Training Center." *Dallas Morning News*, 31 July 1988, sec. G, p. 5.

Biesele, Rudolph Leopold. *The History of the German Settlements in Texas 1831–1861*. Austin: Von Boeckmann-Jones, 1930.

Biffle, Kent. "History Bug Bites Deep in W. Texas." *Dallas Morning News*, 2 September 1990, sec. A, pp. 45, 50.

Bigham, Truman C. "The Desdemona Oil and Gas Field, Texas." Senior thesis, Baylor University, 1919.

"Biographical Sketch of the Late W. B. Ochiltree." In *Texas Almanac for 1870*. Galveston, Tex.: Richardson & Co., 1870.

Bitner, Grace. "The History of Tom Green County, Texas." Master's thesis, University of Texas, 1931.

Black, Steve, and Carolyn Spock. "Caddo Houses in the Dirt and Reconstructed." *Texas Heritage* 18, no. 4 (Fall 2000): 30–31.

Blackwell, Hartal Langford. *Mills County: The Way It Was*. Goldthwaite, Tex.: Eagle Press, 1976.

Blair, E. L. *Early History of Grimes County*. N.p.; privately printed, 1930.

Blasig, Anna J. "The Frontier Experiences of the Wends of Lee County, Texas." Master's thesis, University of Texas, 1951.

Blasig, Anne. *The Wends of Texas*. San Antonio: Naylor Company, 1954.

Block, William T. *East Texas Mill Towns and Ghost Towns*. 3 vols. Lufkin, Tex.: Best of East Texas Publishers, 1994–97.

———. "From Cotton Bales to Black Gold: A History of the Pioneer Wiess Families of Southeastern Texas." *The Texas Gulf Historical and Biographical Record* 8, no. 1 (November 1972: 39–61.

———. *A History of Jefferson County, Texas, from Wilderness to Reconstruction*. Nederland, Tex.: Nederland Publishing Company, 1976.

Boethel, Paul C. *History of Lavaca County*. Rev. ed. Austin: Von Boeckmann-Jones, 1959.

———. *La Baca*. Columbus, Tex.: privately printed, 1993.

Bowers, Eugene W., and Evelyn Oppenheimer. *Red River Dust: True Tales of an American Yesterday*. Waco: Word Books, 1968.

Bowles, Flora Gatlin, ed. *A No Man's Land Becomes a County*. Goldthwaite, Tex.: Mills County Historical Society, 1958.

Bowman, Bob. *The 35 Best Ghost Towns in East Texas and 220 Other Towns We Left Behind*. Lufkin, Tex.: Best of East Texas Publishers, 1988.

———. *This Was East Texas*. Diboll, Tex.: Angelina Free Press, 1966.

———. *The Towns We Left Behind*. Diboll, Tex.: Angelina Free Press, 1972.

———. "Twice a County Seat: Town Bluff, Eastex Ghost Town, Is Revived by Dam B Reservoir." *Houston Chronicle*, 8 May 1966, sec. 3, p. 13.

Boyd, Douglas K., Martha Doty Freeman, Michael D. Blum, Elton R. Prewitt, and J. Michael Quigg. *Phase I Cultural Resources Investigations at Justiceburg Reservoir on the Double Mountain Fork of the Brazos River, Garza and Kent Counties, Texas*. 2 vols. Reports of Investigations, no. 66. Austin: Prewitt and Associates, 1989.

Branda, Eldon Stephen, ed. *The Handbook of Texas: A Supplement*. Austin: Texas State Historical Association, 1976.

Braudaway, Doug. [Unpublished typescript history of Val Verde County, Texas.] Typescript. 2000. Personal research files of Doug Braudaway, Del Rio, Tex.

Brelsford, Bernice. "Sutherland Springs Once a Saratoga and a Long Branch." *Floresville (Tex.) Chronicle-Journal*, 19 January 1989, p. 9.

Brewer, Steve. "Springs Are No Longer Hot Spot: Flow of Ailing Visitors Seeking Relief in Soothing Water Dries Up." *Dallas Morning News*, 14 February 1982, sec. AA, p. 15.

Bridges, Katherine. "Magnolia." *The Junior Historian* 11, no. 4 (January 1951): 3.

Brollier, Anthony. "Place Names in Wichita County." *The Junior Historian* 4, no. 5 (March 1944): 1–9.

Bronstad, Alvin L., ed. *Memoirs of the Rev. John Knudson Rystad, Our Savior's Lutheran Church.* [Clifton, Tex.]: privately printed, [1967].

Brooks County Historical Survey Committee. *The Faith Healer of Los Olmos: Biography of Don Pedrito Jaramillo.* [Falfurrias, Tex.]: Brooks County Historical Survey Committee, 1972.

Brown, Clois Truman. "The History of Deaf Smith County, Texas." Master's thesis, West Texas State College, 1948.

Brown, David O., John A. Peterson, and Amy C. Earls. *Plan for the Identification, Evaluation, and Treatment of Historical and Archaeological Properties and Plan for the Preservation of Architectural Properties.* [El Paso]: Archaeological Research, [ca. 1995].

Brown, Dewey. "Battered Sabine Pass Sets Out to Rebuild: Families to Restore Little Coast Towns." *Port Arthur (Tex.) News*, 11 July 1957, p. 12.

Brown, Kenneth L. "Why Is the Wallisville Townsite Important?" Typescript. [Ca. 1980.] Library, Wallisville Heritage Park, Wallisville, Tex.

Brownwood Civic Association. Papers. [Ca. 1972–79.] "Brownwood Civic Association" vertical files, Baytown Historical Museum, Baytown, Tex.

Bruce, Leona Banister. *They Came in Peace to Coleman County.* Fort Worth: Branch-Smith, 1970.

———. *Trickham, Texas: A Neighborly Chronicle.* Salado, Tex.: Anson Jones Press, 1966.

Brune, Gunnar. *Major and Historical Springs of Texas.* Texas Water Development Board Report, no. 189. Austin: Texas Water Development Board, 1975.

———. *Springs of Texas, Volume I.* Fort Worth: Branch-Smith, 1981.

Bryce, Robert. "All's Well? Candelaria's Only Well Supplied Free Water to All Until the EPA Weighed In." *Texas Monthly* 20, no. 1 (January 1992): 80.

Buckner, Oran Silas. "History of Terry County." Master's thesis, Texas Technological College, 1943.

Burgess, Roger Andrew. "The History of Crosby County, Texas." Master's thesis, University of Texas, 1927.

"Burnett, Crystal, and Scott Bays and Vicinity, Baytown, Texas: Questions and Answers Relating to Evacuation and Relocation of a Flood Plain." Typescript. 1974. "Brownwood" vertical files, Baytown Historical Museum, Baytown, Tex.

Burnett, John. "Prairie Hill Fest Outshines Rain's Dampening Effect." *Waco Tribune-Herald*, 28 September 1980, sec. A, pp. 1, 10.

Burns, Nancy. *The Collapse of Small Towns on the Great Plains: A Bibliography.* Emporia State Research Studies, 31, no. 1. Emporia, Kans.: Emporia State University, 1982.

Bush, W. A. "Washington County." *Austin State Gazette,* 26 March 1859, p. 3.

Caddoan Mounds: Temples and Tombs of an Ancient People. Texas Parks and Wildlife Department Booklet 4000–384. Austin: Texas Parks and Wildlife Department, 1984.

Cadwallader, Robert. "Norse: Town Fit for King: Residents Recall Late Monarch's Visit." *Waco Tribune-Herald*, 19 January 1991, sec. C, pp. 1, 3.

Calderón, Roberto R. *Mexican Coal Mining Labor in Texas and Coahuila, 1880–1930.* College Station: Texas A&M University Press, 2000.

Caldwell, David. "Ghost Towns of Anderson County." *Texas Historian* 32, no. 3 (January 1972): 10–16.

"Candelaria Community Now Has Different Owners." *Presidio (Tex.) International*, 19 August 1994, p. 1.

"Candelaria Water Well Comes in on Second Attempt." *Marfa (Tex.) Big Bend Sentinel*, 27 February 1992, p. 1.

Carmack, George. "Ladies at the Helm." *San Antonio Express-News*, 17 September 1977, sec. B, pp. 1, 4.

———. "A Story of Romance: Serbin Is Born in Texas." *San Antonio Express-News*, 21 April 1973, sec. B, p. 1; sec. C, p. 8.

Case, Peggy. "Quintana's 'Gun Mounds' Conjure Up Memories." *Freeport (Tex.) Brazosport, Facts,* 1 May 1974, sec. A, p. 9.

Casey, Clifford B. *Mirages, Mysteries, and Reality: Brewster County, Texas, the Big Bend of the Rio Grande.* Seagraves, Tex.: Pioneer Book Publishers, 1972.

———. "The Trans-Pecos in Texas History." *West Texas Historical and Scientific Society Publications* 5 (1933): 7–18.

Castillo, Pedro, and Albert Camarillo. *Furia y Muerte: Los Bandidos Chicanos.* University of California, Los Angeles, Chicano Studies Center, Monograph no. 4. Los Angeles: University of California, Los Angeles, 1973.

Castro Colonies Heritage Association. *The History of Medina County, Texas.* Dallas: Curtis Media, 1994.

Chapman, Art. "Healing Water: The Magic of Wizard Wells Has All But Vanished." *Fort Worth Star-Telegram*, 18 September 1996, sec. A, pp. 17, 19.

Chenoweth, Dean. "On Saturday: Ficklin Memorial Ceremony Slated." *San Angelo (Tex.) Standard-Times*, 15 October 1965, evening edition, sec. B, p. 12.

Christiansen, Thomas P. "Danevang, Texas." *Southwestern Historical Quarterly* 32, no. 1 (July 1928): 67–73.

Chubbuck, Beth. "The History of Trickham, Texas, and Its Relationship to the Land." Typescript. [Ca. 1980.] 16 lvs. "Trickham, Texas" vertical file, Texas Collection, Baylor University.

187

"Cities (Quintana)—Brazoria County File" vertical file. Angleton Library, Brazoria County Libraries, Angleton, Tex.

Citizens Bond Committee. "Brownwood's Sunk without Your Vote" [advertisement]. *Baytown (Tex.) Sun*, 14 July 1979, sec. B, p. 2.

Clark, J. Mabel. "War Cry of First Texans to Be Heard as Massacre at Fort Parker Recalled in Centennial Pageant: Capture of Cynthia Ann and Her Brother to Be Depicted This Week." *Dallas Morning News*, 17 May 1936, sec. I, p. 5.

Clemens, Gus. *The Concho Country*. San Angelo, Tex.: Mulberry Avenue Books, 1980.

Coleman County Historical Commission. *A History of Coleman County and Its People*. 2 vols. San Angelo, Tex.: Anchor Publishing Company, 1985.

Collins, Lois A. "The Significance of Oil Company Camps in the Development of the Permian Basin." *The Permian Historical Annual* 28 (1988): 85–109.

Colorado County Historical Commission. *Colorado County Chronicles*. 2 vols. Austin: Nortex Press, 1986.

Colorado County 1986 Sesquicentennial Committee. *Colorado County Sesquicentennial Commemorative Book*. La Grange, Tex.: Hengst Printing & Supplies, [ca. 1986].

Comanche County Centennial Association. *Comanche County Centennial, 1886–1956, July 1 thru 7, Official Souvenir Program*. [Comanche, Tex.]: Comanche County Centennial Association, [1956].

Comstock Study Club. *Comstock: Friends & Neighbors*. [Comstock, Tex.]: privately printed, [1976].

Conkling, Roscoe P., and Margaret B. Conkling. *The Butterfield Overland Mail 1857–1869*. 2 vols. Glendale, Calif.: Arthur H. Clark Company, 1947.

Conn, Jerry. "77 Years Ago Today: 'Fun' in a Flood." *San Angelo (Tex.) Evening Standard*, 24 August 1959, sec. A, p. 1.

Cornett, Steve. "Medicine Mounds Break Horizon on Rolling Ranch Land: Stark, Low Hills Sentinel-like as Town Lives and Dies." *Amarillo (Tex.) Sunday News-Globe*, 11 June 1972, sec. B, p. 1.

Corning, Leavitt, Jr. *Baronial Forts of the Big Bend: Ben Leaton, Milton Faver, and Their Private Forts in Presidio County*. San Antonio: Trinity University Press, 1967.

Coryell County Genealogical Society. *Coryell County, Texas, Families 1854–1985*. 2 vols. Dallas: Taylor Publishing, 1986–87.

"Council Meets Tonight: Brownwood Evacuation Area May Be Reduced." *Baytown (Tex.) Sun*, 26 November 1979, sec. A, p. 1.

Cox, Edwin T. *History of Eastland County, Texas*. San Antonio: Naylor Company, 1950.

Cox, Mary L. *History of Hale County, Texas*. Plainview, Tex.: privately printed, 1937.

Cox, Mike. *Red Rooster Country: A Ragtag Collection of Stories about a Hunk of the Lone Star State Larger Than Ohio*. Hereford, Tex.: Pioneer Book Publishers, 1970.

Craddock, Lelia Davis. "The History of Education in Hamilton County." Master's thesis, Baylor University, 1953.

Crane, R. C. "Ghost Towns of West Texas." *West Texas Historical Association Year Book* 7 (1941): 3–10.

Creighton, James A. *A Narrative History of Brazoria County*. [Angleton, Tex.]: Brazoria County Historical Commission, 1975.

Crews, D'Anne McAdams. *Huntsville and Walker County, Texas: A Bicentennial History*. Huntsville, Tex.: Sam Houston State University Press, 1976.

Crittenden, Pauline. "Texas Tours: Wizardry Returns After Well's Dry Spell." *Dallas Morning News*, 24 September 1978, sec. O, p. 2.

Crocchiola, Stanley Francis Louis [F. Stanley, pseud.]. *The Glenrio, New Mexico, Story*. Nazareth, Tex.: privately printed, 1973.

———. *The Lipscomb, Texas, Story*. Nazareth, Tex.: privately printed, 1975.

Crook, Cornelia English. *Henry Castro: A Study of Early Colonization in Texas*. San Antonio: St. Mary's University Press, 1988.

———. *The Story of D'Hanis*. Hondo, Tex.: Anvil Herald, 1961.

Crosby County Historical Commission. *A History of Crosby County 1876–1977*. [Crosbyton, Tex.]: Crosby County Historical Commission, 1978.

Cross, Mary. Interview by T. Lindsay Baker. Justiceburg, Tex., 20 May 1971. Typescript in possession of author.

Crouch, Carrie J. *A History of Young County, Texas*. Austin: Texas State Historical Association, 1956.

Curtis, Sara Kay. "A History of Gillespie County, Texas, 1846–1900." Master's thesis, University of Texas, 1943.

Dalby, N. L., and Roy Dalby. "Gone with the Wind, Dalby Springs of Old: Sick and Lame Long Gone, but Springs Remain at Once Popular Health Resort." *Texarkana (Tex.) Gazette*, 24 December 1961, sec. B, p. 4–5.

Danevang Community Anniversary, Danevang, Texas, 1894–1944, Translation 1976. N.p., [ca. 1976].

Daniels, James Morris. "I Dig the Past on Wallis Hill." *Texas Historian* 46, no. 1 (September 1985): 1–5.

Dapeer, Barry. "Ghost Towns of Texas." Typescript. 1958. "Ghost Towns" vertical file, Daughters of the Republic of Texas Library, San Antonio.

Davidson, Darrell. "The Town of Washington: Its Place in Texas History and Its Restoration." *Houston Chronicle*, 15 February 1970, magazine section, pp. 18–23.

Davis, E. Mott, and James E. Corbin. *Archeological Investigations at Washington-on-the-Brazos State Park*. State Building Commission Archeological Program Report, no. 5. Austin: State Building Commission, 1967.

Davis, John L. *The Danish Texans.* San Antonio: University of Texas Institute of Texan Cultures at San Antonio, 1979.

Davis, Kathleen M. "Hueco Tanks Rock Art—A Story of Our Past." *Password* 19, no. 2 (Summer 1974): 97–98.

Deaf Smith County Historical Society. *The Land & Its People 1876–1981: Deaf Smith County Texas.* [Hereford, Tex.]: Deaf Smith County Historical Society, 1982.

Deal, Jerry. "Catarina Now Sleeps Quietly as Boom Days of '20's Fade." *San Antonio Express and News*, 17 September 1962, sec. A, p. 14.

Debo, Darrell. *Burnet County History: A Pioneer History 1847–1979.* 2 vols. Burnet: Burnet County Historical Commission, 1979.

"Dedication Slated in Serbin." *Austin American*, 10 April 1970, p. 23.

Deener, Bill. "A King Comes Calling: Norwegian Monarch to Visit Texas Town." *Dallas Morning News*, 1 August 1982, sec. AA, pp. 1, 11.

"Deep in the Dirt of Texas: Hope of a Cure Brings the Sick to Try Out 'Radioactive' Dirt." *Life* 39, no. 17 (24 October 1955): 57–58.

"Descendants Pay Tribute to Pioneer: Centennial of Norwegian Farmer's Voyage to U.S. Is Commemorated." *Fort Worth Star- Telegram*, 15 September 1946, sec. I, p. 11.

DeShields, James T. *Border Wars of Texas.* Edited by Matt Bradley. Tioga, Tex.: Herald Company, 1912.

————. *Cynthia Ann Parker: The Story of Her Capture.* St. Louis: privately printed, 1886.

————, comp. and ed. *Tall Men with Long Rifles: The Glamorous Story of the Texas Revolution, as Told by Captain Creed Taylor, Who Fought in That Heroic Struggle from Gonzales to San Jacinto.* San Antonio: Naylor Company, 1935.

Dickerson, Patricia Wood, Margaret Skeels Stevens, and James Bowie Stevens, eds. *Geology of the Big Bend and Trans-Pecos Region: Field Trip Guidebook of the South Texas Geological Society, San Antonio, Texas.* San Antonio: South Texas Genealogical Society, 1990.

Dietrich, Wilfred O. *The Blazing Story of Washington County.* N.p.: privately printed, 1950.

"Diocese Says Ruidosa Church Should Be Torn Down." *Marfa (Tex.) Big Bend Sentinel*, 21 November 1991, p. 5.

Dixon, Bobby. "Ghost Towns of the South Texas Coast." *The Junior Historian* 7, no. 1 (September 1946): 27–28.

Dobie, Dudley R. "Lagarto Near Vanishing Point, Once Flourishing College Town." *San Antonio Express*, 18 November 1934, sec. D, pp. 1, 5.

"Dolores: Two Ghost Towns." *Laredo (Tex.) Times*, 8 November 1981, centennial edition, sec. HH, p. 2.

Dominguez, Dixie L. "Hueco Tanks: A Vital Resource in Southwestern History." *Password* 31, no. 3 (Fall 1986): 123–36.

Dominy, Myrtis, and Norton Fox. *History of Prairie Hill, a Central Texas Community.* N.p.: Prairie Hill Ex-students Assn., 1981.

Donoghue, Jack Vincent. "Washington on the Brazos." Master's thesis, University of Texas, 1935.

Dooley, Claude W., comp. *Why Stop? Lone Star Legends.* Odessa, Tex.: Lone Star Legends Company, 1978.

Downie, Alice Evans. *Terrell County, Texas, Its Past—Its People.* Sanderson, Tex.: Terrell County Heritage Commission, 1978.

Draeger, Joan. "Don Pedrito—The Great Faith Healer." *The Junior Historian* 24, no. 5 (March 1964): 1–5, 31.

Drago, Harry Sinclair. *Red River Valley: The Mainstream of Frontier History from the Louisiana Bayous to the Texas Panhandle.* New York: Clarkson N. Potter, Inc., 1962.

"Drag Strip Construction Underway." *Monahans (Tex.) Sandhills Free Press*, 14 July 1966, p. 3.

Draughon, Guy. "Ft. Parker Rises as Memorial to Cynthia Ann, Quanah." *Fort Worth Star-Telegram*, 4 April 1965, sec. 1, p. 17.

Duncan, Charles. "Old Mill—Symbol of Eliasville." *The Junior Historian* 13, no. 3 (December 1952): 21–22.

Dworaczyk, Edward J. *The First Polish Colonies of America in Texas.* San Antonio: Naylor Company, 1936.

Early Settlers of Terry: A History of Terry County, Texas. Hereford, Tex.: Pioneer Book Publishers, 1968.

An Economic Survey of Gaines, Terry, and Yoakum Counties, Texas. Lubbock: Division of Business Administration, Texas Technological College, 1953.

Ehresman, Allen. Interview by T. Lindsay Baker. Endee, N. Mex., 6 February 1987. Typescript in possession of author.

1869–1969, Our Savior's Lutheran Church Centennial Celebration, June 28–29, 1969. [Norse, Tex.]: privately printed, [1969].

"Eliasville: Home of UT Presidents." *Wichita Falls (Tex.) Times*, 29 February 1976, sec. E, p. 9.

Elliott, Alline Halliburton. *Rural Schools of Llano County from 1854 to 1948.* N.p.: privately printed, [ca. 1986].

"El Paso Diocese Reviewing Decision on Ruidosa Church." *Marfa (Tex.) Big Bend Sentinel*, 23 November 1991, p. 2.

Embry, Ann Thurston. "Medicine Mound Takes Name from Ancient Indian Legend." *Quanah (Tex.) Tribune-Chief*, 1 May 1958, sec. 2, p. 3.

Engerrand, George C. *The So-called Wends of Germany and Their Colonies in Texas and Australia.* University of Texas Bulletin, no. 3417. Austin: University of Texas, 1934.

Erwin, Ed. "Quintana Beach an Easy Coast." *Houston Chronicle*, 17 December 1995, Texas supplement, p. 6.

Escamilla, Romella G., ed. *The Spirit of Val Verde.* Del Rio, Tex.: Diana Sotelo Vertuche, 1985.

"Faced Flood by Herself: Mrs. D. Q. McCarty Lost Friends in Deluge at Ben Ficklin." *San Angelo (Tex.) Standard-Times*, 3 May 1934, sec. 4, p. 8.

Farris, Frances Bramlette. *From Rattlesnakes to Road Agents: Rough Times on the Frio.* Edited by C. L. Sonnichsen. Fort Worth: Texas Christian University Press, 1985.

———. "Recalls Old Days at Frio Town." *Frontier Times* 25, no. 5 (February 1948): 131–33.

"F. C. Taylor Won for Ben Ficklin." *San Angelo (Tex.) Standard*, 3 May 1924, sec. 1, p. 1.

Federal Emergency Management Agency. *Flood Insurance Study, City of Baytown, Texas, Harris and Chambers Counties, March 4, 1987, Community No. 485456.* [Washington, D.C.]: Federal Management Agency, 1987. Microfiche FEM 1.209: 485456/987.

Ficklen, Mary. "The Midas-rich Town That Might Have Been." *Dallas Morning News*, 23 May 1976, sec. G, pp. 1, 4.

Fiorini, Phillip. "Ghost Towns Only a Memory of Boom Days in Panhandle." *Amarillo (Tex.) Daily News*, 31 October 1985, sec. C, pp. 1–2.

Fisher County Historical Commission and the Sheltons. *History of Fisher County,* Texas. Rotan, Tex.: Fisher County Historical Commission and the Sheltons, 1983.

Fisher, O. C. *It Occurred in Kimble.* Houston: Anson Jones Press, 1937.

Flannery, John Brendan. *The Irish Texans.* San Antonio: University of Texas Institute of Texan Cultures at San Antonio, 1980.

Fohn, Joe. "Like People, Town's Landmark Is Moving." *San Antonio Express*, 27 August 1981, sec. A, p. 2.

Fore, Roger W. "Ghost Playground." *San Antonio Express*, 15 February 1948, magazine section, p. 16.

Fowler, Gene. *Crazy Water: The Story of Mineral Wells and Other Texas Health Resorts.* Fort Worth: Texas Christian University Press, 1991.

Fox, Anne A. "Old Wallisville Town Site." Typescript Nomination to the National Register of Historic Places. 1981. Office of National Register Programs, Texas Historical Commission.

Fox, Anne A., D. William Day, and Lynn Highley. *Archaeological and Historical Investigations at Wallisville Lake, Chambers and Liberty Counties, Texas.* University of Texas at San Antonio Center for Archaeological Research, Archaeological Survey Report, no. 90. San Antonio: University of Texas at San Antonio, 1980.

Fox, Daniel E. *Traces of Texas History: Archeological Evidence of the Past 450 Years.* San Antonio: Corona Publishing Company, 1983.

Freehling, Michael. *Hueco Tanks State Historical Park, El Paso County, Texas.* TSNL Laboratory Index Series, no. 4–76. Austin: Texas System of Natural Laboratories, 1976.

Freeman, Martha Doty. *A History of Civil War Military Activities at Velasco and Quintana, Brazoria County, and at Virginia Point, Galveston County, Texas.* Reports of Investigations, no. 103. Austin: Prewitt and Associates, 1995.

———. *A History of Quintana, a Nineteenth-century Coastal Port in Brazoria County, Texas.* Reports of Investigations, no. 117. Austin: Prewitt and Associates, 1998.

Freeman, Martha Doty, and Douglas K. Boyd. *Phase II Historical Investigations at Justiceburg Reservoir, Garza and Kent Counties, Texas.* Reports of Investigations, no. 72. Austin: Prewitt and Associates, 1990.

Freeman, Martha Doty, Marie E. Blake, and Elton R. Prewitt. *Archival and Archeological Investigations at Quintana Townsite and Fort Terrell, Brazoria County, Texas.* Reports of Investigations, no. 118. Austin: Prewitt and Associates, 1997.

Frio County Centennial Corporation. *Historic Frio County 1871–1971.* Pearsall, Tex.: Frio County Centennial Corporation, [ca. 1971].

Fry, Tillie Badu Moss. "A History of Llano County, Texas." Master's thesis, University of Texas, 1943.

Fuller, Frank. *Subsidized Destruction: The Wallisville Lake Project and Galveston Bay.* Austin: Texas Center for Policy Studies, 1995.

Funderburk, Delva. "Old Fort Parker." *The Junior Historian* 8, no. 3 (December 1947): 5–8.

Fuqua, Debbie L. "Washington-on-the-Brazos: Its History and Relationship with the Land." Manuscript. 1974. "Washington-on-the-Brazos" vertical files, Texas Collection, Baylor University.

Gabrysch, R. K., and C. W. Bonnet. *Land-surface Subsidence in the Area of Burnet, Scott, and Crystal Bays Near Baytown, Texas.* U.S. Geological Survey Water-Resources Investigations, 21–74. Austin: U.S. Geological Survey, 1974.

Gard, Wayne. *The Chisholm Trail.* Norman: University of Oklahoma Press, 1954.

———. *The First 100 Years of Texas Oil and Gas.* Dallas: Texas Mid-Continent Oil & Gas Association, [ca. 1965].

———. "Retracing the Chisholm Trail." *Southwestern Historical Quarterly*, extra number (1 May 1956): 1–24.

Garza County Historical Survey Committee. *Wagon Wheels: A History of Garza County.* Seagraves, Tex.: Pioneer Book Publishers, 1973.

"Gateway to the West:" Eastland County History. [Eastland, Tex.]: Eastland County Book Committee, 1989.

Gay, Beatrice Grady. *"Into the Setting Sun:" A History of Coleman County.* N.p.: privately printed, n.d.

Geiser, Samuel Wood. "Ghost-towns and Lost-towns of Texas, 1840–1880." *The Texas Geographic Magazine* 8, no. 1 (Spring 1944): 9–20.

Ghormley, Pearl. *Eastland County, Texas: A Historical and Biographical Survey.* Austin: Rupegy Publishing Company, 1969.

190

Ghost Towns Scrapbooks. Center for American History, University of Texas at Austin.

Gibson, Joe E. *Old Angelo.* San Angelo, Tex.: Minuteman Press, [ca. 1971].

Gillespie County Historical Society. *Pioneers in God's Hills: A History of Fredericksburg and Gillespie County: People and Events.* 2 vols. Fredericksburg, Tex.: Gillespie County Historical Society, 1960–74.

Glendinning, Jim. "Historic Hot Springs Resort Reopens." *The Desert Candle* (Alpine, Tex.) 12, no. 2 (April–June 1998): 1, 11.

Gómez, Arthur R. "The Glen Springs-Boquillas Raid Reconsidered: Diplomatic Intrigue on the Rio Grande." *The Journal of Big Bend Studies* 4 (1992): 97–113.

————. *A Most Singular Country: A History of Occupation in the Big Bend.* Charles Redd Monographs in Western History, no. 18. Provo: Brigham Young University Charles Redd Center for Western Studies, 1990.

Gone, but Not Forgotten: A Cemetery Survey of Crosby County, Texas. Crosbyton, Tex.: Crosby County Pioneer Memorial, 1983.

Gonzales County Historical Commission. *The History of Gonzales County, Texas.* Dallas: Curtis Media Corporation, 1986.

Goodwin, Mrs. Jack. *"Ghost Towns" We Have Known.* N.p.: Trinity District Texas Federation of Women's Clubs, [ca. 1976].

Graham, Bill. "Ghost Town—S. Texas Style." *San Antonio Sunday Express and News*, 22 August 1971, sec. H, p. 1.

Graham, J. O., comp. *The Book of Wharton County, Texas, Containing Outstanding Facts About Its History, Industries, Resources, Developments and Opportunities.* [Wharton, Tex.]: Philip Rich, [ca. 1926].

"Grapetown Homecoming Set Sunday." *Fredericksburg (Tex.) Standard*, 9 June 1976, p. 9.

"Grapetown Schuetzen Verein 1888." *Fredericksburg (Tex.) Radio Post*, 4 May 1946, sec. D, p. 10.

Green, Boyd. Interview by T. Lindsay Baker. Chillicothe, Tex., 28 February 1987. Manuscript notes in possession of author.

Greene, A. C. "Past Almost Palpable at Redone Fort Parker." *Dallas Morning News*, 13 January 1991, sec. J, p. 9.

————. *A Personal Country.* College Station: Texas A&M University Press, 1969.

Gregg, John Ernest. "The History of Presidio County." Master's thesis, University of Texas, 1933.

Grider, Sylvia Ann. *The Wendish Texas.* San Antonio: University of Texas Institute of Texan Cultures, 1982.

Grimes County Historical Commission. *History of Grimes County, Land of Heritage and Progress.* Dallas: Taylor Publishing Company, 1982.

Grimm, Agnes C. *Llanos Mestenas: Mustang Plains.* Waco: Texian Press, 1968.

Grothe, Randy Eli. "'Honey, We're Sinking.'" *Dallas Morning News*, 9 April 1978, sec. G, p. 1.

Grusendorf, Arthur A. "A Century of Education in Washington County, Texas." Typescript. 1940. Texas Collection, Baylor University.

Guthrie, Keith. *Texas Forgotten Ports.* 3 vols. Austin: Eakin Press, 1988–95.

Habermacher, Ursula. "D'Hanis." *The Junior Historian* 24, no. 3 (December 1963): 24–28, 32.

Hable, Nancy. "Magnolia on the Trinity." *The Junior Historian* 28, no. 4 (January 1968): 22–23.

"Hackberry, Texas" vertical file. Friench Simpson Memorial Library, Hallettsville, Tex.

Hailey, Mike. "Royal Festivity: Norse Plays Host to King of Norway." *Waco Tribune-Herald*, 11 October 1982, sec. A, pp. 1–2.

Haley, J. Evetts. *Charles Goodnight: Cowman and Plainsman.* Norman: University of Oklahoma Press, 1949.

Hall, Margaret Elizabeth. *A History of Van Zandt County.* Austin: Jenkins Publishing Company, Pemberton Press, 1976.

Hamilton County Historical Commission. *A History of Hamilton County, Texas.* Hamilton, Tex.: Hamilton County Historical Commission, 1979.

Hanna, Bill. "Park Restrictions Frustrate Rock Climbers: Hueco Tanks Tries to Protect Ancient Cave Pictographs." *Houston Chronicle*, 30 July 2000, sec. E, p. 5.

Hannum, Helen Kothe. "Cherry Spring, Texas—Its History Seasoned with Legend." *Fredericksburg (Tex.) Radio Post*, 6 May 1971, sec. 4, pp. 4–5.

Hansford County Historical Commission. *Hansford County, Texas.* 2 vols. Spearman, Tex.: Hansford County Historical Commission, [ca. 1980–83].

Hardeman County Agricultural and Industrial Edition. Quanah, Tex.: Quanah Tribune-Chief, [ca. 1928].

Harry, Jewel Horace. *A History of Chambers County.* Dallas: Chambers County Historical Commission, 1981.

Hayes, Robert M. "Excavations Show Mysterious Cherokee County Indian Hills Antedate White Men in Texas." *Dallas Morning News*, 9 March 1941, sec. I, p. 8.

————. "Indian Mound in East Texas Is Excavated: Data of Historical Value Sought by WPA Workers Directed by University Man." *Dallas Morning News*, 10 December 1939, sec. I, p. 14.

Haynes, Emma R. *The History of Polk County.* N.p.: privately printed, 1937.

Hayter, Delmar J. "The Crookedest River in the World: Social and Economic Development of the Pecos River Valley, 1878–1950." Ph.D. diss., Texas Tech University, 1988.

Heard, J. Norman. "Ghost Town Resurrection." *The Lufkin Line* (Lufkin Foundry and Machine Company, Lufkin, Tex.) 24, no. 3 (September-October 1949): 4–9.

"Heart of Texas Marker." *Brady (Tex.) Standard*, 14 May 1976, sec. VII, p. 1.

Hecht, Arthur. *Postal History in the Texas Panhandle: Compiled from Postal Records in the National Archives*. Canyon, Tex.: Panhandle-Plains Historical Society, 1950.

Helton, R. M. "Bob." Interview by T. Lindsay Baker. Burkburnett Oil Field, Wichita County, Texas, 23 April 1987. Typewritten notes in possession of author.

Henry, Christopher D. *1979 Geologic Setting and Geochemistry of Thermal Water and Geothermal Assessment, Trans-Pecos Texas, with Tectonic Map of the Rio Grande Area, Trans- Pecos Texas and Adjacent Mexico*. University of Texas at Austin, Bureau of Economic Geology, Report of Investigations, no. 96. Austin: Bureau of Economic Geology, University of Texas, 1979.

Henson, Margaret Swett. *History of Baytown*. Baytown, Tex.: Bay Area Heritage Society, 1986.

Henson, Margaret Swett, and Kevin Ladd. *Chambers County: A Pictorial History*. Norfolk, Va.: Donning Company, Publishers, 1988.

Heritage Committee of the Polk County Bicentennial Committee and the Polk County Historical Commission. *A Pictorial History of Polk County, Texas (1846–1910)*. Rev. ed. [Livingston, Tex.]: Heritage Committee of the Polk County Bicentennial Committee and the Polk County Historical Commission, 1978.

Heritage Division Committee. *Patchwork Memories: Historical Sketches of Comanche County, Texas*. Comanche, Tex.: Heritage Division of Comanche County Bicentennial Committee, 1976.

Hewitt, William Phillip. "The Czechs in Texas: A Study of the Immigration and the Development of Ethnicity 1850–1920." Ph.D. diss., University of Texas at Austin, 1978.

Higdon, Mrs. Grady. "Obscurity Shrouds Thriving Frio Town Almost Overnight." *San Antonio Sunday Express and News*, 29 September 1963, sec. A, p. 10.

Hill, Frank P. "Plains Names." *Panhandle-Plains Historical Review* 10 (1937): 36–47.

Hillen, Michelle. "Fort Parker Building New Visitors Center: Site Intended to House Artifacts, Give Visitors Shelter." *Waco Tribune-Herald*, 29 August 2000, sec. A, pp. 1, 7.

———. "Local Governments Receive Old Fort Parker, $550,000: Groesbeck, Mexia to Share Operation of Historical Park in Limestone County." *Waco Tribune-Herald*, 2 September 2000, sec. B, pp. 1, 10.

Hines, Margaret Howard, ed. *Archeological Survey of Fort Parker State Park, Limestone County, Texas*. Texas Antiquities Committee Permit, no. 1461. Austin: Cultural Resources Program, Public Lands Division, Texas Parks and Wildlife Department, 1996.

Historic Matagorda County. 2 vols. Houston, Tex.: D. Armstrong, 1986.

History Book Committee of Houston County Historical Commission. *History of Houston County, Texas, 1687–1979*. Tulsa: Heritage Publishing Company, 1979.

"History of Frio Town." Mimeographed. N.d. "Ghost Towns" vertical file, University of Texas Institute of Texan Cultures, San Antonio, Tex.

A History of Post Offices and Communities: First Congressional District of Texas: Lamar County. Texarkana, Tex.: Wright Patman, 1968.

Hohenberger, Cynthia. "The Grapetown Legacy." *The Junior Historian* 26, no. 1 (September 1965): 6–9, 25.

Hole, Frank, ed. *The Quintana Townsite, Brazoria County, Texas*. 4 vols. Yale University, Department of Anthropology, Reports in Archeology, no. 1. [New Haven, Conn.]: Department of Anthropology, Yale University, 1982.

Holland, Paige. "The History of Dam B, Tyler County, Texas, and Its Relationship to the Land." Typescript. 1982. "Dam B, Texas" vertical file, Texas Collection, Baylor University.

Hollenbeck, Alfred, Jr. "Marines, BP Agents Save Candelaria from Grassfires." *Presidio (Tex.) International*, 2 April 1998, pp. 1–2.

Holley, Joe. "Lively in Lipscomb." *Texas Co-op Power* 56, no. 7 (January 2000): 6–9, 12.

Hollingsworth, Tommy. "Rattlesnake Air Force Base." *Texas Historian* 34, no. 5 (May 1974): 31–32.

Horton, Thomas F. *History of Jack County, Being Accounts of Pioneer Times, Excerpts from County Court Records, Indian Stories, Biographical Sketches, and Interesting Events*. Jacksboro, Tex.: Gazette Print, [1932].

House, Boyce. *Roaring Ranger: The World's Biggest Boom*. San Antonio: Naylor Company, 1951.

Housewright, Ed. "Faith in the Country: Award-winning Pastor Knows Joys, Difficulties of Small-town Ministry." *Dallas Morning News*, 9 October 1994, sec. A, pp. 1, 30–31.

Huckabay, Ida Lasater. *Ninety-four Years in Jack County 1854–1948*. Jacksboro, Tex.: privately printed, 1949.

"Hueco Tanks: Epicenter of the Southwest's Pueblo Culture." *Texas Parks & Wildlife* 56, no. 2 (February 1998): 19–21.

Hughes, Alton. *Pecos: A History of the Pioneer West*. 2 vols. Seagraves, Tex.: Pioneer Book Publishers, 1978–81.

Hulbert, Harry. "'Old Trickham' of Cattle Trail Days." *Frontier Times* 27, no. 5 (February 1950): 148–49.

Huson, Hobart. *Texas Coastal Bend Trilogy: Two Sea-captains Johnson, El Copano, St. Mary's of Aransas*. Edited by Kathleen Huson Maxwell. Austin: Eakin Press, 1994.

192

———. *Refugio: A Comprehensive History of Refugio County from Aboriginal Times to 1955.* 2 vols. Woodsboro, Tex.: Rooke Foundation, 1955.

Hutcheson, Barry W. *The Trans-Pecos: A Historical Survey and Guide to Historic Sites.* Texas Tech University, College of Agricultural Sciences, Department of Park Administration, Horticulture, and Entomology, Research Report, no. 3. Lubbock: Texas Tech University, 1970.

Hutcheson, Nita Fran. "Ghost Towns of Texas." *The Junior Historian* 20, no. 4 (January 1960): 9–12, 20.

Jack County Genealogical Society. *The History of Jack County, Texas.* Dallas: Curtis Media Corporation, 1985.

Jackson, A. T. "Many Texas Cities Have Vanished." *Frontier Times* 7, no. 8 (May 1930): 357–59.

James, Vinton L. "Recollections of the Sheep Range." *Frontier Times* 5, no. 9 (June 1928): 356–59.

Jasper County Historical Survey. *Historically Marked Sites in Jasper County.* N.p.: Jasper County Historical Survey Committee, 1973.

Jayne, Linda. "Hurricane Carla and Her Legacy." In *Baytown Vignettes: One Hundred and Fifty Years in the History of a Texas Gulf Coast Community,* compiled and edited by John Britt and Muriel Tyssen. Baytown, Tex.: Lee College, 1992.

Jefferson County Historical Commission. *Dedication of Spanish-American War Foritifcations Historical Marker, 3:00 p.m., June 25, 1983.* [Beaumont, Tex.]: Jefferson County Historical Commission, 1983.

Jefferson County Historical Commission. *Dedication of Texas State Historical Marker, City of Sabine and Sabine Pass, Lions Park, Sabine Pass, Texas, Saturday, April 20, 1991, 11:00 a.m.* [Beaumont, Tex.]: Jefferson County Historical Commission, 1991.

Jenkins, John H., comp. *Cracker Barrel Chronicles: A Bibliography of Texas Towns and County Histories.* Austin: Pemberton Press, 1965.

Johnson, B. B. "Wallisville, Texas." Typescript. [ca. 1935.] Chambers County Materials, Center for American History, University of Texas at Austin.

Jones, Dotty. *A Search for Opportunity: A History of Hansford County.* Gruver, Tex.: Jones Publishing Company, 1965.

Jones, Lawrence T., III. "Cynthia Ann Parker and Pease Ross—The Forgotten Photographs." *Southwestern Historical Quarterly* 93, no. 3 (January 1990): 379–84.

Jones, Marie Beth. "The Quintana Story." *Brazosport (Texas) Facts,* 31 January 1960, p. 1; 3 February 1960, p. 1; 7 February 1960, p. 1; 10 February 1960, p. 1; 14 February 1960, p. 1; 17 February 1960, p. 1; 21 February 1960, p. 1; 24 February 1960, p. 1.

———. "Quintana Tale Revived Memories." *Brazosport Facts,* 6 March 1960, p. 1.

Judd, Donald. "La Mision del Sagrado Corazon." *Marfa (Tex.) Big Bend Sentinel,* 21 November 1991, p. 5.

Justice, Glenn. *Odessa: An Illustrated History.* Chatsworth, Calif.: Windsor Publications, 1991.

———. *Revolution on the Rio Grande: Mexican Raids and Army Pursuits 1916–1919.* Southwestern Studies, no. 95. El Paso: Texas Western Press, 1992.

Kegley, George. *Archeological Investigations at 41EP2, Hueco Tanks State Park, El Paso County, Texas.* Austin: Texas Parks and Wildlife Department, 1980.

Kelley, Dayton. "Serbin Is Wend Heaven." *Houston Chronicle,* 13 April 1958, magazine section, pp. 36–37.

Kelly, Louise, comp. *Wichita County Beginnings.* Burnet, Tex.: Eakin Press; Wichita Falls, Tex.: Wichita County Historical Commission, 1982.

Kelso, John. "At Road's End: Politics Boils Down to Precious Little to Texas Town." *Austin American-Statesman,* 19 September 1989, sec. A, pp. 1, 6.

Kenmotsu, Nancy A., Timothy K. Perttula, Patricia Mercado-Allinger, James E. Bruseth, Sergio Iruegas, and Curtis Tunnell. *Archeological and Documentary Research at Medicine Mounds Ranch, Hardeman County, Texas.* Texas Historical Commission Department of Antiquities Protection Cultural Resource Management Report, no. 4. Austin: Texas Historical Commission, 1994.

Kennedy, Randy. "Much of West Texas Stays Dry, No Matter If It Rains or It Shines." *Waco Tribune-Herald,* 30 November 1997, sec. B, p. 4.

Kerr, Bob. "Death of College Ended Goodnight's Pioneer Boom: Town, School History Take Similar Turn." *Amarillo (Tex.) Sunday News-Globe,* 5 May 1963, sec. D, p. 1.

Kerr, Ralph M. "The Development of the Schools of Archer County, Texas." Master's thesis, Baylor University, 1950.

Kilian, John. *Baptismal Records of St. Paul Lutheran Church, Serbin, Texas, 1854–1883.* Translated and edited by Joseph Wilson. Easley, S.C.: Southern Historical Press, 1985.

Killen, Mrs. James C., ed. *History of Lee County, Texas.* Quanah, Tex.: Nortex Press, 1974.

Kimble County Historical Commission. *Families of Kimble County.* Junction, Tex.: Kimble County Historical Commission, 1985.

Kimble County Historical Survey Committee. *Recorded Landmarks of Kimble County.* Junction, Tex.: Kimble County Historical Survey Committee, 1971.

King, Dick. *Ghost Towns of Texas.* San Antonio: Naylor Company, 1953.

"King of Norway Visits County." *Iredell (Tex.) Times,* 14 October 1982, p. 6.

Kirk, Wylene. "Early Post Offices and Towns in the Permian Basin Area." *Texas Permian Historical Annual* 1 (1961): 11–21.

Klym, Kendall. "The Ways of the Wends." *Austin American-Statesman*, 5 March 2000, sec. D, p. 3.

Koethe, Jim. "Eliasville Still Has Look of Western Town." In *Scrapbook of Young County*, edited by Barbara Neal Ledbetter. Graham, Tex.: Graham News, 1966.

Krisch, Lucille Stewart. "Twigs and Trees: Stories of Ghost Towns." *San Antonio Light*, 28 April 1957, sec. D, p. 20.

Krizak, Jeanette. "Oil, Race Track Keep Penwell on the Map." *Odessa (Tex.) American*, 1 March 1991, sec. B, pp. 1–2.

Krupica, Richard. "An Annotated Bibliography on Ghost Towns in the State of Texas." Typescript. 1974. "Ghost Towns Term Papers" vertical file, Texas Collection, Baylor University.

Ladd, Kevin. "Wallisville: A Crossroads of Cultures." *Touchstone* 11 (1992): 57–61.

La Gesse, David. "Marines Repairing Road, Image: Border Residents Wary After Teen's Death Despite Aid in War on Drugs." *Dallas Morning News*, 15 March 1998, sec. A, pp. 45, 52–53.

"Lamar Cemetery a Place of Peace, Calm." *Rockport (Tex.) Pilot*, 26 October 1991, Winter Visitor's Guide section, pp. 52, 54.

Landrum, Jeff. *Reflections of a Boomtown: A Photographic Essay of the Burkburnett Oil Boom.* Wichita Falls, Tex.: Humphrey Printing Company, 1982.

Langford, J. A., and Fred Gipson. *Big Bend: A Homesteader's Story.* Austin: University of Texas Press, 1955.

Langston, Mrs. George. *History of Eastland County, Texas.* Dallas: A. D. Aldridge & Co., 1904.

La Roche, Clarence. "The Lost Lamar Cemetery." *San Antonio Express*, 6 April 1952, magazine section, p. 21.

Lasater, Dale. *Falfurrias: Ed C. Lasater and the Development of South Texas.* College Station: Texas A&M University Press, 1985.

Lassiter, Berta Clark. *We Come and Go: A Handbook for the Big Bend National Park.* San Antonio: Naylor Company, 1949.

Lee, Steven H. "Ranching Losses Hit Tiny Town: Rural Texans Struggle to Maintain Economy, History, Lifestyle." *Dallas Morning News*, 9 April 1995, sec. A, p. 34.

Leggett, Mike. "State Moves to Halt Damage to Indian Art: Rising Park Use Prompts Protection to Ancient Paintings in West Texas." *Austin American-Statesman*, 23 August 1998, sec. A, pp. 1, 14.

Leshner, William. "The White City on the Sap." *The Texas Magazine* 1, no. 6 (April 1910): 75-76.

Leslie, Candace. "Birthplace of Texas Independence: Washington-on-the-Brazos State Historical Park." *Texas Highways* 46, no. 3 (March 1999): 18–25.

Lewis, Glenn. "Brownwood Bond Vote Scheduled." *Houston Post*, 24 June 1979, sec. A, p. 13.

———. "Plan to Buy Brownwood Lots for Barge Terminal Criticized." *Houston Post*, 3 August 1979, sec. A, p. 7.

Lewis, Holden. "The Challenge of Gravity: Hueco Tanks Chalks Up Marks with Climbers." *Houston Post*, 3 April 1988, sec. H, p. 5.

Limestone County Historical Museum Members. *A Family History of Limestone County.* Dallas: Limestone County Historical Museum Board, [ca. 1986].

Link, Henry. "All Aboard for Magnolia." *The Junior Historian* 17, no. 1 (September 1956): 17–20.

Lipscomb County Historical Survey Committee. *A History of Lipscomb County.* Lipscomb, Tex.: Lipscomb County Historical Survey Committee, 1976.

Live Oak County Centennial Association, Inc. *Live Oak County Centennial Association, Inc., Presents the First Century of Progress, 1856–1956, Celebration: May 2–3–4–5, 1956.* [George West, Tex.]: Live Oak County Centennial Association, Inc., 1956.

Live Oak County Historical Commission. *The History of the People of Live Oak County, Texas, 1856 to 1982.* [Oakville, Tex.]: Live Oak County Historical Commission, [ca. 1982].

Loftin, Jack. *Trails Through Archer: A Centennial History—1880–1980.* Burnet, Tex.: Eakin Publications, 1979.

Lonsdale, John T., and James R. Day. *Geology and Ground-water Resources of Webb County, Texas.* U.S., Department of the Interior, Geological Survey, Water-supply Paper no. 778. Washington, D.C.: Government Printing Office, 1937.

Lyons, Grant. "Livelier Days Recalled: Town of Sabine Evaporates as Post Office Abandoned." *Port Arthur (Tex.) News*, 9 August 1964, sec. C, p. 3.

McAllen, Margaret. *The Heritage Sampler: Selections from the Rich and Colorful History of the Rio Grande Valley.* Rev. ed. Edinburg, Tex.: Hidalgo County Historical Museum, 1992.

McAuliffe, Suzy. "Anniversary of a Tragedy: The Day the Sky Fell on Ben Ficklin." *San Angelo (Tex.) Standard-Times*, 22 August 1982, sec. E, pp. 1–2.

McConal, Jon. "Reunion in Town Famous for Dirt." *Fort Worth Star- Telegram*, 24 May 1988, sec. 1, p. 9.

MacCormack, John. "Isolated Towns Plan New High School: Students Hoping to See End of 80–mile Commute to Classes." *Waco Tribune-Herald*, 27 February 1996, sec. A, p. 3.

McCormick, Darlene. "Innovations Planned for Old Fort Parker: Bed and Breakfast, Cultural Events May Increase Attendance at Historic Site." *Waco Tribune-Herald*, 8 October 1992, sec. D, pp. 1, 5.

———. "2 Area State Parks Set to Close: Agency Wants Limestone County Facilities Shut Down." *Waco Tribune-Herald*, 31 July 1992, sec. C, pp. 1–2.

McCully, John. "A Place Where Time Stood Still: Old Hotel Houses a Family of Five." *San Antonio Sunday Light*, 7 May 1939, sec. 1, p. 15.

194

M'Dermett, Mrs. D. R. P. "Texas Planter 'Carries on' for Great Grandfather." *Dallas Daily Times Herald*, 3 October 1926, sec. 4, p. 1.

McElgunn, Jim. "Preservation: Wallisville Heritage Project." *Texas Heritage* 1, no. 4 (Fall 1984): 15–17.

[McGregor, Stuart.] "Texas Towns of Historic Interest That Have Been Abandoned or Remain Small Towns Today.—'Ghost' Towns and 'Lost' Towns." In *The Texas Almanac and State Industrial Guide*. Dallas: A. H. Belo Corporation, 1936.

[———.] "Texas Towns of Historic Interest That Have Been Abandoned or Remain Small Today. 'Ghost' Towns and 'Lost' Towns." Mimeographed. 1936. "Ghost Towns" vertical file, Center for American History, University of Texas at Austin.

McGrew, Bill Judson. "Petrography of Candelaria Area, Presidio County, Trans-Pecos Texas." Master's thesis, University of Texas, 1955.

McNally, Lori. "The History of Rock Island, Colorado County, Texas, and Its Relationship to the Land." Typescript. 1983. "Rock Island, Texas, Term Papers" vertical file, Texas Collection, Baylor University.

McWilliams, Margaret. "Ghost Town of Red Gold." *The Junior Historian* 18, no. 2 (November 1957): 8–10.

Madison, Virginia, and Hallie Stilwell. *How Come It's Called That? Place Names in the Big Bend Country*. Albuquerque: University of New Mexico Press, 1958.

[Magnolia Town Company, Magnolia, Tex.] *Town of Magnolia*. San Augustine, Tex.: A. W. Canfield, Printer, [1840]. Handbill. Beinecke Library, Yale University, New Haven, Conn.

Mahoney, Richard B., Roger G. Moore, and Sue Winton Moss. *Cultural Resource Investigations and Archeological Inventory of the Baytown Nature Center Park, City of Baytown, Harris County, Texas*. Report of Investigations, no. 243. N.p.: Moore Archeological Consulting, 1999.

Martin, Madeline. "Ghost Towns of the Lower Sabine River." *The Texas Gulf Historical and Biographical Record* 2, no. 1 (November 1966): 7–22; 3, no. 1 (November 1967): 15–25.

Martínez, Arnulfo Simeón. "History of Education in Starr County." Ph.D. diss., University of Texas, 1966.

Martinez, Ronalee S. "Brownwood: From Devastation to Restoration." Typescript. [Ca. 1997.] Webb Historical Society files, Lee College.

Massengill, Fred I. *Texas Towns: Origin of Name and Location of Each of the 2,140 Post Offices in Texas*. Terrell, Tex.: privately printed, 1936.

Maxwell, Ross A. *Big Bend Country: A History of Big Bend National Park*. Big Bend National Park, Tex.: Big Bend Natural History Association, 1985.

———. *The Big Bend of the Rio Grande: A Guide to the Rocks, Landscape, Geologic History, and Settlers of the Area of the Big Bend National Park.* University of Texas Bureau of Economic Geology Guidebook, no. 7. Austin: University of Texas, 1968.

———. *Mineral Resources of South Texas: Region Served Through the Port of Corpus Christi*. University of Texas Bureau of Economic Geology Report of Investigations, no. 43. Austin: University of Texas, 1962.

Mayes, May Louise. "Wallisville." *The Junior Historian* 5, no. 4 (January 1945): 5–6.

Mays, Christi. "Hard Work Pays Off: Men Who Toiled to Build Fort Parker Get Token of Thanks." *Waco Tribune-Herald*, 8 March 1998, sec. B, pp. 1, 10.

Meadows, Emma Lou. *DeKalb and Bowie County: History and Genealogy*. DeKalb, Tex.: privately printed, 1968.

Meadows, John B. Interview by T. Lindsay Baker. Austin, Texas, 12 May 2000. Typewritten notes in possession of author.

"Medicine Mounds Deemed Historically Important." *The Medallion* 31, no. 3–4 (May–June 1994): 3.

Mertz, Richard J. "'No One Can Arrest Me': The Story of Gregorio Cortez." *The Journal of South Texas* 1 (1974): 1–17.

Mewhinney, H. "Old Waverly Inhabitants Disagree on Whereabouts." *Houston Post*, 26 August 1963, sec. 3, p. 9.

Miles, Bob. "Hueco Tanks: Desert Oasis." *Password* 29, no. 2 (Summer 1984): 64–71, 104.

Miles, Elton. *Tales of the Big Bend*. College Station: Texas A&M University Press, 1976.

Miles, Susan, and Mary Bain Spence. "Major Ben Ficklin." *West Texas Historical Association Year Book* 27 (1951): 58–77.

Miller, Mrs. S. G. *Sixty Years in the Nueces Valley, 1870 to 1930*. San Antonio: Naylor Company, 1930.

Miller, Nita. "South Bend Boom Town." In *Scrapbook of Young County*, edited by Barbara Neal Ledbetter. Graham, Tex.: Graham News, 1966.

Miller, Ray. *Ray Miller's Texas Parks: A History and Guide*. Houston: Cordova Press, 1984.

Mills County Historical Commission. *Mills County Memories*. Goldthwaite, Tex.: Mills County Historical Commission, 1994.

Mills, W. S. *History of Van Zandt County*. Canton, Tex.: privately printed, 1950.

Minard, Rosemary. "Romantic Remnant of a Vanished Town: Waverly Cemetery." *Texas Highways* 30, no. 1 (January 1983): 44–47.

Mohon, Monty, and Michelle Mohon. *Gillespie County: A View of Its Past*. Virginia Beach, Va.: Donning Company/Publishers, 1996.

Monahans Junior Chamber of Commerce. *Water, Oil, Sand, and Sky: A History of Ward County, Texas*. Monahans, Tex.: Monahans Junior Chamber of Commerce, [ca.1962].

Moncos, Mary Linn, and Marian Farmer Knapp. *Quay County*. Lubbock: Craftsman Printers, 1985.

195

Montoya, Susan. "2-room Schoolhouse Closes Doors: Parents Say Long, Bumpy Ride Sickening Students." *Harlingen (Tex.) Valley Morning Star*, 15 August 1998, sec. A, p. 5.

Moore, Carolyn. "Annotated Bibliography, Ghost Towns." Typescript. [Ca. 1971.] "Ghost Towns Term Papers" vertical file, Texas Collection, Baylor University.

Moore, Roger G. *Archeological and Historical Investigation of a 5-acre Petroleum and Terminal Corporation Dredge Spoil Disposal Area, Quintana, Brazoria County, Texas.* Report of Investigations no. 124. Houston: Moore Archeological Consulting, 1996.

Moorman, Travis. "Only the Cemetery Remains: Once-Thriving Gussettville Now Overgrown with Weeds." *Corpus Christi (Tex.) Caller-Times*, 7 July 1957, sec. B, p. 10.

Moran, Rhonda. "Quintana's Past Told in 'Jigsaw' Recovery." *Angleton (Tex.) Times* (Angleton, Tex.), 19 December 1979, pp. 1, 14.

Morgan, Lee. Interview by T. Lindsay Baker. Lake Justiceburg, Justiceburg, Texas, 20 May 1971. Typewritten notes in the possession of author.

Morton, Dorothy Virginia. "A History of Quay County, New Mexico." Master's thesis, University of Colorado, 1938.

Moseley, Lou Ella. *Pioneer Days of Tyler County.* Fort Worth: Miran Publishers, 1975.

Most, Melissa M. "D'Hanis, Texas, and Its Relationship to the Land." Typescript. 1981. "D'Hanis, Texas" vertical file, Texas Collection, Baylor University.

Myres, Samuel D. *The Permian Basin: Petroleum Empire of the Southwest.* 2 vols. El Paso: Permian Press, 1973–77.

Nacogdoches Jaycees. *The Bicentennial Commemorative History of Nacogdoches.* [Nacogdoches, Tex.]: Nacogdoches Jaycees, 1976.

Nagle, J. C. *Irrigation in Texas.* U.S., Department of Agriculture, Office of Experiment Stations, Bulletin no. 222. Washington, D.C.: Government Printing Office, 1910.

Neal, Bill. *The Last Frontier: The Story of Hardeman County.* Quanah, Tex.: Quanah Tribune-Chief, 1966.

Neighbors, Camille Yeamans. "The Old Town Saint Mary's on Copano Bay and Some Interesting People Who Once Lived There." Master's thesis, Southwest Texas State Teachers College, 1942.

"Nervy Express Messenger Killed Two Train Robbers." *Frontier Times* 4, no. 11 (August 1927): 52–55.

Nesterowicz, S. *Notatki z Podróży* (Travel Notes). Toledo, Ohio: A. A. Paryski, 1909.

Nethaway, Rowland. "Futile to Seal This Border: Miles of Fence Wouldn't Keep People from Crossing." *Waco Tribune-Herald*, 29 November 1996, sec. A, p. 12.

New, Hattie Mae Hinnant. *Lagarto, a Collection of Remembrances: The History, the People, the Stories.* Kingsville, Tex.: Kathy's Kopies, [2000].

Newell, H. Perry, and Alex D. Krieger. *The George C. Davis Site, Cherokee County, Texas.* Memoirs of the Society for American Archaeology, no. 5. Menasha, Wis.: Society for American Archaeology, 1949.

"New Town in Ector Derrick Shadows." Typescript. N.d. "Penwell, Texas" vertical file, Petroleum Museum, Midland, Tex.

Nielsen, George R. *In Search of a Home: Nineteenth-century Wendish Immigration.* College Station: Texas A&M University Press, 1989.

Nocona's Bicentennial Heritage '76 Committee. *Panorama of Nocona's Trade Area.* Saint Jo, Tex.: Nocona's Bicentennial Heritage '76 Committee, 1976.

Nunley, Parker. *A Field Guide to Archeological Sites of Texas.* Austin: Texas Monthly Press, 1989.

Oatman, Wilburn. *Llano, Gem of the Hill Country: A History of Llano County, Texas.* Hereford, Tex.: Pioneer Book Publishers, 1970.

Ochiltree County Historical Survey Committee. *Wheatheart of the Plains: An Early History of Ochiltree County.* N.p.: Ochiltree County Historical Survey Committee, 1969.

"Oil Town of Orla Not Quite Boom or Bust Kind of Place: Located in Busy Area, It Manages to Hang On." *Houston Post*, 7 August 1994, sec. A, p. 34.

Olien, Diana Davids, and Roger M. Olien. "Oil and Community Development in Ector County, Texas, 1920–1960." *The Permian Historical Annual* 35 (1995): 31–50.

Olien, Roger M. "Boom Town Business: The Permian Basin Experience." *The Permian Historical Annual* 19 (1979): 3–11.

"Once Cowboy Capital: Old Courthouse, Graves Only Signs of Frio Town." *Corpus Christi (Tex.) Times*, 4 May 1962, sec. C, p. 14.

"Once-thriving Neches River Settlement Now 'Ghost Town.'" *Houston Post*, 22 November 1970, sec. B, p. 3.

Ormsby, Waterman L. *The Butterfield Overland Mail.* Edited by Lyle H. Wright and Josephine M. Bynum. San Marino, Calif.: Huntington Library, 1954.

Orton, Wanda. "Baytonian Urges Brownwood Evacuation Plan Be Changed." *Baytown (Tex.) Sun*, 26 August 1979, sec. A, pp. 1–2.

———. "Brownwood Bond Election Call by Petition Ruled 'Probably Illegal.'" *Baytown (Tex.) Sun*, 24 August 1979, sec. A, p. 1, sec. B, p. 3.

———. "Brownwood Cost More Than Doubled: Increase In Values is Blamed." *Baytown (Tex.) Sun*, 22 June 1979, sec. A, pp. 1, 2.

———. "Brownwood Move May Begin in Spring of '80." *Baytown (Tex.) Sun*, 5 December 1979, sec. A, p. 1, sec. D, p. 4.

————. "Brownwood Perimeter Road: Replacement Needed: Mayor." *Baytown (Tex.) Sun*, 15 July 1979, sec. A, pp. 1, 7.

————. "Brownwood Project Can Be Reduced, Eckhardt Tells Council." *Baytown (Tex.) Sun*, 5 September 1979, sec. A, p. 1, sec. C, p. 8.

————. "Brownwood Renters' Plan Is Defended." *Baytown (Tex.) Sun*, 7 December 1979, sec. A, p. 1, sec. B, p. 4.

————. "City to Chart Course on Brownwood's 'Evacuation:' Workshop Session Planned." *Baytown (Tex.) Sun*, 3 May 1979, sec. A, pp. 1–2.

————. "'Do Something' About Brownwood, City Asked: Council to Discuss Problem." *Baytown (Tex.) Sun*, 13 November 1979, sec. A, pp. 1–2.

————. "$5 Million for Brownwood Given OK by House Panel." *Baytown (Tex.) Sun*, 11 May 1979, sec. A, p. 1, sec. B, p. 2.

————. "Maintenance Price Tag High: Cost to Keep Brownwood Estimated at $7 Million." *Baytown (Tex.) Sun*, 27 June 1979, sec. A, p. 1.

————. "No Tax Increase Here If Bond Issues Approved." *Baytown (Tex.) Sun*, 6 July 1979, sec. A, pp. 1–2.

————. "2nd Brownwood Bond Vote Plan Challenged." *Baytown (Tex.) Sun*, 23 August 1979, sec. A, pp. 1–2.

————. "Second Brownwood Bond Vote Set Jan. 8." *Baytown (Tex.) Sun*, 21 November 1979, sec. A, p. 1, sec. B, p. 4.

————. Sewer Woes Less Known: Most Publicized Problem at Brownwood—Flooding." *Baytown (Tex.) Sun*, 28 July 1979, sec. A, p. 1.

————. "Sponsor of Barge Terminal in Brownwood Delays Plans: Proposal Draws Ire of Leaders." *Baytown (Tex.) Sun*, 3 August 1979, sec. A, pp. 1–2.

————. "Wooster, Portions of Lakewood Deleted from B'Wood Move-out." *Baytown (Tex.) Sun*, 27 November 1979, sec. A, pp. 1, 18.

Orton, Wanda, and Susan C. Hastie. "Council Ponders Next Move After Brownwood Bonds Fail: Airport Issue Also Loses." *Baytown (Tex.) Sun*, 25 July 1979, sec. A, pp. 1–2.

Osborn, William. Austin, Texas. Typewritten letter to author, 24 June 1997, in possession of author.

"Our Savior's Lutheran Church to Celebrate 125th Anniversary: Historic Norse Church to Mark Event on June 26." *Clifton (Tex.) Record*, 8 June 1994, pp. 1, 7.

Palmer, John D. "Glimpses of the Desdemona Oil Boom." *West Texas Historical Association Year Book* 15 (1939): 48–53.

————. "A History of the Desdemona Oil Boom." Master's thesis, Hardin-Simmons University, 1938.

Paredes, Américo. *"With His Pistol in His Hand": a Border Ballad and Its Hero*. Austin: University of Texas, 1958.

Parent, Laurence. *Hiking Big Bend National Park*. Helena, Mont.: Falcon Publishing, 1996.

————. *Official Guide to Texas State Parks*. Austin: University of Texas Press, 1997.

"Parks Transferred." *Texas Highways* 47, no. 12 (December 2000): 45.

Pasztor, David. "Ghost Towns: Dusty, Dying Communities Are Quickly Becoming Familiar Site in West Texas." *Galveston (Tex.) Daily News*, 17 August 1985, sec. A, p. 9.

Patterson, Bessie. "Hereford Man Recalls Life and Death of Prairie Town." *Amarillo (Tex.) Sunday News-Globe*, 1 June 1958, p. 8.

————. *A History of Deaf Smith County Featuring Pioneer Families*. Hereford, Tex.: Pioneer Publishers, 1964.

Patterson, Larry. "Memorandum, August 26, 1982." Photocopy of signed typescript. "Baytown Subdivision Report, August 26, 1982" vertical file (Accession #88.59.7). Baytown Historical Museum, Baytown, Tex.

Payne, L. W., Jr. "How Medicine Mounds of Hardeman County Got Their Name." In *Legends of Texas*, edited by J. Frank Dobie. Publications of the Texas Folklore Society, no. 3. Austin: Texas Folklore Society, 1924.

Pearce, John. "Committee Visits: Logs to Restore Fort Already Cut." *Waco News-Tribune*, 24 June 1966, sec. A, pp. 1, 7.

Pearson, Charles E., William Louis Fullen, Margaret S. Henson, and George J. Castille. *Cultural Resources Evaluation of the J. J. Mayes Farm and the Cummings Lumber Mill, Wallisville Lake Project Area, Texas*. U.S. Army Corps of Engineers, Galveston District, Contract no. DACW 64-84-P-0020 Work Order 0001. Baton Rouge: Coastal Environments, 1985.

Pennington, Mrs. E. E. *The History of Brenham and Washington County*. Houston: Standard Printing & Lithographing Company, 1915.

Perez, Nicole D. "Faith Healer's Shrine Attracts Followers: Hundreds Still Travel to Falfurrias Site 89 Years After Death." *Harlingen (Tex.) Valley Morning Star*, 3 August 1966, sec. A, p. 8.

Petersen, Dennis. "Danevang." *The Junior Historian* 27, no. 4 (January 1967): 20–21, 28.

Peterson, John A., and David O. Brown, eds. *El Valle Bajo: The Culture History of the Lower Rio Grande Valley of El Paso*. 3 vols. El Paso: Archaeological Research; Austin: Hicks and Company, 1994.

Phillips, William Battle. *Coal, Lignite, and Asphalt Rocks*. University of Texas, Mineral Survey, Bulletin, no. 3. Austin: University of Texas, 1902.

————. "The Quicksilver Deposits of Brewster County, Texas." *Economic Geology* 1, no. 2 (November–December 1905): 155–62.

Picquet, Jimmie Ruth. "Some Ghost Towns in South Texas." Master's thesis, Texas A&I University, 1972.

Pierson, Oris Emerald. "Norwegian Settlements in Bosque County, Texas." Master's thesis, University of Texas, 1947.

197

Pitts, John Paul. "Oil Towns Come and Go: And Then There's Orla: Permian Basin Town, Population 6, Has Staying Power." *Dallas Morning News*, 11 September 1994, sec. A, pp. 50–51.

"'Plastic Envelopes' Protect Big Bombers from Weather." *San Angelo (Tex.) Standard-Times*, 3 February 1948, p. 4.

Poe, Charlsie. *Runnels Is My County*. San Antonio: Naylor Company, 1970.

"Ponton Buys Candelaria." *Marfa (Tex.) Big Bend Sentinel*, 20 January 1994, p. 1.

Pool, William C. *Bosque County, Texas*. San Marcos, Tex.: San Marcos Record Press, 1954.

————. *Bosque Territory: A History of an Agrarian Community*. Clifton, Tex.: Bosque Memorial Museum, 1964.

Porter, Jack. "For Knowledge and Character: Goodnight Baptist College Training Launched in 1898." *Amarillo (Tex.) Sunday News-Globe*, 14 August 1966, sec. D, p. 16.

Porter, Millie Jones. *Memory Cups of Panhandle Pioneers*. Clarendon, Tex.: Clarendon Press, 1945.

Potts, Marisue Burleson. *Motley County Roundup: Over One Hundred Years of Gathering*. 2nd ed. Floydada, Tex.: privately printed, 1991.

Powers, Kay. "Wendish Still Flavors Speech of Serbin Folk." *Austin American-Statesman*, 12 June 1975, sec. A, p. 17.

"Prisoners Missed Death by Minutes in Flood of 1882." *San Angelo (Tex.) Standard-Times*, 3 May 1934, sec. 2, p. 3.

Pryor, Belinda. "Kanawaha and Kiomatia Boast Long Histories." *Detroit (Tex.) News*, 21 July 1983, pp. 1, 4.

Pryor, David. "Newburg, Texas: The Relationship Between the Town and Its Environment." Typescript. 1981. "Newburg, Texas" vertical file, Texas Collection, Baylor University.

Przygoda, Jacek. "New Light on the Poles in Texas." *Polish American Studies* 27, no. 1–2 (Spring–Autumn 1970): 80–86.

————. *Texas Pioneers from Poland: A Study in the Ethnic History*. Waco: Texian Press, 1971.

"Pyote—Supply Base of Worlds Greatest Oil Pool." *Texas Commercial News* 16, no. 7 (July 1928): 20.

Quillin, Gayle L. "Desdemona." Typescript. 1979. 23 lvs. "Desdemona, Texas, Term Papers" vertical file, Texas Collection, Baylor University.

"Quintana Park Dedicated in Broad Community Fete." *Lake Jackson (Tex.) Brazorian News*, 2 September 1982, pp. 1, 4.

"Quintana, Texas vertical file. Brazoria County (Tex.) Historical Museum.

"Quintana, Texas" vertical file. Center for American History, University of Texas at Austin.

Ragsdale, Kenneth B. *Big Bend Country: Land of the Unexpected*. College Station: Texas A&M University Press, 1998.

————. *Quicksilver: Terlingua and the Chisos Mining Company*. College Station: Texas A&M University Press, 1976.

Ramsey, Grover Cleveland. Papers. Center for American History, University of Texas at Austin.

Randel, Jo Stewart, and Hobart Ebey Stocking, eds. *A Time to Purpose: A Chronicle of Carson County and Area*. 4 vols. Hereford, Tex.: Pioneer Book Publishers, 1966–72.

"Readers' Views." *Baytown (Tex.) Sun*, 20 July 1979, sec. A, p. 6.

Recer, Paul. "Battle Against Creeping Submersion: Life on Texas Coast Now Nightmare." *Waco News-Tribune*, 2 October 1972, sec. B, p. 1.

Refugio County History Book Committee of the Texas Extension Homemakers Council of Refugio County. *The History of Refugio County, Texas*. Dallas: Curtis Media Corporation, 1985.

Reindorp, Reginald C., trans. "The Founding of Missions at La Junta de los Rios." *Supplemental Studies of the Texas Catholic Historical Society* 1, no. 1 (April 1938): 1–28.

Richardson, T. C. "When the Norsemen Came to Texas: After Eight Centuries a Mild-mannered Quaker Leads His Race to New Homes in Land Discovered by Viking Ancestors." *Farm and Ranch* (Dallas) 45, no. 34 (21 August 1926): 1, 10.

Rister, Carl Coke. *Oil! Titan of the Southwest*. Norman: University of Oklahoma Press, 1949.

Rivas, Maggie. "Tiny Candelaria May Lose Its Heart: Residents Fear School Closing Could Kill Town." *Dallas Morning News*, 6 August 1989, sec. A, pp. 45, 48.

Roberts, Mrs. W. A. "Frio County Has a Colorful History." *Frontier Times* 8, no. 8 (June 1935): 453–59.

Rock, James L., and W. I. Smith. *Southern and Western Texas Guide for 1878*. St. Louis: A. H. Granger, 1878.

Rode, Rosalind. "Still Sits the Schoolhouse by the Road." *The Junior Historian* 15, no. 5 (March 1955): 21–22, 25.

Rogers, Matthew Alan. "Not My House! The Government's Right of Eminent Domain." Typescript. 1991. Baytown (Tex.) Historical Museum.

Roy, Janet. "The Life and Times of Minera, Texas." *Southwestern Historical Quarterly* 49, no. 4 (April 1946): 510–17.

Rushing, Kathy. "The History of Penwell, Texas, in Ector County and Its Relationship to the Land." Typescript. 1983. "Penwell, Texas, Term Papers" vertical file, Texas Collection, Baylor University.

Russell, T. J. *Pioneer Reminiscences of Jefferson County*. Edited by Bertie Holmes Boodry. Beaumont, Tex.: Southeast Texas Genealogical & Historical Society, 1987.

Sabine Pass and the Interests Requiring That It Be Made a Deep Water Port of the First Class. Beaumont, Tex.: Journal Print, 1889.

Sabine Pass in the Texas Coast Country. Sabine Pass, Tex.: Sabine Land and Improvement Country, [ca. 1897].

Sabine, Texas. Company of the City. *Certificate of Stock in the City of Sabine, Republic of Texas.* Houston: Telegraph Press, 1839. Beinecke Library, Yale University.

Sabine, Texas. Company of the City. "Constitution of the Company of the City of the Sabine." Typescript. N.d. Beinecke Library, Yale University.

St. Clair, Kathleen, and Clifton R. St. Clair. *Little Towns of Texas.* Jacksonville, Tex.: Jayroe Graphic Arts, 1982.

Salcedo, Myra Lee. "Best: The Worst Little Town in Texas." *Midland (Tex.) Reporter-Telegram,* 28 June 1987, sec. F, pp. 1–2.

Sale, Mark "Haughk." *Archaeological Monitoring of a Joint Task Force-Six Road Improvement Project Along the International Border in West Texas: The Candelaria Road Segment.* El Paso: Lone Mountain Archaeological Services, 1999.

Salter, Bill. "Gonzales County Town Photographer's Delight." *San Antonio Sunday Express and News,* 28 December 1969, sec. B, p. 4.

____. "Old Sutherland Springs Once Held Title as South's Resort Center." *San Antonio Sunday Express and News,* 27 October 1968, sec. B, p. 2.

Sanders, Olga Flores. "End of Highway Opens World of Learning." *Waco Tribune-Herald,* 2 May 1986, sec. B, pp. 1, 9.

Santa Fe Splinters. 34 vols. Microfilm. Southwest Collection, Texas Tech University.

"Save the Church." *Marfa (Tex.) Big Bend Sentinel,* 21 November 1991, p. 3.

Schlachter, Barry. "Expect a Small Class Reunion: Big Bend High School Class of '98 Numbers 2." *Harlingen (Tex.) Valley Morning Star,* 30 May 1998, sec. A, p. 6.

Schmidt, Charles F. *History of Washington County.* San Antonio: Naylor Company, 1949.

"Schoenstatt Shrine Is 'a Beautiful Place.'" *Rockport (Tex.) Pilot,* 26 October 1991, Winter Visitor's Guide section, p. 55.

"Schutzenfests—Marksmanship Tourney—Prominent Sporting Events and Custom." *Fredericksburg (Tex.) Radio Post,* 6 May 1971, sec. 7, p. 2.

Scott, Bess Whitehead. "Quintana and Velasco Forts Gone." *Houston Post-Dispatch,* 6 December 1931, magazine section, p. 3.

Scott, Karen West. "An Interpretive Plan for Caddoan Mounds State Historic Site (The George C. Davis Site), Cherokee County, Texas." Master's thesis, Stephen F. Austin State University, 1984.

Scott, Quintana. *Along Route 66.* Norman: University of Oklahoma Press, 2000.

Scott, Quintana, and Susan Croce Kelly. *Route 66: The Highway and Its People.* Norman: University of Oklahoma Press, 1998.

Scott, Zelma. *A History of Coryell County, Texas.* Austin: Texas State Historical Association, 1965.

Seguilia, Frances. *Moments in Time: A History of the Tornillo Community and Its People.* Tornillo, Tex.: Cayote Publishing Company, 1981.

Severin, Emilie B. "Letters to the Editor." *Marfa (Tex.) Big Bend Sentinel,* 3 December 1991, p. 3.

Shafer, Harry Joe. "Lithic Technology at the George C. Davis Site, Cherokee County, Texas." Ph.D. diss., University of Texas at Austin, 1973.

Siegel, Stanley. *Big Men Walked Here! The Story of Washington-on- the-Brazos.* Austin: Jenkins Publishing Company, Pemberton Press, 1971.

Siekman, Bob. Interview by T. Lindsay Baker. Pyote, Texas, 25 May 1987. Typewritten notes in possession of author.

"Sinking Subdivision Causes Controversy." *Waco Tribune-Herald,* 26 August 1984, sec. A, p. 17.

Sitton, Thad, and James H. Conrad. *Nameless Towns: Texas Sawmill Communities, 1880–1942.* Austin: University of Texas Press, 1998.

Skaggs, Stella Shaffer. *Deep in the Heart of Texas.* Waco: Davis Bros. Publishing, 1971.

Smith, Betty. "125 Years of Service Celebrated by Our Savior's Lutheran Church." *Clifton (Tex.) Record,* 6 July 1994, sec. A, pp. 1, 7.

Smith, Mark G. "Baytown's for the Birds." *Southern Living* May 2000, Texas Living section.

Smith, Nancy. "History and Environment of Prairie Hill, Texas." Typescript. 1976. "Prairie Hill, Texas, Term Papers" vertical file, Texas Collection, Baylor University.

Smith, Norman. *Ballinger Bicentennial Rural Heritage.* [Ballinger, Tex.]: Ballinger Bicentennial Commission, [ca. 1976].

Smith, Ruth, and Fay Pannell. "Oak Hill: A Vanished Community." *Sayersville Historical Association Bulletin* no. 5 (Spring 1984): 6–12.

Smith, W. C., III. Interview by T. Lindsay Baker. Baytown, Texas, 3 November 2000. Typewritten notes in possession of author.

Smithers, W. D. *Chronicles of the Big Bend: Photographic Memoir of Life on the Border.* Austin: Madrona Press, 1976.

———. *Pancho Villa's Last Hangout: On Both Sides of the Rio Grande in the Big Bend Country.* Edited by Dudley R. Dobie, [Alpine, Tex.]: privately printed, [ca. 1964].

Solis, Rosaline. "Sabine Pass—Retrospect and Prospect." *The Junior Historian* 25, no. 5 (March 1965): 1–6, 32.

"So Long Ago? Or Was It?" *Fredericksburg (Tex.) Radio Post,* 15 April 1976, p. 9.

Sparkman, Ervin L. *The People's History of Live Oak County, Texas.* Edited by Mary Sparkman Roberts. Mesquite, Tex.: Ide House, 1981.

Speer, Cindy. "Quintana—Its History and Relationship to the Land." Typescript. 1977. "Quintana, Texas, Term Papers" vertical file, Texas Collection, Baylor University.

Spence, Mary Bain. "The Story of Benficklin, First County Seat of Tom Green County, Texas." *West*

Texas Historical Association Year Book 22 (1946): 27–46.

Spies, Eldor E. *Rural Schools of Lavaca County.* N.p.: privately printed, 1995.

Spikes, Nellie Witt. *The Early Days on the South Plains.* N.p.; n.d.

Spikes, Nellie Witt, and Temple Ann Ellis. *Through the Years: A History of Crosby County, Texas.* San Antonio: Naylor Company, 1952.

Sprague, Karen, and Steve Sprague. "Texas Ghost Towns: Sutherland Springs." Typescript. 1998. "County Files-Wilson County-Sutherland Springs" vertical file, Daughters of the Republic of Texas Library, San Antonio.

Stacy, Dennis. "All's Well at Wizard Wells: A Couple Digs in to Revive a Legend." *Texas Weekly* 1, no. 19 (19 January 1986): 12.

"State Opens Fort Leaton." *San Antonio Sunday Express and News*, 25 October 1970, sec. L, p. 7.

Steely, Skipper. Paris, Tex. Typewritten letter to author, [2 June 1985], in possession of author.

"Stella Maris Chapel Was First Church." *Rockport (Tex.) Pilot*, 26 October 1991, Winter Visitor's Guide section, pp. 53–54.

Stiff, Edward. *The Texan Emigrant.* Cincinnati: George Conclin, 1840.

Stoker, W. M. (Fred). *A Pictorial History of Higher Education in the Texas Panhandle.* Canyon, Tex.: West Texas State University, 1976.

Straach, Kathryn. "Lone Star Ghost Towns: Former State Backbones Are Now Mere Skeletons." *Dallas Morning News*, 26 October 1997, sec. G, pp. 8, 11.

Stroud, Martha Sue. *Gateway to Texas: History of Red River County.* Austin: Nortex Press, 1997.

Sullivan, Quaidie. "Neches Dam 'B' Offers Year-Round Recreation." *Houston Chronicle*, 19 July 1959, sec. 2, p. 2.

"Survivor of Flood Had No Fear at First: Mrs. Hardy Jones Saw Entire Town Wash Away." *San Angelo (Tex.) Standard-Times*, 3 May 1934, Sec. 3, p. 4.

"Survivors Recall Ben Ficklin Flood." *Frontier Times* 10, no. 2 (November 1932): 54–56.

Sutherland Springs Development Company. *Why Not Know Why?* Sutherland Springs, Tex.: Sutherland Springs Development Company, [ca. 1909]. Daughters of the Republic of Texas Library, San Antonio.

Svrcek, V. A., trans. and ed. *A History of the Czech-Moravian Communities of Texas.* Waco: Texian Press, 1974.

Syers, William Edward. "Off the Beaten Trail: The Mines' Ghosts: Better Not Follow!" *San Antonio Sunday News and Express*, 8 December 1963, sec. B, p. 9.

———. "A Graveyard for Memories." *San Angelo (Tex.) Standard-Times*, 26 November 1961, sec. B, p. 4.

———. *Off the Beaten Trail.* Waco: Texian Press, 1971.

Syversen, Odd Magnar, and Derwood Johnson. *Norge: Texas: Et Bidrag til Norsk Emigrasjonshistorie.* N.p.: Stange Historielag, 1982.

Tarpley, Fred. *1001 Texas Place Names.* Austin: University of Texas Press, 1980.

Taylor, Thomas U. *Irrigation Systems of Texas.* U.S., Department of the Interior, Geological Survey, Water-supply and Irrigation Paper, no. 71. Washington, D.C.: Government Printing Office, 1902.

———. *The Water Powers of Texas.* U.S., Department of the Interior, Geological Survey, Water-supply and Irrigation Paper, no. 105. Washington, D.C.: Government Printing Office, 1904.

"Terrific Flood! Great Destruction of Life." *San Angela (Tex.) Tom Green Times,* 26 August 1882, p. 1.

Tevis, Dean. "Fuss Over Hog Law Cost Wallisville County Seat: Rusting Hinges on Decayed Doors and Crumbling Walls of Once Beautiful Courthouse Vague Reminders of Chambers County Town of 30 Years Ago." *Beaumont (Tex.) Sunday Enterprise*, 22 July 1934, sec. B, p. 8.

Texas Forest Service. *Famous Trees of Texas.* 3rd ed. [College Station]: Texas Forest Service, 1985.

Texas Ghost Towns. Vol. 4, 2nd. ed., 9 April 2001. <www.TexasGhostTowns.com> (8 October 2002).

Texas Parks and Wildlife Department. *Caddoan Mounds: Temples and Tombs of an Ancient People.* Texas Parks and Wildlife Department Booklet 4000–384. Austin: Texas Parks and Wildlife Department, 1984.

Texas State Highway Department. *A Guide to the South Plains of Texas.* Lubbock: Texas State Highway Department, Division No. 5, 1935.

Thompson, Bill. "Gone Are Slaves, Indians: Old Kiomatia Plantation Still Rises Above River." *Paris (Tex.) News*, 5 September 1954, sec. II, p. 5.

———. "The Red River Valley—V: Kiomatia Plantation, Reminder of the Wright Family." *Paris (Tex.) News*, 10 July 1960, p. 6.

Thompson, Cecilia. *History of Marfa and Presidio County, Texas, 1535–1946.* 2 vols. Austin: Nortex Press, 1985.

Tidwell, Laura Knowlton. *Dimmit County Mesquite Roots.* N.p.: Wind River Press, 1984.

"To Fund Civic Center: Prairie Hill Readies Fall Festival." *Waco Tribune-Herald*, 14 October 1977, morning ed., sec. B, p. 1.

Tolbert, Frank X. "A Boom Town at Rest: Trees Cloak Texas' First Oil Site." *Dallas Morning News*, 14 January 1962, sec. 1, p. 22.

———. "Deep in Texas, a Bit of Norway." *Dallas Morning News*, 16 June 1962, sec. 1, p. 18.

———. "Films Help Keep Goodnight Alive." *Dallas Morning News*, 11 December 1966, sec. A, p. 32.

———. "Fort Parker Looms as Courage Shrine." *Dallas Morning News*, 5 April 1953, sec. 4, p. 1.

———. "A 'Hero Hobo' from Norway." *Dallas Morning News*, 21 March 1981, sec. A, p. 31.

————. *The Story of Lyne Taliaferro (Tol) Barret, Who Drilled Texas' First Oil Well.* Dallas: Texas Mid-Continent Oil & Gas Association, 1966.

————. "Tolbert's Texas: Artists and Deer 'Haunt' the Wells." *Dallas Morning News*, 15 February 1964, sec. 4, p. 1.

————. "Tolbert's Texas: The Black Spring Would Not Freeze." *Dallas Morning News*, 29 August 1961, sec. 4, p. 1.

————. "Tolbert's Texas: Cities of Pluck, Soda Pop Visited." *Dallas Morning News*, 14 September 1965, sec. D, p. 1.

————. "Tolbert's Texas: Complaints About Juno, Old Alton." *Dallas Morning News*, 8 May 1963, sec. 4, p. 1.

————. "Tolbert's Texas: Not Just Legend at Indian Springs." *Dallas Morning News*, 25 September 1967, sec. D, p. 1.

Toth, Sharon Allen. "Obscure Quintana Cemetery Fragment of Boom Town That Storms Destroyed." *Freeport (Tex.) Light*, 27 March 1985, pp. 1, 9.

"Towns Fade in West Texas, Scientists Told." *El Paso Herald Post*, 14 September 1956, p. 7.

Traweek, Eleanor Mitchell. *Of Such as These: A History of Motley County and Its Families.* Quanah, Tex.: Nortex Offset Publications, 1973.

Tunnell, Curtis D., and J. Richard Ambler. *Archeological Excavations at Presidio San Augustin de Ahumada.* State Building Commission, Archeological Program, Report, no. 6. Austin: State Building Commission, 1967.

Tyler, Ron, ed. *The New Handbook of Texas.* 6 vols. Austin: Texas State Historical Association, 1996.

Tyler, Ronnie C. *The Big Bend: A History of the Last Texas Frontier.* Washington, D.C.: Government Printing Office, 1975.

U.S. Department of Commerce, Bureau of the Census. *The Eighteenth Decennial Census of the United States: Census of Population: 1960.* Vol. I, part A. Washington, D.C.: Government Printing Office, 1961.

————. *Fifteenth Census of the United States: 1930: Population.* Vol. I. Washington, D.C.: Government Printing Office, 1931.

————. *Fourteenth Census of the United States Taken in the Year 1920: Population.* Vol. 1. Washington, D.C.: Government Printing Office, 1921.

————. *A Report of the Seventeenth Decennial Census of the United States: Census of Population: 1950.* Vol. 1. Washington, D.C.: Government Printing Office, 1952.

————. *Sixteenth Census of the United States: 1940: Population.* Vol. 1. Washington, D.C.: Government Printing Office, 1942.

————. *Thirteenth Census of the United States Taken in the Year 1910: Population.* Vol. 3. Washington, D.C.: Government Printing Office, 1913.

U.S. Department of the Interior. Census Office. *Ninth Census of the United States: Statistics of Population.* Washington, D.C.: Government Printing Office, 1872.

————. *Population of the United States in 1860: Compiled from the Original Returns of the Eighth Census.* Washington, D.C.: Government Printing Office, 1864.

————. *Report on the Population of the United States at the Eleventh Census: 1890: Part I.* Vol. 15. Washington, D.C.: Government Printing Office, 1895.

————. *Statistics of the Population of the United States at the Tenth Census (June 1, 1880).* Vol. 1. Washington, D.C.: Government Printing Office, 1883.

————. *Twelfth Census of the United States, Taken in the Year 1900: Population: Part I.* Vol. 1. Washington, D.C.: Government Printing Office, 1901.

U.S. Department of War, Secretary. *Letter from the Secretary of War, Relative to the Improvement of the Navigation of the Harbor and Bar at Sabine Pass, Texas.* U.S., 43rd Cong., 2nd Sess., House Executive Document no. 116. Washington, D.C.: Government Printing Office, 1875.

————. *Letter from the Secretary of War, Transmitting a Report from the Chief of Engineers of the Results of a Survey of the Entrance to Sabine Pass, Texas.* U.S., 47th Cong., 1st Sess., House Executive Document no. 147. Washington, D.C.: Government Printing Office, 1882.

Valenza, Janet Mace. *Taking the Waters in Texas: Springs, Spas, and Fountains of Youth.* Austin: University of Texas Press, 2000.

Valley By-liners. *Rio Grande Roundup: Story of Texas Tropical Borderland.* Mission, Tex.: Border Kingdom Press, 1980.

Vaughn, Thomas Wayland. *Reconnaissance of the Rio Grande Coal Fields of Texas.* U.S. Department of the Interior, Geological Survey, Bulletin, no. 164. Washington, D.C.: Government Printing Office, 1900.

"Vote is 5–1: Brownwood Evacuation Is Endorsed by Council." *Baytown (Tex.) Sun*, 5 May 1979, sec. A, pp. 1, 2.

VT. [pseud.] "People and Places." *Dallas Morning News*, 17 August 1930, feature section, p. 6.

Wallisville Lake Project Dedication Ceremony, November 1, 1999, 10:30 a.m., Wallisville, Texas. N.p.: U.S. Army Corps of Engineers, 1999. Library, Wallisville Heritage Park.

"Wallisville Townsite." Typescript. [Ca. 1980.] Library, Wallisville Heritage Park.

Walter, Ray A. *A History of Limestone County.* Austin: Von Boeckmann-Jones, 1959.

Ward County 1887–1977. Dallas: Taylor Publishing Company, [ca. 1977].

Waring, Margaret. Comanche, Tex. Typewritten letter to author, 13 April 1999, in the possession of author.

Waring, Margaret, and Samuel J. C. Waring, comps. *Comanche County Gravestone Inscriptions.* Vols. I and IV. Comanche, Tex.: privately printed, 1976, 1983.

Warner, C. A. *Texas Oil and Gas Since 1543.* Houston: Gulf Publishing Company, 1939.

Warren, Laura. "Norway's King Olav V to Visit Centex Church." *Waco Tribune-Herald,* 2 August 1982, sec. B, p. 1.

Washington, Texas. *Certificate of Stock in the Town of Washington.* Houston: Telegraph Press, [ca. 1839]. Beinecke Library, Yale University.

"The Waters of Concho Swept Away County Seat: Ben Ficklin Flood Greatest Disaster." *San Angelo (Tex.) Standard,* 3 May 1924, sec. 3, p. 1.

Watson, Lee. "In Ben Ficklin Flood 80 Years Ago He Perched in Tree, Saw Homes Disappear." *San Angelo (Tex.) Standard-Times,* 24 August 1962, morning edition, sec. B, p. 1.

Watthuber, Kristie. "Faithful Gather to Preserve Fort Parker." *Waco Tribune-Herald,* 23 August 1992, sec. C, pp. 1, 7.

———. "Groesbeck Plans to Take Over Park: State-local Accord Would Allow Site to Remain Open." *Waco Tribune-Herald,* 30 September 1992, sec. A, pp. 1, 6.

Weaver, Bobby D. *Castro's Colony: Empresario Development in Texas, 1842–1865.* College Station: Texas A&M University Press, 1985.

Webb, Perry. "Ireland: Its People and Land." Typescript. N.d. "Ireland, Texas" vertical file, Texas Collection, Baylor University.

Webb, Walter Prescott, ed. *The Handbook of Texas.* 2 vols. Austin: Texas State Historical Association, 1952.

Welch, June Rayfield. *Historic Sites of Texas.* Waco: Texian Press, 1972.

Wharton County Historical Commission. *Wharton County Pictorial History 1846–1946: Our First 100 Years.* Austin: Eakin Press, 1993.

Wharton, David. *The Soul of a Small Texas Town: Photographs, Memories, and History from McDade.* Norman: University of Oklahoma Press, 2000.

Wheat, Jim. *More Ghost Towns of Texas.* Garland, Tex.: The Lost & Found, 1971.

Where Healing Waters Flow: White Sulphur Water, 80 Feet Deep, Sutherland Springs, Texas. Sutherland Springs, Tex.: H. A. Speer, [ca. 1910]. Texas Collection, Baylor University.

White, Edna McDaniel. *East Texas Riverboat Era and Its Decline.* Beaumont, Tex.: LaBelle Printing & Engraving Company, 1965.

Whitehead Memorial Museum and Val Verde Historical Commission. *La Hacienda: An Official Bicentennial Publication.* [Del Rio, Tex.]: Whitehead Memorial Museum, [1976].

Wichita Historical Society. Wichita Falls, Tex. "Red River Station: The 'Jumping-off' Point on the Chisholm Trail." Mimeographed. 1956. "Ghost Towns" vertical file, Center for American History, University of Texas at Austin.

Williams, Annie Lee. *A History of Wharton County 1846–1961.* Austin: Von Boeckmann-Jones, 1964.

Williams, J. W. "The National Road of the Republic of Texas." *Southwestern Historical Quarterly* 47, no. 3 (January 1944): 207–24.

Winchester, Mrs. J. M. "The Deans at La Plata." *Amarillo (Tex.) Sunday News and Globe,* 14 August 1938, sec. C, p. 32.

Wofford, Verna Dean, ed. *Hale County Facts and Folklore.* 3 vols. Lubbock: Pica Publishing Company, 1978–86.

"Won't Somebody Save Me?" *Presidio (Tex.) International,* 15 February 1996, p. 1.

Wood, Alpha Kennedy. *Texas Coastal Bend: People and Places.* San Antonio: Naylor Company, 1971.

Wood, Harry. "Growth from 5 to 65: In Study Butte, That's Booming." *San Angelo (Tex.) Standard-Times,* 22 January 1967, sec. C, p. 11.

Worcester, Don. *The Chisholm Trail: High Road of the Cattle Kingdom.* Lincoln: University of Nebraska Press, 1980.

Wright, Bill. *Portraits from the Desert: Bill Wright's Big Bend.* Austin: University of Texas Press, 1998.

Wright, Mildred Sulser, and William D. Quick. *United States Spanish-American War Fortifications at the Sabine Pass, Texas.* Decorah, Iowa: Anundsen Publishing, 1982.

Yeats, Angela. "The Environment and History of Wizzard [sic] Wells, Jack County, Texas." Typescript. 1982. "Wizzard [sic] Wells, Texas" vertical file, Texas Collection, Baylor University.

Yeats, E. L., and E. H. Sheldon. *History of Fisher County, Texas.* N.p.: privately printed, 1971.

Yelvington, Henry. "Minera, for Years a Mining Camp, now Ghost Town on Border." *San Antonio Express,* 25 November 1934, sec. D, pp. 1, 3.

Yoakum County Historical Commission. *Yoakum County from Sod to 1985.* [Dallas]: Taylor Publishing Company, [ca. 1986].

Young, Buck A. *The Making of a City: Baytown, Texas, Since Consolidation 1948–1998.* Baytown, Tex.: Lee College, 1997.

Young County Federation of Women's Clubs. *Scrapbook of Young County: A Pictorial History.* [Graham, Tex.]: Young County Federation of Women's Clubs, [ca. 1945].

Young County Historical Commission. *Roots in Young County.* [Graham, Tex.]: Young County Historical Commission, 1978.

Zachry, Juanita Daniel. *The Settling of a Frontier: A History of Rural Taylor County.* Burnet, Tex.: Nortex Press, 1980.

Ziegelt, Wanda. "The Environment and History of Carlton, Texas." Typescript. 1977. "Carlton, Texas" vertical file, Texas Collection, Baylor University.

Zientek, Marion. "St. Francis, 'Polish Village:' Symbol of the Past, Dear to Some." *The Texas Catholic Herald* 6 (December 1968): 2.

Index

203

Doebbler, Friedrich, 69
Dolores, Tex., 104–106
Drought, at La Plata, 92
Dryden, Eugene E., 43
Dryden, Tex., 43–45
Dublin, Tex., 27
Dudley, Dick S., 101–102

East Direct, Tex., 43
Eastern Texas Railroad, 138
Eastland, Tex., 41
Eastland County, Tex., ghost towns in, 40–41
Ector County, Tex., ghost towns in, 128–29
Edinburg, Tex., 94
Edmondson, Tex., 150
Edmondson, W. W., 150
El Campo, Tex., 38, 39, 40
Electric City, Tex., 45–47
Electricity, at Electric City, 46–47
Elephants, at Mankins, 101
Elgin, Tex., 114–16
Eliasville, Tex., 47–49
Elkhart, Tex., 100
El Paso, Tex., 59, 77–78; railroads to, 43, 124, 133; roads to, 8, 159
El Paso County, Tex., ghost towns in, 75–78
Emma, Tex., 49–51
Enola Gay, 135
Ernst, Max A., 14
Eskota, Tex., 52–54
Estacado, Tex., 50
Evadale, Tex., 181
Everett, J. H., 25–26

Fairfield, Tex., 100
Fairland, Tex., 54–55
Falfurrias, Tex., 93, 97–98
Farley, Beverly Caster, 44
Farrier, J. W., 37
Farris, Frances Bramlette, 63
Faskin Mound, Tex., 87–88
Ficklin, Benjamin F., 8
Field, Herschel Robert ("Gravy"), 18–19
Field, Mattie E. Chambers, 19
Fires: at Lipscomb, 96; at Medicine Mound, 103; at Newtown, 109–10; at Ogden, 119; at Rock Island, 143; at Stoneham, 162–63
Fisher County, Tex., ghost towns in, 52–54
Flomot, Tex., 55–57
Floods: at Ben Ficklin, 8–9; at Minera, 105; at Sutherland Springs, 168
Follett, Tex., 96
Forrester, S. W., 28
Fort Concho, Tex., 8–9
Fort Davis, Tex., 24, 60, 147
Fort Leaton, Tex., 57–60

Fort Leaton State Historical Park, Tex., 60
Fort Lincoln, Tex., 123–24
Fort Mason, Tex., 31
Fort Parker, Tex., 60–62
Fort Parker Memorial Park, Tex., 61–62
Fort Stockton, Tex., 24, 147
Fort Worth, Tex., 118, 133, 158
Fort Worth and Denver Railway, 66, 149–50
4–C Company, 138–40
Fowler, S. L., 107
Fox Nation, Tex., 71
Franks, Bill, 173–74
Fredericksburg, Tex., 31, 32, 69–70, 127
Fredericksburg and Northern Railway, 70
Frederickson, Emil, 111
Freeport, Tex., 136–37
Frenchmen: at Old D'Hanis, 123; at Wallisville, 174–75
Frio City, Tex. See Frio Town, Tex.
Frio County, Tex., ghost towns in, 62–64
Frio River, 62–64
Frio Town, Tex., 62–64

Gallagher, N. A., 153
Galveston, Harrisburg and San Antonio Railway, 6, 43–45, 122, 124
Galveston, Tex., 136, 181; as destination for cotton, 98–99; hurricane at, 39; as port of entry, 153, 157
García, Julia Cuellar de, 98
Garza County, Tex., ghost towns in, 84–85
Gatesville, Tex., 81–82
Gentiliz, Theodore, 123–24
George West, Tex., 72
Germans: at Cherry Spring, 31–32; in Diocese of Galveston, 153; at Grapetown, 69–70; at Old D'Hanis, 122–24; at Wiess's Bluff, 80–81
Ghost towns, causes of death for: agricultural consolidation, 4, 7, 12, 16, 27, 30, 34, 35, 39, 43, 48, 57, 67–68, 72, 73, 85, 87–88, 89, 94, 102, 103, 106, 131, 132, 143, 157–58, 161, 162–63, 171, 182; agricultural production more efficient elsewhere, 25, 148; American Indians, destruction by, 61; coal, reduced demand for, 105; county seat, loss of, 51, 64, 92, 171–72; fire damage, 103, 109–10, 119–20, 143, 162–63; flood damage, 8–9, 168, 175; highways, bypassing, 6, 12, 34, 53, 70;

highways, improved, 12, 27, 39, 45, 57, 67–68, 87–88, 94, 102, 103, 106, 127, 157–58, 162, 174; land subsidence, 20–22; military base closings, 135; mineral resources, depletion of, 14; oil depletion, 10, 41, 47, 48, 85, 121–22, 126, 134–35, 145, 161; railways, abandonment of, 27, 81; railways, bypassing, 51, 63–64, 72, 74–75, 89, 92, 118, 122, 124, 177, 179, 181, 182; timber resources, exhaustion of, 130–31; U.S. Army, destruction by, 114–16; water, lack of, 5, 29, 101, 124; wool and mohair prices, decline of, 83
Giddings, Tex., 157, 158
Gillespie County, Tex., 13; ghost towns in, 31–32, 69–70
Glazier, Tex., 97
Glenn Springs, Tex., 14–15
Glenrio, Tex., 64–66
Glover, Robert M., 7
Goldthwaite, Tex., 29, 107
Gonzales, Tex., 6–7, 73
Gonzales County, Tex., ghost towns in, 6–7
Goodnight, Charles, 66–69
Goodnight, Mary Ann Dyer, 66–67, 69
Goodnight, Tex., 66–69
Goodnight College, 66–69
Goose Island State Park, 91
Gorman, Tex., 41
Graham, Tex., 49, 162
Grandfalls, Tex., 143–45
Grand Saline, Tex., 159, 160
Grange. See Patrons of Husbandry
Greeks, at Desdemona, Tex., 41
Grenada, Tex. See La Plata, Tex.
Grimes County, Tex., ghost towns in, 162–64
Gristmill, at Eliasville, Tex., 47–49
Groesbeck, Tex., 62
Groundwater extraction, 20
Gruver, Tex., 75
Guadalupe River, 6
Guadalupe Peak, Tex., 126
Guerra, Antonia, 93
Guerra, Arcadio, 93–94
Gulf, Beaumont and Kansas City Railway, 181
Gulf Intracoastal Waterway, 137
Gussett, Norwick, 71
Gussettville, Tex., 71–72

Hackberry, Tex., 72–74
Hale County, Tex., ghost towns in, 149–50
Hall, Edward, 59
Hall, John W., 176
Hallettsville, Tex., 74

206